Advance Praise for
JEWISH PRIDE

"Contrarian Michael Steinhardt has used his wealth to launch innovations to help make the Jewish world become as vibrant and committed as possible. A strong believer in data and evaluation, he is a harsh critic of how the organized Jewish community uses its resources. Not afraid to admit failure, he turns to each new idea with undiminished enthusiasm. This is a book of a secular and proud Jew who loves the Jewish people and the joy of experiencing Jewish life."

> —**Jehuda Reinharz**, President Emeritus of Brandeis University, President and CEO of the Jack, Joseph, and Morton Mandel Foundation

"In this book Michael Steinhardt describes among other projects, his brilliant and innovative idea of Birthright. Birthright is successful in bringing American and Israeli young people together for the sake of advocating the relationship between the US, Israel and other countries. And I know that even some marriage proposals and weddings resulted. This book should be read by all people of good will who advocate for the relationship between Israel, the US and other countries."

> —**Ruth K. Westheimer**, Ed.D, co-author (with Jonathan Mark) of *Heavenly Sex: Sex In The Jewish Tradition* (NYU Press)

"Here is the view from the inside—not of the Jewish religious world, but the Jewish philanthropic and institutional and political world. It is astute, candid, and could only have been written by someone whose access and contributions have made a difference in the lives of countless Jews."

> —**Rabbi David Wolpe**, Max Webb Senior Rabbi, Sinai Temple, Los Angeles

"For the twenty some years that we've been friends, Michael has demonstrated by word and deed his deep caring for the Jewish People. This book, written with full heart, reflects not only that caring, but also his concerns and his hopes for our future. It is a welcome addition to our ongoing debate."

> —**Charles Bronfman**, Co-Founder, Birthright Israel

JEWISH PRIDE

JEWISH PRIDE

MICHAEL STEINHARDT

WICKED SON

A WICKED SON BOOK
An Imprint of Post Hill Press

Jewish Pride
© 2022 by Michael Steinhardt
All Rights Reserved

ISBN: 978-1-63758-002-8
ISBN (eBook): 978-1-63758-003-5

Cover design by Richard Ljoenes
Interior design and composition by Greg Johnson, Textbook Perfect

Post Hill Press
New York ✦ Nashville
posthillpress.com

Published in the United States of America
1 2 3 4 5 6 7 8 9 10

For my wife
Judy

Our children
David, Daniel, and Sara

And our grandchildren
Jacob, Josh, Kira, Aatein, Talia,
Lila, Anceena, Nate, Theo, Halean,
Aaliyah, Eli, and Leo

Contents

Acknowledgments

This book took me almost a decade to write. I'm not sure why it was such a struggle. It may have something to do with my intensely conflicted feelings about my people, the Jewish people. On the one hand, I have been critical about the way many Jewish communal institutions work—and about the future we face under their continued leadership. On the other, I feel immense affection for Jews everywhere. I love old Jews and young Jews, rich Jews and poor Jews, Russian Jews and Ethiopian Jews, Uruguayan Jews and Moroccan Jews, American Jews and Israeli Jews. I consider all Jews a part of my family—and writing about family is complicated.

When you make money and start to give it away, you quickly discover the limits of your ability to have an impact and create change. Sometimes when I look back on the years I spent trying to engage secular young Americans in the richness of Jewish life, I feel I've made a difference; at other times, not so much. This book represents my best effort to offer an honest reckoning of my successes and failures. I hope that both—the things that worked and the lessons I learned from those that didn't—will inspire others to think about the Jewish future and to take risks in order to try and make a lasting difference in Jewish life.

Across my philanthropic career, I rarely acted alone. I was deeply fortunate to find like-minded people of means to join me in both more and less successful efforts to build a Jewish identity. Among major philanthropists, I will forever be grateful to Len Abramson, Sheldon (z"l) and Miri Adelson, Charles Bronfman, Edgar Bronfman (z"l), Bill Davidson, Harold Grinspoon, Tom Kaplan, Charles (z"l) and Lynn Schusterman, Paul Singer and Terry Kassel, and so many others who felt as I did about what needed to be done and how to do it and put their money and time on the line.

Many people assisted in creating this book.

Seymour Epstein, David Foreman, and Len Saxe helped me begin to untangle my ideas about Jewish values and my vision for the future of Diaspora Jews.

Wendy Belzberg, Jacob Berman, Daniel Bonner, Shira Dicker, Tova Dorfman, Abe Foxman, David Goldin, Felicia Herman, Ezra Merkin, Charlie Melman, Eli Schapp, and Jordan Singer were early readers of parts or the whole of the book. Their insights made a tremendous difference to the finished product. Laurie Blitzer, Josh Elkin, Alon Futterman, Hayim Herring, Valerie Khaytina, Aliza Kline, Gidi Mark, and Barry Shrage also offered their recollections at various points in the process.

David Gedzelman single-handedly brought together the people and forces that made this project succeed. He has played a central role in my philanthropic work for more than twenty-five years, offered innumerable recollections and suggestions when he reviewed the manuscript at various points, and acted as a valuable sounding board throughout the process.

This book would not have been written without my writing partner, David Hazony. He did much of the research and helped me put words and ideas to paper. I am grateful for his good humor, patience, and dogged determination to make this book a reality.

Acknowledgments

My editor, Adam Bellow, publisher of Wicked Son, believed in this book when I wasn't so sure it would ever be more than a dream. He steered this ship, and I am grateful for his stewardship.

I have been married to the love of my life, Judy, for fifty-three years, and I could not ask for a more committed, optimistic, and steadfast life partner. Judy's warmth and grace shine brighter as the years pass, and I am eternally grateful for her support and wisdom. She offered crucial insights on the manuscript as well.

My three children, David, Daniel, and Sara, their spouses Sarah, Tanata, and Mark, and our thirteen grandchildren, are truly the lights of my life. I turned eighty last year, and in my ninth decade, my interests and passions have narrowed. At some point, politics interested me; today, not so much. The art world once fascinated me but not today. I still have areas of deep interest: Horticulture and animals stand out. But my children and grandchildren—they are my future and on my mind nearly all the time. My daughter Sara dedicated many hours in helping review and formulate my memories and thoughts that appear throughout the book.

This book is not an academic work of history. It is a memoir. It is a recollection of my personal journey, filled with my encounters, observations, and memories. I have tried to tell this story as faithfully as I could, and I accept all errors as my own.

To some extent, it is also a call for action and a vision for the future, and it is my hope that, even if not every prescription is as feasible or wise as I would want it to be, the central message of the book—that Jewish identity can be a source of inspiration and pride for Jews everywhere, regardless of their background or religious outlook—has been delivered in a way that can both explain my story and inspire a new generation of Jews.

Prologue

In December 1995, at the age of fifty-five, I left a successful career on Wall Street. I could have retired comfortably. I could have become a normal philanthropist, giving money to worthy charities while spending my energies on family, social life, and hobbies. Instead, for the last two and a half decades, I have thrown my time, passion, experience, resources, and reputation into the task of improving Jewish life.

Why did I do this? It's not a simple question. After all, it is, on balance, good to be an American Jew in the twenty-first century. We do not face anything like the persecution, discrimination, or other hardships the generations before us suffered.

And yet, despite all the good things we American Jews have received, there is a problem.

Our community has been, for decades, stuck in a kind of malaise. On the whole, we are not fired up. We are not in love. We are not, as a community, showing courage or creativity or heroism. If anything, the opposite is true. Every year, more and more young Jews seem to just drift away. However you want to measure it—participation in Jewish educational institutions, philanthropic dollars given to Jewish causes, Jewish books purchased, synagogue membership, support for Israel—our sense of Jewish purpose seems to be dissipating.

Of course, there are pockets of strong attachment, especially among more traditional communities, and this fact often distracts us from the disturbing reality of declining Jewish identity among the secular majority. Not everyone wants to build their Jewish identity on religious rituals, faith, or single "issues" like Holocaust remembrance or support for Israel. Being Jewish has always meant something deeper and more complex—a product of centuries of collective experience—yet, also immediate and personal.

I grew up in a traditional home but, early in life, became an atheist. My overwhelming attachment to being Jewish has nothing to do with divine commandments, rabbinical teachings, or halachic practice. It is a thoroughly secular pride in being Jewish.

"Pride" might seem like an obvious thing. Who wouldn't want Jews to be proud? But it's not obvious, and it hasn't been for a long time. It turns out that there are forces that have been working hard to undermine our pride.

One big problem is the character of many major Jewish institutions, which seem to care a lot more about raising money than making your Jewish life rich, inspiring, and important. Another is the barrage of anti-Semitic and anti-Zionist noise that gets under our skin and makes us second-guess ourselves. Another is apathy and distraction: We are too busy worrying about other things to see our flagging Jewish pride as a priority.

If the phrase "Jewish pride" makes you uncomfortable, if you're not sure why it's important, or if you're embarrassed because you don't know all the Jewish holidays, or who Maimonides was, or how to speak Hebrew, or what to do at a Shabbat dinner—this is not your fault. It is, to a large degree, the fault of our institutions and leaders, and of the generations that came before you, which failed to provide what you, as a Jew, truly deserve: a core of knowledge, personal heroic examples, a powerful bond to the Jewish people, a tool kit for living a confident Jewish life, and a sense of the incomparable joy of being Jewish.

Jewish pride, once you have tapped into it, is an incredible thing. It's invigorating, it's life-changing, and it's beautiful. But if you cut off the oxygen to pride, it withers. It becomes something stale and stunted, and you don't really want it anymore. Many of us have come to feel exactly that.

Over the last two and a half decades, I've helped launch programs aimed at solving this problem in different ways. Programs like Birthright Israel, which offers free, ten-day trips to Israel for young Jews from around the world. Or OneTable, which offers Shabbat experiences in your home with your friends. I've helped build Jewish schools and cultural centers as well. Some of these projects were more successful than others.

When the Covid-19 pandemic swept through our world in the spring of 2020, few of us understood how long it would last. For engaged Jews, it brought a deep disruption of every institution that our Jewish lives were built on: From synagogue worship to life cycle events, from communal celebrations to visits to the JCC, from family gatherings to gala dinners to trips to Israel— nearly every piece of our Jewish lives was reinvented, canceled, or moved online.

But with crisis comes opportunity. We have known for a long time that our institutions were not delivering the kind of multigenerational Jewish pride that we needed. Now we have a real chance to take stock as a community, to think new thoughts about where we are going, and to make new plans, without the onerous burden of institutional inertia and old habits holding us back.

I chose to write this book because I know that for many, Jewish pride has become, in recent decades, a question that needs answering—much more so than for my generation.

When I was growing up, we knew we were Jewish, we had a chip on our shoulder, and we took pride in the achievements of Jewish scientists, movie stars, ballplayers, and the heroes who built the State of Israel. We didn't question our connection to, and responsibility for, each other. We were aware of a certain kind of Jewish excellence, and we were not ashamed to say so.

Today, it seems, we take Jewish achievements for granted, and we often don't feel like we are a part of them. And because we do not feel ownership in the achievements of other Jews, or in our history and our unique Jewish qualities, we cut off the oxygen that fuels our pride.

We are in the process of losing something unbelievably precious—the core of what a non-Orthodox, secular Jewish life in the Diaspora once was and can still be. And the burden of solving this problem will soon be shifting to the next generation.

The good news is that once we have put our finger on the problem, we have taken a crucial first step in solving it. And from everything I've seen and done, I know we already have many of the tools we need to solve it. But do we have the courage?

Michael Steinhardt
Bedford, N.Y., April 2022

CHAPTER 1

A Jew from Bensonhurst

Have you ever held an Uzi in your hands?

We all have moments that we look back on as powerful and formative. For me, that moment occurred sixty years ago, in the summer of 1962, on a kibbutz in northern Israel. I was twenty-one years old, visiting the young country for the first time. I was all alone in the dark of night, and I was holding a rifle.

I'm not sure why the kibbutz trusted me, a stranger from America, to perform guard duty. Maybe it was my bright red hair and confident grin. Or the fact that I'd previously spent six months on active duty in the U.S. Army, which meant that I probably wouldn't accidentally shoot someone. Or maybe they were impressed that I had left behind two of my friends, with whom I'd traveled to Europe for a vacation between jobs, and come to visit the Jewish state by myself.

Whatever it was, they asked me to spend the night patrolling the perimeter of the kibbutz on foot, and they handed me an Uzi. It had a heavy wooden stock and smelled like gun oil. We hadn't seen any Uzis at Fort Dix, and I wasn't completely sure I'd know how to use it. But I didn't care.

Although my memories of the kibbutz have faded with time, what stands out is the color. I had arrived in the late afternoon, and everything seemed shrouded in a deep brown—the earth and limited vegetation reflecting, I suppose, the passage of summer months without rainfall. It was dusty and hot. The few structures of the kibbutz were little more than glorified Quonset huts. I had walked with the kibbutz's leaders along the soft brown paths. Their English was not bad. They invited me to stand guard the same night.

And so, I found myself patrolling alone for hours along the edge of the kibbutz, beside the Jordan River. I looked out into the moonlit barren valley across the river into the Kingdom of Jordan—enemy territory. And as I walked, I felt an unfamiliar sense of pride welling up inside me. Pride in being entrusted with the safety of the sleeping kibbutz. Pride in my own willingness to face whatever dangers might confront me in the night. Pride and awe in walking the banks of this storied biblical stream.

I thought about my buddies who would meet up with me later in Paris, about my friends back home, about my parents, and about how this moment fit in the long, twisted trail of Jewish history. Other than the crunch of my own footsteps and the breeze blowing through the eucalyptus trees, there was little to hear.

This was before the Six-Day War, before the peace treaties with Egypt and Jordan, before the United States became Israel's patron and protector. Israel had barely survived its birth and was under constant threat of invasion by more powerful nations around it. Terrorist bands, known as *fedayeen*, had routinely attacked civilian communities along the border, like this kibbutz.

It was also a poor country. Economically it was in severe distress, and most of the funds it received came not from foreign investments but donations from Diaspora Jews. By the time I got there, this little plot of barren land had already absorbed more than a million immigrants, including refugees from Europe and hundreds of thousands of Jews from across the Middle East, most of them expelled from Arab countries after Israel's victory in 1948.

Many people thought Israel wouldn't survive its next war. But for me that night, with the strap of the heavy Uzi cutting into my shoulder, this moment meant something profound. The experience somehow went to the core of my being as a Jew.

For the first time in my life, I was directly contributing to the physical self-defense of the Jewish people. I had come to Israel as a tourist. Yet here I was a few days later holding a weapon, entrusted with the safety of the vulnerable kibbutz. What was I willing to do with this gun? If suddenly we were attacked, how would I react? I had served in the military but had never seen battle. Now I felt like I was entrusted with protecting a young Jewish community against a real threat of violence.

It was as though I had stepped out of one world and into another, a world where the word "Jewish" suddenly meant something entirely new and different. Back in New York, being "Jewish" was a passive reality, something I was born into and was reflexively proud of. The risks and sacrifices demanded by that world were limited, as were the possibilities for what Jews could achieve. Like so many Diaspora communities over the centuries, we had relied on police, the military, laws, and government leaders who were not really our own. They set the rules of the game, the limits of what being Jewish could mean.

Now, in Israel for the first time, I found myself in a realm where "Jewish" wasn't just a religious or ethnic modifier, a stroke of paint on a broader American canvas. Here, being Jewish suffused one's entire life. And it demanded a willingness to put one's life on the line. But it also opened up unimagined possibilities. And the kinds of people who had built this world and continued to define it—pioneers, warriors, statesmen—were, in spirit and action, wholly different from the Jews I had known all my life.

My lifelong fascination with Israel began on that trip. Like so many other American Jews, I never saw moving there as an active possibility, and I never was destined to master the Hebrew language. For reasons I cannot fully explain, my connection to Israel would always be filtered through a lens of translation. But I would try to make up for it, to a degree, by visiting there often and getting to know as many Israelis as I could from a wide variety of political, religious, and industrial backgrounds. That trip, as so often happens to people in early adulthood, opened a door in my life that would express itself in an endless stream of questions.

What kind of Jew did I want to be? What did Jewish pride really mean? These questions, having suddenly overwhelmed my thoughts, continue to resonate in me to this day.

IN ORDER TO UNDERSTAND WHY I chose, at the height of my career, to leave it behind and dedicate my life to launching pride-building programs for Diaspora Jews, you need to know a few things about the world I grew up in.

To begin with, I was born into a world without a Jewish homeland. There was no State of Israel when I was born. There were only Jews, living in different kinds of communities around the world. Some were better off, others worse. Some were more traditional and insular, while others wanted to live modern, secular lives as successful citizens of their country.

When I was born on December 7, 1940, one year to the day before Pearl Harbor, there were probably close to ten million Jews still alive in Europe. The Jews of the United States were second, with under five million. Of these, more than two million lived in the five boroughs of New York City.

But by the time I was five years old, the most cataclysmic war in human history had changed the world, and the Jews of Europe had nearly vanished. Most were dead. The rest became impoverished refugees scrambling for a new life elsewhere. America became the center of world Jewry, and New York was the center of American Jewry.

Bensonhurst, however, was not the center of Jewish New York. It was a lower-middle-class immigrant neighborhood in Brooklyn, which we Jews shared with Italians. We played stickball and basketball, and some of us got into fights. We were not wealthy, but it was, on the whole, a good life. We had friends, went to public school, and had a very strong sense of ourselves as Jews and of our place in the larger scheme of American life.

The New York I grew up in was filled with immigrant Jews who had a sense that you didn't have to be embarrassed about your Jewishness to succeed. Every Jewish denomination had its own rabbinical seminary in New York. Jewish culture had a big impact on the city as a whole, from its delis to its comedy clubs to its Broadway theaters. And while we still had difficulty getting into Ivy League schools, City College attracted the best minds that New York's Jews had to offer.

The Jews of Bensonhurst were not terribly concerned with their "identity." We lived largely in a world of our own making. Like other ethnic groups, we had our own stores and restaurants where Jewish businessmen, artists, and mobsters mingled freely. We had Jews of all classes: from financiers to shopkeepers to garment workers to furriers and tradesmen. "Being Jewish" in Bensonhurst was not a *problem*. We knew who we were, and we were proud of it.

Immigrant neighborhoods like Bensonhurst were much more of a mosaic than a melting pot. Each immigrant group forged powerful internal bonds and built a vibrant life of its own, apart from others. We Jews had little to do with the Italian kids. For starters, we were afraid of them. When they walked down the street, the metal heels on their shoes made a menacing noise announcing their approach. It was widely believed, rightly or wrongly, that many of them had familial ties to the mob. It wasn't worth getting into fights with them, we thought, because you never knew if one of their fathers was a Mafia lieutenant.

We also did not have the same approach to education as the Italian kids. At the Seth Low Junior High School, I was in a merit-based class called SP, or "special progress," in which academically advanced kids skipped directly from seventh to ninth grade. Almost all the SP kids were Jews. Once our class played softball in the schoolyard against a shop class almost entirely made up of Italian kids. I was playing third base, and a big Italian kid hit a ball deep into the outfield. He lumbered around first, then passed second base, and headed to third. At that moment, the ball was coming toward me from the outfield. I managed to catch it and tag him out just in time for him to slam me, at full force, into the wall behind third base.

More than a decade later, that same kid was found with a bullet in his head, sitting in a car outside a cemetery.

We didn't think much about anti-Semitism, either. Violence against Jews had many sources: The Nazis were one, the Stalinists in the Soviet Union were another, as were the Arabs who attacked Jewish communities in Palestine, and closer to home, the Italian kids who beat us up every Easter in Bensonhurst. We knew very well that Jews had been subjected to violence around the world from the beginning of time. In America, there were plenty of opportunities to get beaten up for being Jewish. But it didn't feel so different from what the Italians and Irish and Puerto Ricans went through.

We Jews had one huge advantage over other groups, however. Our parents taught us to care about doing well in school.

No single factor explains Jewish success in America more than our habits of learning and study—habits ingrained in us for centuries. Knowledge and education were consistently viewed by Jews as the keys to a better future. If one generation of Jews had been tailors and shopkeepers, the next would be lawyers and doctors. Like every group of immigrants, we had our own codes and language and foods. But the main thing that set us apart was the unwritten commandment that even the poorest Jews held sacred: Do thy homework.

ALTHOUGH I LATER BECAME AN unusually successful Wall Street money manager, I didn't come from a Jewish banking family, like some of those who could trace their success back to Germany. My father's family had come from Russia, and he was born and raised in the tough Brooklyn neighborhood of Brownsville.

Sol Steinhardt never finished high school, and he made an erratic living through questionable activities—mainly gambling and selling jewelry of dubious origin. He wasn't particularly warm, but he was smart and aggressive, and would often be seen with his friends walking down Broadway, stopping at Lindy's for cheesecake, finding out where the floating crap games were, or cruising the Diamond District. A redhead like me, he was given the Irish-sounding nickname "Red McGee." Like Sky Masterson in *Guys and Dolls*, he almost always had a large wad of cash in his pocket.

Sol divorced my mother when I was not even a year old, and after that, I didn't see him all that much. I was raised by my mother and grandmother in a modest apartment on 72nd Street, between Bay Parkway and 21st Avenue. My mother, Claire Steinhardt, was also born in Brooklyn after her parents emigrated from Poland. Early each morning she would ride the subway to the wholesale fruit market on what was then called the Lower West Side of Manhattan, where she helped out with the bookkeeping for my Uncle Louie's apple business. She worked long hours, coming home in the early evening.

My relationship with my father was complicated. I can't say I was proud of him, neither for his professional choices nor for his having divorced my mother. But I did learn a few important things from him. For one, he was extremely generous. When he wasn't broke, he helped out his brother and sister financially as well as my mother. And he did his best to be a caring father, within the limits of his ability.

It was my mother who raised me, and it was she who taught me, both explicitly and through her example, how to be Jewish. Like me, she didn't keep all the laws. On Shabbat, we would often celebrate with Chinese takeout that she snuck into the house when my more pious grandmother wasn't looking.

It was also my mother who made sure I attended Hebrew school every afternoon—a torturous failure as far as educational experiences go—and that we observed all the holidays according to tradition as best we could. The Bnai Isaac synagogue, where I had my bar mitzvah, was a cavernous, lifeless place where hunched-over, white-haired men in long prayer shawls passed around smelling salts to stay awake during the Yom Kippur services. The prayer books were all in Hebrew, and for most of the year very few people showed up.

Then one of my closest friends, Marty Taubman, took me to a different kind of synagogue. It was called a *shtiebel*, and it held its services in the basement of a four-story apartment building. From the entrance, you walked down half a flight of stairs into a room with makeshift tables and chairs and a Torah scroll. Here I understood even less of what was going on—even the conversations were all in Yiddish. But I nonetheless discovered a warmer, livelier, and more intimate place of worship, where there was no operatic cantor, and prayers were led by ordinary folks. In the *shtiebel*, I tasted, for the first time, a powerful, welcoming, vibrant Jewish spirit that I did not later forget.

I did not know it at the time, but it was in that *shtiebel* that I first encountered, in distilled form, a kind of Jewish joy that I have always looked for ways to recreate, both in my life and in the broader Jewish community. A warm fire, an urgent energy that connects Jews across time and space, not just those who live today but also across many generations in history, through song and dance and love and prayer. A powerful intimacy and a binding commitment of a people through time and across oceans and cultures.

But even as we felt the pull of tradition, we were also in the process of assimilating into American life. Like other Jews of that era, we took special pride in holding up for admiration certain figures who had succeeded in terms the mainstream society admired.

A few of these were athletes. Sandy Koufax, the ace pitcher for the Dodgers who made Jewish history when he refused to play on Yom Kippur, was the most famous graduate of my Bensonhurst high school. Indeed, in my neighborhood, the only sin greater than rejecting God was disrespecting the Brooklyn Dodgers. Ever the contrarian, I preferred the New York Giants, and I often made my mother schlep me on the subway all the way to the Polo Grounds, in the northern reaches of Manhattan, to watch my favorite team.

Most of our heroes, however, had names like Albert Einstein, Louis Brandeis, George Gershwin, and Leonard Bernstein. Famous Jewish scientists, jurists, and artists made up our communal pantheon. We took pride in their accomplishments. And in a way, their accomplishments were our own.

Indeed, one of the clearest signs of the dwindling fire of Jewish pride in our time is the marked absence of Jewish heroes in our world. It's not that Jews aren't achieving incredible success in politics, business, media, science, or the arts. It's that we have grown so accustomed to their success, and have lost the feeling that their success really means something to us personally, that we can no longer really put our finger on almost anyone to hold up as exemplary *as* Jews. We lack Jewish heroes—and without a distinct sense of Jewish heroism, there can be no Jewish pride.

I WAS FIVE OR SIX years old when the refugees started coming to Bensonhurst. Thousands of them, with bluish numbers tattooed on their forearms and a ghostly look in their eyes. They spoke mainly Yiddish and other European languages. They were poor and needed jobs and places to live. But they had an immense impact on my sense of what it meant to be a Jew.

The refugees brought home to me the reality of the Holocaust in a way that movies and exhibits never could. Each of these Jews was a uniquely broken shell carrying memories—a destroyed village, murdered loved ones, horrific images of concentration camps— that could never be erased. My whole generation felt the heat of the ovens on our necks through the survivors in our midst.

For me and many others, however, they also signified something else: the weakness of religion and the failure of faith. Where had

God been during the Holocaust? He had promised to make the Jews "as plentiful as the sands of the sea and the stars in Heaven." But he had apparently neglected to tell Hitler. In the face of this unmitigated horror, many of us struggled with the problem of how to believe in a God who had abandoned the Jews to their fate. In what way could they have possibly deserved it? What kind of God would allow that to happen?

By the time I was a teenager, my turn toward atheism was complete. I respected religious people, and in some ways, I admired and even envied their profound and joyful spirituality. But I couldn't accept the core premise on which it was all based.

Two months before I turned sixteen, I made a point of eating a meal on Yom Kippur, the Jewish day of fasting and atonement. What's more, I did it publicly, in front of my scandalized mother. It wasn't enough to reject the idea of God in my mind. I had to show the world that I was no longer on board.

At the same time, I was still proud to be a Jew. My Jewish identity simply had no need for, or dependence on, religion. In this regard, I turned out to be part of a larger trend. Like many other American Jews, my identity sharply diverged from my religious beliefs. And while I have maintained a healthy sense of pride in being Jewish, it has nothing to do with religion.

More and more Jews today are not Jews of faith. These include what some sociologists call "Jews of no religion," but also many Jews who in practice feel much more strongly about their Jewish ethnicity, in a secular-cultural way, than they do about God or religion. Even those who do attend synagogues often see religion as less important than other aspects of Jewish identity. Today, more than half of American Jews see religion as not very important in their lives.

Does this mean they lack a strong Jewish identity? Not necessarily. The problem is that for most of these Jews a strong ethnic

and cultural identity doesn't transfer easily to the next generation. They are often at a loss to explain to their kids why Jewish
education, communal involvement, or marrying another Jew is
important. Recent studies suggest that while Orthodoxy is mostly
holding steady, non-Orthodox Jews are moving inexorably toward
a post-religious Jewish identity. I prefer to call it "secular" Judaism.

What we can do with that secular Jewish identity—how we can
support it, deepen it, and, most importantly, transmit it to the next
generation—has been the main focus of my philanthropic work.
And nothing supports this secular Jewish identity more clearly and
directly than a healthy pride in being Jewish.

Of course, the kind of Jewish pride I grew up with was the
product of many factors and influences that no longer exist today.
We are no longer an immigrant community packed into dense
urban neighborhoods, working and socializing mainly with each
other and reveling in the successes of our fellow Jews. We also no
longer have the same obstacles to social and professional success
and no longer face the existential threats and collective traumas
that hovered over Jewish life back then.

At the same time, I am convinced that the central elements of
pride—caring about other Jews, knowledge of our history, commitment to education and achievement, and simple joy in being
Jewish—can be kindled into a powerful secular Jewish identity
that can be passed to the next generation. We just need to decide
that we want it.

As I've said, my father wasn't around very much, but when he
did show up he had an outsized impact. For example, at my bar
mitzvah, he gave me $5,300 worth of stock. Even today, that's a

large gift for a thirteen-year-old. Back then, it was a fortune. Not surprisingly, it made me intensely curious about stocks, and by the time I was sixteen I had become consumed with the goal of mastering the markets.

I worked hard in high school and finished at the age of sixteen. I was ready for college and had planned on enrolling in Bernard Baruch School of Business at City College. Not only was it named after a renowned Jewish financier, but it was also free of charge.

Then my father invited me out to dinner at a place on the Upper West Side called Mrs. J's Sacred Cow, known for its prime rib and steaks and also for its waiters who aspired to sing and act on Broadway. As we were finishing up, he asked me where I was planning to go to college. When I told him, he looked down and shook his head.

"I don't think you should go there," he said.

"Well, where should I go?"

"You should go—" and then he paused, as if to search his mind for a fleeting fact, and then finally caught it: "You should go to the Wharton School at the University of Pennsylvania."

Wharton had not even been on my radar. Not only was it in Philadelphia, which seemed like a different planet, but it was also unthinkably expensive.

But he told me that if I got accepted, he would cover the costs. And after submitting a last-minute application, I got in. Soon I found myself on a train to Philadelphia, unexpectedly setting off on a new path.

While there were plenty of other Jewish students at Wharton, I wasn't quite like them. My background was humbler than theirs. They were more sophisticated and seemed to know instinctively how to comport themselves at an Ivy League school. They knew how to dress, how to talk, and other basic habits that took me two full years to figure out. Nevertheless, I was an excellent student and finished my degree in three years.

After graduating, I returned to New York and landed a job at Calvin Bullock, Ltd., an old-school Manhattan investment firm where almost everyone wore custom-made suits and finished work at 5:30 p.m.—and where the clients felt satisfied with modest returns and a genteel atmosphere. The lobby was adorned with a model of a grand old sailing vessel as its centerpiece. The nautical theme was everywhere, and it was central to their image. Like a good captain, Calvin Bullock would steward your money, with a steady hand, through whatever storms might come.

I was the only Jew at Calvin Bullock. They probably didn't realize it when they hired me. Steinhardt ("hard stone" in German) is not an obviously Jewish name. The firm hosted an annual gala for staff and top investors, and every year Hugh Bullock, the son of the firm's founder, gave the same speech, describing it as "a firm of Christian gentlemen, where like attracts like."

At a certain point, I had made enough of a mark for Hugh Bullock to notice me, and he was surprised to learn that I was Jewish. At the next year's dinner, as he gave the speech, his eyes locked on mine, and he deliberately skipped the word "Christian." "A firm of gentlemen," he said, "where like attracts like."

Today, this might be seen as an expression of WASP anti-Semitism. It's hard to imagine a CEO today so blithely excluding people of other faiths. But I didn't see it that way. Instead, I felt immensely proud that I, a Jew from Bensonhurst, had used my skills to work my way into the upper echelons of Protestant society. I felt like I'd made it in America.

I left the firm in 1961, at the age of twenty, when I was drafted into the U.S. Army. I spent six months on active duty at Fort Dix in southern New Jersey and, later, six years in the Army reserves.

The following summer, in 1962, I took a trip to Europe with a couple of friends touring France, Italy, and Greece. Naturally, I was amazed by the beauty, history, and grandeur of Western civilization.

And then, at a moment when our climb up to the Parthenon in Athens seemed to make the whole trip feel complete, I decided to break away and spend two weeks in Israel by myself. My life would never be the same.

THE ESTABLISHMENT OF ISRAEL IN 1948 was a pivotal moment in my young life. In the wake of the Holocaust, this was our people's first real miracle. Like Jews all over the world, the Jews of Benson-hurst did their best to follow the news coming out of the Middle East, and as I grew older, I would read the weekly *Jerusalem Post*, International Edition, from cover to cover. Throughout the years of my youth, I internalized the new state's successes, its failures, and its fears as if they were my own.

Though I hardly felt it at the time, not all Jews reacted to the founding of Israel the way we did in Bensonhurst. Some Orthodox groups saw the secular and political foundations of Zionism as a threat to their religious principles. This attitude persists today among some ultra-Orthodox Jews, many of whom view Zionism as a secular distraction from their faith or even a form of idolatry.

But opposition came from the other end of the religious spec-trum as well. Decades earlier, the Reform movement had set the tone for many non-Orthodox Jews in their Pittsburgh Platform of 1885: "We consider ourselves no longer a nation, but a religious community, and therefore expect [no] return to Palestine." Although an increasing number of Reform rabbis publicly embraced Zionism in the early twentieth century—most famously Stephen Wise and

Abba Hillel Silver—opposition to Jewish statehood remained the movement's official doctrine until 1937. After 1948 this attitude changed decisively, but the discomfort with Zionism as a proud national movement is sometimes felt in certain quarters even today.

Nor was Jewish opposition to Zionism limited to religious groups. A certain set of elite American Jews also expressed ambivalence about the notion of a Jewish state. The publisher of the *New York Times*, Arthur Hays Sulzberger, had for decades been an anti-Zionist Jew. Unlike most Reform Jews, however, Sulzberger continued to oppose Zionism even *after* the Holocaust and blamed the murder of European Jews, at least in part, on the Zionists' demand for statehood. "It is my judgment," Sulzberger said in 1946, "that thousands dead might now be alive [if] the Zionists [had put] less emphasis on statehood."[1] Indeed, much has been written about an implicit anti-Israel bias prevailing at the *Times* over many decades, as ownership has been handed down within the family. As we shall see, I've certainly felt an undercurrent of hostility from that august paper, directed both at me personally and at some of the programs I've helped create.

Sulzberger was not alone. Indeed, his outlook was typical of a certain elite set of assimilated American Jews who had made it in America and didn't want to be accused of dual loyalty. For many influential Jews, being Jewish wasn't about supporting the creation of a different country on foreign soil. For them, the mission of Jews was to be a successful class, dedicating themselves to living an ethical life, and making America a better place, not just for Jews but for others as well. In 1942, in the middle of the Holocaust, a small

---

1 Rafael Medoff, "*New York Times* Column on Anti-Zionism a Reminder of its Own Publisher's Past," *The Algemeiner* (February 18, 2014), http://www.algemeiner.com /2014/02/18/new-york-times-column-on-anti-zionism-a-reminder-of-its-own-publisher%E2%80%99s-past/.

but outspoken group called the American Council for Judaism was founded, declaring that Zionism "tends to confuse our fellowmen about our place and function in society and diverts our own attention from our historic role to live as a religious community wherever we may dwell."

Most Jews, however, believed that Zionism embodied a raw heroic spirit that had to be supported—or, at a minimum, they identified the need for a refuge from persecution that only a sovereign homeland could offer. Supreme Court Justice Louis Brandeis, one of our great heroes, embraced Zionism in the 1910s and, along with some other Jewish leaders, made it acceptable for mainstream Jews to support it. By the time I was growing up, a clear majority of Jews in America had adopted this view.

I was always baffled by Jews who insisted we were merely a community of faith. After all, to define being Jewish this way would mean that I, as an atheist, would not be included—and neither would a large proportion of American Jews today. On the contrary, I knew with all my being that I was part of a people and proud of it. A people that had a right to fight for themselves and to live in their homeland, with or without God's help.

PEOPLE WHO VISIT ISRAEL TODAY can have little conception of what the country was like in its early years. At the time of my first visit in 1962, Israel was a poor country that had until quite recently been obliged to ration basic foods. It was surrounded by large Arab armies that were still smarting from military humiliations in 1948 and 1956 and were just waiting for the right time to invade again.

Everything felt sloppy and provisional. The cities were full of litter, with groaning Mercedes-Benz buses, received as part of the reparations package from Germany, belching black diesel smoke. The country had more than tripled its population in a decade and a half, and the difficulty of absorbing so many penniless immigrants weighed on everything. Most of them had come from Arabic-speaking countries like Morocco, Algeria, Libya, Syria, and Iraq, where the culture was completely different from that of the mostly European Jews who had founded the country.

The climate was harsh and uncooperative as well. Desert winds blew dry heat from the south and east, the rains fell only in winter, and water was a scarce resource. As a budding investor, I also appraised the country somewhat unfavorably. The economy was mostly controlled by the state, per the socialist leanings of its founders, so there weren't a lot of foreigners lining up to invest in private companies. The culture, too, seemed strange. Hebrew was an alien language to me, as it was to most of the Arabic- and Yiddish-speaking newcomers.

Still, I could sense among the citizens of this young nation an inner strength and vibrancy, a confident boldness expressed in a living language that was completely different from the calcified Hebrew of the prayers I had heard at Congregation Bnai Isaac.

As I traveled around the country, mostly by bus, I managed to find other young people who spoke English and spent some time with them. I met a group of young French Jews and strained my high school French to converse with them.

After my visit to the kibbutz, I caught a ride with someone, and we stopped for gas outside of Beit She'an, a steamy development town housing immigrants from North Africa and best known for its archaeological treasures. I walked into a little convenience store at the gas station. At the time, you couldn't get American products like Coca-Cola because the Arab states would boycott any international company doing business in Israel. So everything was locally made, and it wasn't very good. I tentatively approached the shop-keeper, a redhead like myself who also spoke some English. We began chatting.

"What happens," I said, "when all those Arab armies decide to invade Israel, again, like they did in 1948?"

He took a drag on his cigarette and looked at me grimly. "We will cut their heads off," he deadpanned. "We will kill them. They won't stand a chance."

I had never heard a Jew speak that way. And in the face of legitimate, existential fears with the Holocaust being a recent memory, hearing this kind of talk sent a jolt of respect up my spine. We'd spent centuries running away from our enemies. But this guy wasn't going anywhere.

Not long afterward, I saw a deeply moving film called *Hill 24 Doesn't Answer*. It was Israel's first feature film, released in 1955, about a group of foreign-born Jews who come to Israel to fight in the War of Independence. By the end of the movie, all the main characters have died defending a hill overlooking the road to Jerusalem.

I was struck by the courage and commitment of Jews who had left behind everything they knew in their home countries, settled in a harsh and alien land, learned a new language, and embraced the obligation to defend themselves without relying on anyone else.

In Brooklyn, some Jews liked to talk tough. In Israel, they were the real deal.

These experiences left a major impression on me. I soon became preoccupied with the idea of dying a heroic death. I would have dreams at night in which I battled against Arab marauders. I always lost. But a heroic death, I felt, would give my life a greater meaning totally unlike the track it was on.

On that trip, and others that followed, I saw many different sides of what the Zionists were accomplishing in Israel. Despite the challenges of fending off military threats and bringing together Jews from so many countries in a state of ongoing economic crisis, there was also a profound joy, a romantic sense that people were willing to sacrifice—to struggle, overcome, and live a mutually supportive Jewish life in a full and open way—that was foreign to me and most other American Jews. Israelis knew how to dance and sing and celebrate life with an intensity I had not seen outside the Orthodox community of Bensonhurst. They possessed a powerful spirit that hid nothing and apologized to no one.

Today we take Israel's success and survival for granted. Back then, it was stunning to encounter these Israeli Jews doing their own construction, building roads and schools, farms and factories, and a uniquely Jewish army. Some of what I saw, like the kibbutz, was driven by a creative, universal vision of how humans could live differently. But for much of Israel, it was just about Jews coming together to live a thoroughly Jewish national life.

It was as if all the centuries of Jewish creativity and excellence, which in America and Europe had been expressed through science and the arts as well as law, business, and finance, were being fermented in a country-sized petri dish and channeled into every aspect of human existence.

Israel, I began to realize, was nothing less than *a living Jewish ideal*: intense, proud, joyful, comprehensive, and full of fire. The contrast with Jewish communal life in America could not have been more striking.

After I returned to New York I landed my next job at Loeb, Rhoades & Co., a venerable Jewish investment bank whose atmosphere was worlds apart from what I'd seen at Calvin Bullock.

We worked much longer hours, covering multiple markets, and constantly brainstormed new investment strategies to make bolder bets and achieve greater returns. I was earning a lot more, working with incredibly sharp and creative people, and making some very good friends.

This was the dawn of the age of hedge funds. Investors had discovered they could do extremely well through an aggressive approach that employed risky bets, sometimes offsetting each other, to produce consistently higher returns. It turned out I was very good at it, and by the spring of 1967, I and a few friends had decided to launch our own fund. We secured a modest office at 67 Beaver Street, near Wall Street, and started with $7.7 million in capital. I was twenty-six years old and already making more money than I had ever imagined.

Something happened, however, that delayed the launch of Steinhardt, Fine, Berkowitz & Company by a month.

Egypt, led by the Soviet-backed nationalist Gamal Abdel Nasser, had forged an alliance with Jordan and Syria that was openly threatening to invade and destroy Israel. War was in the air, and deep anxiety could be seen on the face of almost every Jew I knew. For several harrowing weeks in May 1967, the possibility of a second Holocaust was on everyone's mind. Trenches were dug in Tel Aviv to accommodate the mass graves they were expecting to need. The rhetoric of the Arab leaders was all about Jewish blood. Nasser ordered the evacuation of U.N. peacekeeping forces from the Sinai Peninsula and, in a clear act of war, closed the Straits of Tiran, Israel's economic lifeline to its Red Sea port in Eilat.

The war finally broke out on June 5, and American Jews were left in the dark for several unbearably long days as to what was really happening. The Arab governments were claiming victory, but Israel remained silent as its air and ground forces devastated the Arab armies. We had no idea, however, and feared Israel's end was near.

I went to a rally of support near the U.N. building. Rabbi Shlomo Carlebach, a bearded Orthodox hippie famously known as "the singing rabbi," was amped up with his acoustic guitar on a flatbed truck between First and Second Avenues. The songs were taken from classical Jewish texts and Hasidic sayings, but there was something deeply resonant about them. His serene baritone wasn't operatic like the cantors in the synagogues. It was folksy, not always on pitch, and somehow pulled me into a trance. I found myself staring, along with everybody else, into an eternal Jewish campfire.

At a certain point, he abruptly stopped and said, "The only song appropriate to sing now is the song for the dead soldiers in Israel." And then he began to chant the traditional Jewish prayer for the dead—"El Malei Rachamim," "O God, full of mercy." As he sang, he began to cry. And his cries reverberated among the buildings of the East Side of Manhattan.

I spoke with him afterward. We had known each other for a few years, and he wanted my help in getting on a plane to Israel to support the troops. I was more than happy to pay for it, but what I really wanted was to go myself. How could I not? We didn't yet know if Israel would survive, but if we were headed for catastrophe, I wanted to be there.

It was hard to book a flight—turns out I wasn't the only Jew who felt as I did—and by the time I found one, the war was already over.

THE SIX-DAY WAR ENDED WITH a monumental victory that few of us believed possible. It was a moment of pride in being a Jew unlike anything in my life, before or since. Things changed for

American Jews, especially in New York. Non-Jews began to see us through the lens of Israel's victory. It is deeply ingrained in human nature: People respect a winner. The Jews had shown an ability to fight that resonated with many Americans.

It also changed how many Jews saw themselves. Men who would never have worn a *yarmulke* in public started doing it. Men and women alike started wearing necklaces with a Jewish star. The idea of a modern Hebrew warrior captured the American imagination. A photo of an Israeli soldier taking a swim in the Suez Canal with a rifle in his hand and a toothy Jewish grin appeared on the cover of *Life* magazine.

Although many Jews would not have agreed at the time, to me, it seemed that within non-Orthodox American Jewry, below the surface, there were two clear, opposing forces, and every Jew would ultimately have to choose between them.

One force, born of the fear of persecution and social rejection that we had faced for centuries, pushed Jews to downplay their ethnic heritage and minimize their difference. Much of American Jewish life had been built on this tacit assumption, and a great many Jews, it seemed, cared more about how to make it in America than how to make sure their children remained committed Jews.

Was it working? The more Jews became accepted in American society, what would keep them from relinquishing their Jewish identity entirely? Why should parents teach their children to be Jewish, if being "Jewish" was nothing more than an obstacle or a historical vestige?

Intuitively, I never liked the idea of hiding who I was. It struck me as deeply unhealthy. I also knew that if Jews continued to feel this way, then America would, within a generation or two, become the place where millions of Jews simply disappeared.

The second force, which I saw as embodied in the Zionist movement, encouraged secular Jews to embrace our uniqueness and wear it with pride—just as many Orthodox, and especially ultra-Orthodox, Jews did. The basic human need for self-respect, honor, and physical strength wasn't just true for individuals—communities and nations needed them too. The more Israel succeeded, the more you could see Jews around the world feeling the pull of pride.

Of course, "Zionism" and "assimilationism" are imprecise, and in some sense unfair, labels for these two forces. On the level of political and ideological commitments, the vast majority of non-Orthodox Jews were, by this time, avowed Zionists. The leaders of the community described themselves as proud Jews who supported Israel. Many synagogues put up an Israeli flag alongside an American one.

Yet beneath the surface, at a level I would call spiritual, I felt like this fight was still raging, and that it wasn't going well. A great many nominally pro-Israel leaders and institutions behaved in ways that suggested they still cared a lot more about gaining acceptance in America than defending Jewish honor or ensuring that the next generation would remain committed to their identity. It would be a long time before studies would prove me right, but it struck me that whether you looked at the quality of Jewish schools, the boredom triggered by our houses of worship, the increasing rate of intermarriages, the general lack of Jewish knowledge, or the insistence on trying not to stick out too much in American life—it all felt like Jewish pride was in retreat, and we would pay a heavy price in the next generation.

I understood that in America, assimilation was in its essence a force of nature, whereas pride had to be actively cultivated and defended—and the more accepting America became of its Jews, the more powerful would be the forces that Jewish pride would have to array itself against.

Why did I associate Jewish pride with Zionism? Part of it was instinctive—my experience in visiting Israel and meeting Israelis had triggered a sense that the very essence of Zionism had something to do with the assertion of Jewish pride. And as I learned more, I discovered that my instinct was right. Zionism had indeed started out, even before Theodor Herzl turned it into a political movement in the 1890s, as a spiritual critique of what Diaspora life had done to the Jews of Europe, a rebuttal to the centuries-long evisceration of the Jewish spirit. For decades, well into the twentieth century, Zionist thinkers argued about how to best instill a defiant pride in the Jewish soul—whether through farming, or warfare, or the Hebrew language, or the arts, or sovereign statehood.

The truth is, every Jew—whether Orthodox or secular, Diaspora or Israeli—makes choices about how "Jewish" their lives will be. The battle rages in all of us. I know some people will argue that because I'm a secular Jew living in America and because I've invested my best energies in reaching unengaged Jews without trying to get them to be observant or to make *aliyah*, I actually am just another highly assimilated Jew who is part of the force of assimilation. For decades, many Zionists called for the "negation of the Diaspora," claiming that Jewish pride was fundamentally impossible without actually living in our sovereign homeland.

I have never believed that to be true. But I do think that as long as we remain in the Diaspora, assimilation will act on us like the force of gravity and pride will be something akin to learning how to fly. It won't happen on its own. It will require investment, training, technology, and above all the will to be Jewish and to ensure the commitment of our children.

Pride, in other words, is not just where you are on the map—it's also about where you're going. It's a spiritual vector, a force within you that intuitively influences decisions you make throughout your life.

In America of the 1960s, Zionist-style pride and assimilationist-style self-effacement became, in my mind, two forces locked in a battle for the soul of non-Orthodox Jews. The following year, these forces came to a head at a most unexpected moment in my life—on the day of my wedding.

I met Judy Abrams soon after launching my hedge fund. She had come from Scranton, Pennsylvania, to New York City, and, as the fortuitous result of a skiing accident in which she sprained her ankle, she was unable to take the subway downtown to City Hall where she worked. Through her roommate, a mutual friend, she asked to join my carpool. So every morning, I'd leave my apartment on East 79th Street, pick her up in my navy blue Plymouth Fury convertible at her place on York Avenue, and, along with a few other friends, we'd head downtown.

Once her ankle healed, Judy and I started taking long walks and talking into the night. Within months, we were engaged.

But the clash between our backgrounds could not have been greater. Judy's father had done well with his business supplying drugstore products to supermarkets, and he ultimately sold it to A&P. He was now a leader of the Jewish community in Scranton. Judy's mother insisted on hosting the wedding at the Glen Oak Country Club, not far from their home.

The wedding was held on April 28, 1968. Here I was, with an entourage of my closest friends from Bensonhurst and Penn, along with my best friend from the army, a tough Irish kid named Joe Flaherty, as my groomsmen. We had dressed ourselves up as best we could but, compared to Judy's family and their guests, we looked like a gang of ruffians who had wandered in off the street.

Sparing no expense, Judy's mom had hired one of the most famous bands in America, the Lester Lanin Orchestra. Lanin, born to a family of Russian-Jewish immigrants, had performed with his band at presidential inaugural balls in Washington and the Waldorf Astoria's Starlight Roof in New York. They were a go-to for entertaining upper-crust WASPs along the East Coast, and especially on the Upper East Side of Manhattan. There was perhaps nobody more symbolic of the successful assimilated Jew than Lester Lanin.

My father, however, had his own ideas. After Lanin's orchestra had been playing all kinds of trendy dance music, he walked over to the bandleader and barked at him, "Hey, play some Jewish music."

The band leader said that he had been given explicit instructions *not* to play Jewish music.

So my father did what he usually did, which was to pull out a hundred-dollar bill and try to hand it to him. "Now play some Jewish music," he said. But the band leader refused to take the money.

At that point, Judy's mother came over, quickly sized up the problem, and turned to face my father. "I'm in charge of this wedding, Mr. Steinhardt, and there will be no Jewish music. Now that's that."

As if to distill this cosmic clash into a single image, consider that our wedding was officiated by two rabbis: The local Conservative rabbi revered by Judy's mother and their community—and Shlomo Carlebach. Carlebach, with his crazy beard and his guitar, sang in a way that gripped the younger people who flocked around him, piercing them with an unalloyed joy that seemed to pour directly from centuries of Jewish feeling.

Meanwhile, the older guests from Scranton's Jewish elite looked on with acute discomfort.

Judy and I made a home in Manhattan, and I built my career. We had three children: David, born in 1969; Daniel, in 1971; and Sara, in 1975. I asked Judy to find an apartment, and I gave her a list of specific things we preferred, including a view of Central Park. But she was new to the city and unfamiliar with the unwritten rules of affluent life in Manhattan at the time. She found something perfect for us, which happened to be on 97th Street and Fifth Avenue, one block north of the invisible border that ran along 96th Street separating the fashionable Upper East Side from the outskirts of Spanish Harlem. I didn't care. We bought it anyway, and life was good.

Like other affluent Jews, I was invited to take part in Jewish philanthropic activities. I didn't mind making donations. My father, whenever he had money, had often given it away to people in need. I had also begun to feel a powerful sense of responsibility for Jews less fortunate than myself. Childhood memories of the refugees in Bensonhurst, which had been the impetus for my atheism, now took on a different meaning. Jewish life, I understood, was precious.

My problem had to do with Jewish organizations. By all appearances, they seemed to care more about raising money than making sure it was put to good use. I attended lavish dinners where honors were bestowed and big donors were publicly praised, with dollar amounts talked about openly—and it struck me as grotesque. I had been taught that the Jewish tradition of *tzedakah*, or charity, was best done anonymously. Yet here was a whole world where people seemed to wear their checkbooks on their sleeves.

The problem didn't end there. The programs being run by these organizations seemed lifeless. There didn't seem to be very much that was bold, creative, or vibrant coming out of the hundreds of federations, synagogue-based schools, and national organizations. Nothing that might convince young Jews to remain Jewish, let alone make them feel proud of it.

I had come from a demanding business world where we measured success by results, calculated to the penny. You knew exactly what returns you were making for your clients, how well your investments did, and how much money you made. If you didn't perform, you were out.

In the world of Jewish organizations, to my astonishment, nobody seemed to care about performance. It didn't matter whether you ran a good or bad school, or whether the Jewish life these organizations produced was rich and fertile or dry and dull. Instead, everybody seemed to be measured by how much money they gave or raised. Even salaries for organizational leaders were set not by the impact they made but by their fundraising prowess. The incentives were all wrong.

The upshot was that while Jewish donors were being piled high with honors, and hundreds of millions of dollars were poured into organizations with honorable-sounding goals, the situation of American Jews did not seem to be improving.

Back then, we didn't have clear statistics about assimilation. That would come later. What seemed clear to me, though, was that outside of the Orthodox world, Jewish life was becoming so thoroughly "Americanized" that younger Jews were discarding their identity as soon as it was practical to do so.

I decided I didn't want anything to do with it.

Meanwhile, I continued to be drawn to Israeli Jews who filled me with a sense of hope and admiration. Judy and I visited frequently, at least once a year every year of our married life, and I met many different Israelis. We went there on our honeymoon and stayed in an Arab-owned hotel in the newly liberated part of Jerusalem for Israel's Independence Day, or Yom Ha'atzmaut, celebrations.

It was the first time the holiday was celebrated in the united capital city, and the exuberance was intoxicating. Judy and I found ourselves dancing in the streets with so many other Israelis, holding hands in traditional Israeli circle dances, loudspeakers blaring, flags waving, a celebration that continued all across the city.

These Jews were infused with a ferocious joy that established American Jewry could scarcely imagine. The contrast between the two became more striking to me, and increasingly unnerving, after I went back to New York. And as my career took off, I started to feel a growing sense of unease.

THIS MAY SOUND A LITTLE strange, but my career in finance was never driven by a desire to get rich. I was more like a major league ballplayer: Trading was my sport, returns were my win-loss column, and I was determined to become nothing less than the best money manager on earth. I loved the game.

At least, I loved winning. I hated losing. My worst days were when I had made a bad bet and failed my clients. Nothing devastated me as much as losing. But it was a great game, and I was playing in the major leagues.

However, at some point in my late thirties, I started to feel that this was not everything I wanted from life. Yes, I had succeeded, but I had done nothing particularly meaningful. Who were my heroes? Not other money managers. Indeed, many of the Jews I knew on Wall Street behaved in ways I did not find especially admirable. My

34

heroes were people like Albert Einstein and David Ben-Gurion—people who had made a major contribution to the world and the Jewish people.

What was missing from my life, amid the endless tally of wins and losses, was a sense of anything truly admirable, of greatness, of having any enduring legacy for the benefit of my people or of the world. Nothing I had accomplished made me feel the least bit *heroic* in my own eyes.

I thought about quitting entirely, but I didn't have much of a clue as to what I would do. So in the fall of 1978, I decided to pull back and take a year off, starting with a few months in Israel.

I did know that I wanted to help build up the Jewish state by investing in its industries. I met a real estate developer named Lihu Veisser, a quiet, lumbering giant of a man whose fervent Zionism was as axiomatic for him as my Jewish identity was for me. He lived in Ashkelon along the southern coast, and he was consumed with a single problem: How to provide jobs for the hundreds of thousands of working-class Jews who had arrived from Northern Africa and especially Morocco in the 1950s and 1960s.

Lihu enlisted me into his project to create industrial parks that would provide the infrastructure for companies to locate themselves in southern development towns like Kiryat Gat, Netivot, and Ofakim. These weren't fancy office buildings with manicured lawns, but they provided exactly the right kind of spaces for the factories and warehouses these companies needed. These projects ended up creating thousands of jobs for local, mostly North African immigrant, residents.

It was through Lihu that I came to understand something few American Jews were aware of at the time: That unlike the United States, where the vast majority of Jews were descended from Yiddish- and German-speaking Europeans, Israel had absorbed so many Jews from non-European countries, and especially Muslim countries, that it offered a much more diverse representation of the Jewish people as a whole. I felt a personal connection to these Sephardic or "Mizrachi" Jews, as to a long-lost brother: I didn't really know them, but I nonetheless loved them as my own, and I wanted to help them where I could.

I also got to know a banker named Shimon Topor, who became my guide for investing in Israeli companies. Later I started investing in the films of Amos Kollek, the son of Jerusalem's legendary mayor, Teddy Kollek. Amos's films won critical acclaim but, on the whole, they were not commercially successful.

I first met Teddy Kollek during the honeymoon trip Judy and I took in 1968. But I got to know him well during my sabbatical in Israel a decade later. He wasn't especially warm. Educated in Vienna, Kollek was direct, intelligent, moderately tall and overweight, and always wore a sports jacket in a country known for its informality. If he saw people picking any of the flowers he'd had planted in the city, he would scream—"Don't pick the flowers! Jerusalem has to be beautiful!"

Not all of my Israeli investments made money, and some of them would have made me a lot more if I had stayed in them longer. But by helping to develop Israeli industries, I felt that I was doing something genuinely Zionist while other American Jews were planting trees through the Jewish National Fund. Israel may or may not have needed trees, and I had nothing against planting more. But the effort to build an economy that could sustain the Jewish homeland was central to what I saw as the true spirit of Zionism.

During that sabbatical year, I also bought a wonderful property on sixteen acres in Bedford, New York, north of the city in Westchester County. It had a stream right behind the house. I discovered a passion for growing plants and raising animals, and I began learning about horticulture and zoology. I built a nature reserve, a menagerie of flora and fauna that gives me immense pleasure to this day.

I joined the prestigious Century Country Club in Purchase, New York, which had been founded by elite German Jews and included members from some of the most famous assimilated Jewish banking families. For a long time, this was the apex of Jewish high society of a certain kind, one that set its eyes on complete "Americanization" as a kind of holy grail.

I also explored a range of hobbies, from yoga and piano lessons to Torah study. I was still an avowed atheist. But as a Jew, I felt a need to deepen my Jewish knowledge, and I felt a strange attraction to the spirit embedded in our ancient texts, which I studied, using my minimal childhood Hebrew education, with Shlomo Carlebach's twin brother Eli.

THROUGHOUT THE MONTHS OF MY sabbatical, my mind swept over everything I had seen and felt and done with my life to this point. What was it that kept pulling me back to Israel? I marveled at the difference between the vigorous, virile world that Israelis had created and the ossified Jewish world I saw around me in America. But what did it mean?

The whole point of life, its day-to-day essence, seemed different in Israel. It wasn't just the military self-reliance that had struck me on my first visit to Israel when I was handed the Uzi and told to stand guard by the river. Every time I landed at Ben-Gurion Airport, I felt like Judy Garland alighting in the Land of Oz, where suddenly a black-and-white vista becomes filled with Technicolor.

Jewish life in America struck me as intolerably gray—the mundane social goals, the droning temple services, and dreary Hebrew school experience. We American Jews had set as our supreme aim to gain acceptance, success, and wealth in the American context. And to a large degree, we had succeeded.

Israelis, in contrast, were relatively poor, imperiled, inefficient, and frankly had many wrong ideas, especially about capitalism and economic policy. But on the other hand, they were alive. They held a secret close to their hearts that American Jews seemed oblivious to.

Israelis, it seemed, possessed a profound will to live. Not just to survive individually and collectively, but to embrace lofty goals and aspirations, to change history every day, and to enjoy every moment of it without letting the traumas of war and poverty get in the way. They invented kibbutzim to prove to the world that there was a better way to live. They reignited the Hebrew language and built a sovereign state to prove to the world that there was a better way to be a Jew. They reclaimed the biblical landscape and built a thriving modern society just to prove it was possible. Everywhere you turned, Israelis were revolutionizing something—agriculture, water use, the military, immigrant absorption, and on and on. Of course, I had no idea how many further revolutions Israelis would create in the decades ahead, as their scientific and technological abilities took off.

What kind of profound confidence was required to live in a constant state of change and risk-taking? To reinvent everything again and again, not just out of fear but also out of passion? Israel was, already in the 1970s, a magnet for Jews from around the world, either to live or to visit. Certainly, Jews in distress saw it as a refuge and the promise of a better life. But there was more to it than that. Seeing the Star of David on the national flag, having an army of one's own, a land of one's own, and a government and language and school system, in short having a sense of Jewish *sovereignty*—all this made life different in ways that Jews in the Diaspora had never really understood and didn't even realize they might want or need.

All of these thoughts pointed me to a single word: pride. It wasn't just about saying we were "proud to be Jewish." It was an unspoken dignity, an absolute determination to live a Jewish life without compromise, to harness some inner Jewish excellence—the dynamic, intellectual, creative, funny, and mutually caring qualities we often saw in ourselves—and to amplify it a thousandfold without having to worry about how the non-Jewish world might react. David Ben-Gurion put it in words that you could hardly imagine being said by a non-Orthodox leader in the Diaspora: "It matters not what the *goyim* think, but what the Jews do."

To be clear, my goal was not to become Israeli myself. I wouldn't presume to try and, anyway, that was not what I was looking for. I never had any serious intention of moving to Israel, though I have plenty of respect for those who do.

I felt about Israelis much the way I felt about the Orthodox Jews I had met: I admired them, I respected them, I knew I could never *be* one of them, but they had something that secular Jewish life in America was missing. A certainty of purpose, an inner confidence in one's Jewishness, that acted as a prism through which all of life was interpreted and fashioned.

But there was one major difference between the Zionists and the Orthodox, which seemed to get to the heart of my inquiry. Orthodoxy at its core was all about preservation. Their goal was to build a vast constellation of rules and rituals aimed at holding tight to an ancient message and an ancient approach to life. And in this, they appeared to be very successful. (I would later discover, through countless attempts to bring together Orthodox and secular leaders in creating schools or other projects, just how intractable were the barriers they had set up for themselves.)

Zionists, on the other hand, were all about taking this ancient truth and moving it forward. They shared the belief in *progress* that had defined secular Jews ever since their emancipation in the European Enlightenment. In this view, the most important innovation of Judaism is the belief that history is not, as the pagans believed, an endless cycle of conflict and struggle. It is, rather, linear. It moves forward toward a better future. That's why the secular Jews of Europe and America became enamored with rationalism and science in the nineteenth century, socialism in the early twentieth, and progressivism and human rights in the late twentieth. The idea that the world needed to move toward a better age for all humanity resonated deeply with most secular Jews—including me.

In Israel, I saw this idea being applied with a ferocity, creativity, and determination that went beyond anything I had seen. It was as though this secular Jewish belief in possibility and progress had somehow been injected into the drinking water of a whole nation.

But what struck me even more powerfully was that these Jews had mostly come from the same shtetls and towns and shared the same underlying old-world culture and assumptions as did their American Jewish cousins. The unique Israeli edge was therefore something that American Jews should theoretically be able to tap into. What could be done, I wondered, to infuse Diaspora life with some of that spirit?

This simple question would come, in my later years, to dictate the course of my life.

I knew that I was a proud Jew, but I didn't know exactly what that meant. For thousands of years, Jews believed they were a "chosen people," but as a committed atheist, I could not accept that.

For me, it was not about being somehow superior or graced with a certain divinity. The humanist in me would never buy into that.

But I was grateful for my identity as a Jew, proud of the quick-thinking, curious, mutually responsible aspects of our character, and fully cognizant of the incredible achievements in science and the arts that we had produced as a result. I also felt a bond with other Jews that may have been forged in centuries of sorrow but was experienced first and foremost as a kind of joy.

My pride as a Jew was certainly sharpened by the historical context in which I grew up. In the wake of the horrors of the twentieth century, from the pogroms to the Holocaust, being Jewish was an act of defiance. Just by living and breathing and calling yourself a Jew, you were defeating all those who had wanted us dead. Yet all those persecutions, all that suffering, would be meaningless if the new generation was willing to let go of its unique Jewish identity in order to blend in and "make it" in America.

I had already "made it" in America, and I was acutely aware of how unfulfilling a goal that had turned out to be. I knew that the meaning of my life could not just be the sum total of my family, my earnings, and my status. If I were going to undertake a task that was somehow more meaningful, even heroic, it would have to involve translating the deep, distilled Jewish spirit I had encountered in Israel into the lives of non-Orthodox, Diaspora Jews.

The term I later settled on to capture all of this in my mind was "Jewish pride." It would become the North Star of my philanthropic career.

I HAD NO IDEA, at this stage, what such a mission might entail. One thing, however, was clear: I was not going to be a major donor to the American Jewish establishment. The donors and professionals involved deserved credit for dedicating their lives to the welfare of fellow Jews. But everything about the world they had built rubbed me the wrong way. Moreover, it seemed that these organizations were failing in their most important purpose: To guarantee the transmission of a healthy sense of pride in being Jewish from one generation to the next.

Military leaders are often criticized for "planning for the last war." Warfare evolves, new weapons and strategies are invented, and if you want to win, you need to anticipate how the next war is going to be fought rather than simply learning from past failures.

Jewish survival is analogous. In the past, it had been about protecting ourselves from violent anti-Semitism or fighting bigotry and social exclusion. To be sure, there was some of that in America. But the real threat wasn't from Nazis or Nasser's armies or the prejudice of WASP institutions. It was from assimilation. And if the central question was how to get younger Jews to remain Jewish in an America that was increasingly willing to accept them—how to get them to *want* to be Jewish—I couldn't see what concrete results these organizations were achieving.

I didn't know it at the time, but I was far from alone. My profound unease was shared by quite a few other philanthropists, many of whom had chosen to keep their thoughts to themselves. And yet, I knew that changing Jewish life in America would require a willingness to publicly criticize our institutions and philanthropic culture.

Some argued then—and argue now—that donors should have relatively little say in what is done with their philanthropic dollars, and that the nonprofit leaders who raise the funds should have the freedom to make spending decisions with minimal input from those who write the checks.

My criticism of this attitude comes from what might be called a capitalistic perspective. Every thousand dollars I deployed in Jewish nonprofits was a thousand dollars I had earned through my own efforts. It represented the time, talent, skill, sweat, and risk that I had undertaken. Jewish institutions, I sometimes felt, tended to act as though their money just appeared out of a magical process called "fundraising," with little respect for what it took to earn it in the first place.

Ultimately, I concluded that if I was going to use the wealth I had earned for the benefit of my people, it would have to be on my own terms.

I SPENT A YEAR TRYING to understand my life and think about my future, and it was a good thing I did. But like a boxer coming out of retirement, I felt an irresistible force pulling me back into the ring.

I returned to the firm in October 1979, armed with a much clearer sense of where I was headed. Meanwhile, in the years that followed, two significant events deepened my focus on Jewish causes.

One was the rise of the movement to free the Jews of the Soviet Union. I had been involved with Soviet Jewry since the early 1970s when I was introduced to Roman Brackman. Heavyset with curly black hair, a broad face, and slitted eyes that turned down when he smiled, Roman had grown up during Stalin's Great Purges and survived three years in the Gulag. Freed after Stalin's death, he left Russia in 1959 for Warsaw where he married his wife Rita and then immigrated to Israel. But they found it too constricting at the time and ended up in New York where I was introduced to him.

Roman was like a character out of a Russian novel. The more I learned about his story—how he led an uprising in a Siberian camp, how he had sought to escape the Soviet Union by trying to walk to the Black Sea and swim to Turkey—the more I was amazed by his courage and that of other dissidents.

Roman wrote books. None of them became bestsellers, but they reflected his contrarian spirit and outsized personality. He detested Jimmy Carter and wrote a book to explain why. He was convinced that Watergate was a hoax and wrote a book about that too. He was, in short, an amazing character, one whose views, for better or worse, were the product of staring down the Soviet regime decades before more famous dissidents like Natan Sharansky or Ida Nudel made it a fashionable cause. His autobiography, *From Hell to Paradise*, tells the story of a heroic Jew, unlike anyone I have ever met.

He and Rita settled in Chappaqua, New York, where he met other Soviet dissidents, and together they plotted the overthrow of the Soviet Union. He built a bunker near Lake George in Upstate New York and tried to convince me to send my kids there to protect them from the coming Armageddon. And yes, he drank vodka and liked to pound his massive fist on the table to emphasize his points.

Under Soviet Communism, more than two million Jews could not live Jewish lives in any meaningful way. Jewish schools and synagogues were either shut down or saturated with KGB agents. The study of Yiddish and Hebrew was banned. Jewish prayer books, shawls, phylacteries, and Torah scrolls were contraband that Western visitors would smuggle in, at significant personal risk. And if the authorities found out you were engaged in "subversive" Jewish activities, you went straight to the Gulag.

You also couldn't leave. Those who applied for exit visas immediately lost their jobs and rights.

Like the sixteenth-century Spanish Jews who pretended to be Catholics, many Soviet Jews tried to preserve their identity in secret. But others did not. A dissident movement, known as refuseniks, vocally opposed the crushing of Jewish freedom. Some of these Jews were executed or sent to the Gulag.

In America, a small number of Jews began working to build public awareness. The first major protest on behalf of Soviet Jewry was held in Madison Square Garden in 1964. This was a grassroots movement led by younger people taking inspiration from the civil rights and anti-war movements. For years, the Jewish establishment evinced no interest in publicly supporting them. In response, these young Jews, through renegade organizations like the Student Struggle for Soviet Jewry and the Jewish Defense League, took to the streets.

My own involvement in this issue was mostly behind the scenes. I worked directly with Roman to help the dissidents, using both money and connections. Later, in the late 1980s, I traveled to Moscow to meet with them. Sharansky, Nudel, and other famous refuseniks became personal friends. All of them saw Roman as a hero.

What I came to realize was that the phenomenal heroism of these Jews was directly connected to the heroic spirit I had seen in Zionism. It also corresponded to the proud, unapologetic affirmation of Jewish identity that I had seen among Orthodox Jews in America.

In time, the American Jewish establishment came around and embraced the movement. Partly as a result of Jewish activism, Congress passed the Jackson-Vanik Amendment in 1974, which restricted trade with countries that didn't allow free emigration. The campaign culminated in a mass rally, Freedom Sunday for Soviet Jews, held on the National Mall in Washington, D.C., on December 6, 1987. A quarter-million people showed up. Peter, Paul and Mary performed. Former refuseniks Yosef Mendelevitch and Natan Sharansky spoke, as did James Wright, the Speaker of the House, and Shoshana Cardin, president of the Council of Jewish Federations.

The success of this effort was easy to measure. Jews had pulled together, protested in huge numbers, and convinced the Reagan administration to put freedom for Soviet Jews high on the agenda for negotiations with the Soviets. If the U.S.S.R. wanted arms-reduction treaties, they'd have to free their Jews. Immediately, the Soviet regime began allowing tens of thousands of Jews to emigrate. Soon it became hundreds of thousands. Within a few years, the Soviet regime collapsed altogether, and upwards of two million Jews resettled in Israel, the United States, and around the world.

This was an amazing expression—and achievement—of Jewish pride. But it came to pass despite, not because of, the American Jewish establishment, which preferred quiet diplomacy to public outcries. Also, 1987 was a long time ago, and I can't help noticing that almost nothing like it has happened since. American Jews are involved in politics, of course. They will come out in numbers to protest the treatment of African Americans or for gay rights. They know as well as anybody how to mobilize on behalf of universal causes and the suffering of underprivileged people outside their community. But what about their own?

The biggest Jewish-focused protest I can remember in recent years was a hastily organized march in January 2020 against the rise of violent anti-Semitic acts across the country. Twenty-five thousand people marched across the Brooklyn Bridge. A nice turnout to be sure, especially given how quickly it was put together.

But the haphazard nature of that march is part of the point. Why is there no constant, permanent, organized protest movement against anti-Semitism in America? According to FBI statistics, Jews have been by far the leading victims of religious hate crimes in America for many years. And this is nothing compared to what

French and British Jews have endured in recent years. Any Jewish traveler in Europe will discover tight security at every synagogue, with armed guards who ask you personal questions to make sure you're not a terrorist. Jews have been institutionally intimidated in the United Kingdom, slaughtered in France, imprisoned in Iran, and their small but ancient community in Yemen destroyed. This is happening now, not a generation ago.

Why do American Jews tolerate this? Why aren't the protests larger, better planned, more frequent? Why aren't Jews in America visibly and vocally outraged by the open threats of violence faced by their brethren in other countries for the crime of being Jewish?

The absence of such mobilization is an unfortunate symptom of a deeper malady. To address that, a deeper change is needed, one we will take up later on.

THE OTHER SIGNIFICANT EVENT WAS the publication of the 1990 National Jewish Population Survey. This was not the first attempt to paint a statistical picture of American Jewry. There had been another back in 1970. But this one was asking different questions. By the 1980s, people were worried enough about assimilation that pressure mounted for a new survey to study trends in religious observance, affiliation, and intermarriage.

What most people remember about the survey was the revelation that 52 percent of American Jews who got married between 1985 and 1990 had married non-Jews. In 1965–1974, the number had been 25 percent. Before that, it was 9 percent.

I wasn't particularly surprised. The decline of American Jewry was something I could see all around me, an inevitable result, as I thought, of the prevailing assimilationism of secular Jewish culture and the transparent failure of Jewish communal institutions—from synagogues to schools to federations—to maintain and support a healthy sense of Jewish identity. I didn't need a study to tell me that. I saw it every weekend in the Sunday *New York Times*, as I looked at the wedding announcements and saw how the number of weddings officiated by rabbis declined, and the number of apparently interfaith weddings steadily grew. But many other Jews were horrified.

Intermarriage is a sensitive subject. Nobody wants to be told whom they can or cannot marry, especially in a liberal Jewish community. Many Jews who in the 1960s fought for racial intermarriage, and later for gay marriage, have never felt comfortable telling their own children whom to marry.

But if you agree that being Jewish does not just mean being part of a faith community but of a living people; if you see value in building a Jewish family, raising Jewish children, and passing a powerful sense of identity to the next generation, then it is much harder to do that if you marry a non-Jewish spouse. When you marry another Jew, your household is "Jewish" almost by default, whether you are observant or not. When you intermarry, being Jewish becomes one of several options for your children, instead of being the singular defining framework of their lives. We will return to this sensitive topic in greater depth later on.

Intermarriage wasn't the only troublesome statistic. Pretty much every measurement of Jewish commitment—synagogue membership, traditional practice, enrollment in Jewish schools—painted the same picture. While the Orthodox community continued to thrive, other expressions of Jewish identity were in free fall.

I had barely started thinking about how to tackle the question of secular Jewish identity. But the more I focused on it, the more outraged I became. How could we justify the evaporation of

American Jewry? No Jewish community in history had ever had it so good—an absence of large-scale physical threats, unparalleled economic opportunity, unmitigated success in terms of equality, rights, wealth, freedom, achievement—and Jews respond by abandoning their heritage and birthright?

Didn't they understand that *being Jewish* was the very thing that had given them the keys to their success? Wouldn't they want to continue that in their children and grandchildren?

Since the dawn of modern times, Jews have been at the forefront of science, business, law, and the arts—in America more than anywhere else—all because of a "secret sauce" of spiritual and intellectual excellence that is inextricable from their upbringing, their culture, and their identity as Jews. Now it looked as though a majority of American Jews were choosing to abandon this legacy. Jewish life in America, it seemed, was headed for a sad, quiet end.

Part of the problem, I thought, was ideological. The old assimilationist instinct had taken on new forms after the 1960s. The civil rights and anti-war protests had won their battles, and liberal Jews looked for a new way to express their universalist ethical teachings while giving them a Jewish veneer. They ultimately found it in the idea of *Tikkun Olam*, or "repairing the world."

There was a time when *Tikkun Olam*, a theological term borrowed from Jewish mysticism and the rabbinic tradition, simply meant expressing your Judaism not only through religious practice, social association, or the study of Jewish texts and history but also through activism in non-Jewish causes. Jews who embraced this ethical imperative usually maintained a strong foothold in traditional faith and practice. Gradually, however, *Tikkun Olam* evolved from a small part of one's Jewish identity into what can only be called a substitute religion—a way of being "Jewish" in a world that did not set Jews apart in any way.

Perhaps the most concrete example is the emergence of the American Jewish World Service, a kind of Jewish Peace Corps, founded in the mid-80s by American Jews who "wanted to join together as global citizens to help some of the poorest and most oppressed people around the globe." This project, and others like it, put "global justice" at the center of Jewish identity, expressed even in "mitzvah projects" for teens that were largely about helping people who were not themselves Jewish. As a result, Judaism itself became, at least for many secular Jews, almost entirely subordinate to the progressive school of politics.

But even without the left-wing politics, the problem with defining *Tikkun Olam* as the ethical core of Judaism should be self-evident: If your Jewish identity revolves entirely around universal concerns, then you don't really need the Jewish part of your identity at all. You don't need to invest time and effort in ensuring the Jewish commitment of your children for the simple reason that *Jewish identity, while it contains universalist elements, is not itself a universal value.* It is, rather, the specific identity of a particular people in history. By emphasizing only what we may give to others, *Tikkun Olam* distracts us from what we owe ourselves.

This ideological shift was certainly an issue, but it wasn't the only culprit. A much bigger problem was the obvious incompetence of Jewish institutions. Because they were not results- and performance-driven, they were also not accountable for the state of the Jews. My friend Charles Bronfman, who partnered with me in launching Birthright Israel, has written that the American Jewish community is not like a government or corporation, which answer to voters and shareholders, but "a series of fiefdoms, each run by very powerful lords," whose main preoccupation is the maintenance of their own position, rather than the positive impact they might have.[2]

The proof of this was easy to discern from the reaction to the 1990 survey. Every Jewish newspaper and rabbinic sermon cried *gevalt!* when the survey came out. But did anyone lose their job? Was a single federation president, school principal, organizational leader, or pulpit rabbi forced to resign in disgrace? Of course not. The best way to keep a failing system in place is to make sure that nobody is held accountable for its failures.

AND SO, BY THE EARLY 1990s, I started to get restless again.

I had done everything I wanted to do in my finance career. But I wanted my life to mean more. I felt I had been sitting on the sidelines, watching as American Jews frittered away their precious heritage. Meanwhile, I had seen how powerful the spirit of pride could be—in the people who built Israel, in Orthodox rabbis like Shlomo Carlebach, and in refuseniks like Roman Brackman who stood up to a powerful totalitarian regime.

The immense crisis facing American Jews was not helped by the reaction to the population survey: there was much hand-wringing but no commitment to changing how the community functioned. The crisis had been caused in large part by ineffective leaders and institutions—yet these same leaders and institutions were somehow expected to solve it.

I started to search for people who thought the way I did. I became particularly close to Irving Greenberg, known to his

---

2 Charles Bronfman and Howard Green, *Distilled: A Memoir of Family, Seagram, Baseball, and Philanthropy* (Toronto, Ontario, Canada: HarperCollins Publishers Ltd, 2016), 250.

friends and admirers as "Yitz"—a liberal Orthodox rabbi from Riverdale who shared my understanding of what was wrong with Jewish institutions. Yitz was a real intellectual, with a Ph.D. in American History from Harvard, and he had unconventional ideas that appealed to me.

In 1994, I asked Yitz to become president of a new foundation called the Jewish Life Network, later renamed the Steinhardt Foundation for Jewish Life. The idea was to support projects that made Jewish life engaging, educational, exciting, and above all, driven by an emphasis on cultivating pride in being Jewish.

Although we still had much to learn, we knew from the beginning that we wanted to focus on younger Jews, preferably the least engaged ones, because they are at an age when they develop the habits and attitudes that set the tone for their whole Jewish lives. Just as important, we wanted to be able to measure the impact of what we were doing.

It happened that in 1994, I also had my worst year ever as a money manager and felt obligated to stay in the business for at least an extra year to try to recover the losses my clients had suffered.

And so, on December 31, 1995, I retired and closed down my firm. My career as a manager of other people's money was over. From that day forward, I would dedicate not just my capital but also my time and creative energy to solving the problem that lurked beneath everything I felt had gone wrong with American Jewry.

The great majority of young secular Jews were not being given either the knowledge or the experiences that I had received. Because of this, they didn't really care about the rates of assimilation or the dysfunction of the community's institutions. And this would have to change if non-Orthodox Jewish life were to survive over time in America.

So I embarked on a new career, armed with only the fortune I'd made on Wall Street, some personal connections and business experience, and a strong sense for what I knew *wasn't* working.

I had no idea what I was getting myself into.

Interlude: What Is Pride?

Where does Jewish pride come from?

The first step is acknowledging that you are part of a people. Something special and distinct, with its own history. A unique tribe, a team, a nation.

Being a member of the Jewish people is a lot like having a big family.

It begins with caring for our own. If you're a progressive Jew, then Jewish pride means seeing violent anti-Semitic attacks on Orthodox Jews in Borough Park, or Poway, or Paris, as an attack on yourself. It means supporting Israel, not because the Israeli government is always right—it definitely isn't—but because it's a country of your people. If you're an Orthodox Jew, or an Israeli, Jewish pride means seeing progressive and Reform Jews in the Diaspora as part of your family, making them feel accepted and supporting them when they're attacked in Pittsburgh or London or Charlottesville, or even at the Western Wall.

And it means learning about the Holocaust—not just as a universal, detached horror that is meant to teach the world that genocide is bad and tolerance is good, but first of all as our own personal, collective catastrophe. To mourn everything we lost. To get angry at those who murdered our fellow Jews. To resolve that we will never allow it to happen to us again.

But Jewish pride is not just about coming together at the worst moments and accepting the differences among us or sharing our collective tragedy. It's also about celebrating each other's achievements. If a Jew wins a Nobel Prize, or builds an enormous company like Google, or becomes a famous movie actor or musical artist—this should give you pride, just as you would feel proud of a cousin who succeeds. You are thrilled at their success.

Of course, you'll feel a lot more proud if they, too, show a Jewish commitment. When Sandy Koufax refused to play on Yom Kippur, it meant something a lot deeper than if he hadn't. It was like you could reach across and feel the kinship—the knowledge that they, too, see themselves as part of you.

It is not enough, of course, to assert the existence of a bond that you may not really feel. For many of us, other Jews—especially those in far-off countries or whose Jewish lives look very different from our own—are like distant relatives we barely know and may feel little connection to. The question is: Where do feelings of peoplehood come from?

It may sound trite, but it really does all begin with education. Jewish pride cannot exist without knowing about what we have been through together, seen together, the rituals and values and texts we have created together, the long and twisted path of joy and suffering and collective enterprise that made us who we are.

And we Jews have lived through so much, seen so much, and accomplished so much over the last few thousand years, it's hard even to scratch the surface. We have always been a bit edgy: The Bible was a revolutionary book that changed the world, for better or worse. I'm not sure why, but our survival over all those centuries, studying our books and sticking together, seems to have bothered a lot of people, in both Christian and Muslim lands, through the ages.

But once emancipation came in Europe, more than two centuries ago, Jewish edginess was unleashed on the world. The much-maligned Jews were suddenly succeeding at the top levels in so many different fields. We shouldn't be surprised at anti-Semitism: We were competing so far beyond our numbers that it almost looked like the game was rigged. The only way anti-Semites could explain our success was to imagine a mystical, evil Jewish conspiracy.

There was no conspiracy. We were just collectively more creative, more diligent, more interconnected than other people—skills we had developed over many centuries in order to survive. We had no army to protect us. We had to make ourselves useful to those in power just to avoid being massacred. That's why anti-Semitism has never bothered me as some scary cosmic injustice. It's just the way of the world, the price you pay for success: Others will be jealous and do everything to stop you.

Pride means being willing to say, out loud and without qualification, that being Jewish is a wonderful thing. That for whatever reason, we have certain things we're very good at. Every successful nation, every ethnic group, celebrates its strengths. Why shouldn't we? Our contributions to the world span every field from science to the arts, to philosophy and entertainment, to business and finance. All of these areas make the world better. (Sometimes we excel at things that make the world less good, too. We're not perfect, even when we excel.)

But to feel that kind of pride, you have to know something about our history, our contributions, and our particular areas of excellence. Without knowledge and education, there can be no pride.

And so, I started my activism for Jewish pride by focusing on the institutions of Jewish education.

What I found was an absolute mess.

CHAPTER 2

Reinventing Jewish Schools

I don't know if everybody had as awful a time in Hebrew school as I did. For five days a week, Monday through Thursday afternoons plus Sundays, I dragged myself to the school run by our Orthodox synagogue in Bensonhurst. Sweaty and exhausted from a full day of secular school, jealous of the kids who were out playing ball as any normal sixth-grader would, I did not learn much.

The school did its part, too, to make sure I didn't learn much. A joyless institution in which joyless teachers purported to educate miserable, bored kids. Subjects that could have been interesting were presented like they were a recital of the phone book in a heavy Yiddish accent. It was a conspiracy of Jewish indolence: Teachers pretended to teach, we pretended to learn, and everyone went home.

Needless to say, I skipped Hebrew school whenever I thought I could get away with it.

Most of us have gone through some formal Jewish education, and some of us put our kids through it too because we assume that things really can't be any other way. Later in life, whatever Jewish education we may have received is usually forgotten.

How did Jews, the people who value education above everything else, manage to create such terrible schools and keep them running generation after generation?

Part of it has to do with the basic lack of accountability or results-driven standards that have ailed the entire non-Orthodox establishment. There are no standardized tests for Jewish knowledge, no agreed-upon sense of what a Jewish education looks like, and no highly developed, professionalized teacher training system for Jewish subjects.

In the Orthodox world today—about 10 percent of the Jewish population in America—things are different. Almost all Orthodox kids go to day schools. Some of these are excellent, others less so. Regardless of their quality, however, they are part of an insular world. Parents want their children to go to a school where the food is certified kosher, the other kids are Orthodox, and their families are part of a single social framework. These schools are tightly integrated into family and community life. Many of them won't even let children from non-Orthodox homes attend. As a result, there is little competitive pressure from either public or non-Orthodox schools.

For these young students, in other words, pride is not really an issue. The pride of young Orthodox Jews is amply sustained by what we may call an "envelope" of mutually reinforcing experiences, institutions, networks, and exemplars—in which the school plays a central role.

We will return later to the question of how to build an appropriate "envelope" to enhance identity and commitment among non-Orthodox Jews throughout their lives.

My first focus was on formal Jewish education, which was supposed to infuse our children with the core knowledge of who we are, what we have been through, and what we have achieved.

When it comes to schooling, the secular Jewish child faces a far greater degree of competitive pressure from non-Jewish forces than does the Orthodox child. In the non-Orthodox world, every parent has a choice, and every child sees their friends come and go from different kinds of public and private schools. After-school Jewish education competes with other important extracurricular activities which are often more enjoyable and whose benefits are more apparent. And increasingly, families are choosing to avoid Jewish schooling entirely.

In 1990, a few years before I threw myself into the world of Jewish life, a report called "A Time to Act" was issued by a group called the Commission on Jewish Education in North America to explore just how badly non-Orthodox Jewish schools were failing. The commission was started by the industrial magnate and veteran philanthropist Morton Mandel, and it had some very good people on it—including Charles Bronfman and Yitz Greenberg. It also included major scholars, rabbis, and communal, educational, and philanthropic leaders from across the Jewish spectrum.

By the time I launched my foundation in 1994, my sense that Jewish education was terrible had already been backed up by research. The Commission examined Jewish schooling from every possible angle, brought important data, and analyzed the flaws. Their report covered every aspect of the Jewish educational experience, including day schools, supplementary ("Hebrew") schools, campus education, adult education, and summer camps.

What they produced was one of the most blistering indictments of Jewish communal life that has ever been written. Their conclusion, bluntly, was this:

Despite the extensive range of activities, Jewish education is not achieving its mission. Exposure to existing Jewish educational programs leaves many North American Jews indifferent to Judaism, and unwilling or unable to take an active part in Jewish communal living.[3]

Harsh, but true. American Jews were spending more than a billion dollars a year for an educational system that was a complete bust. As one member of the commission put it, as long as Hebrew school "is something you have to live through rather than enjoy, it cannot be valuable. So many Jewish-Americans have had an impoverished supplementary school experience as their only Jewish education."

Of course, there are always points of light. Individual fantastic schools and stellar teachers and administrators could be found. But they were nothing more than that—points of light in a sea of darkness.

On the whole, the commission identified five major issues which, taken together, created a swampland of mediocrity:

1. Only a small percentage of school-age kids were actually attending Jewish schools.

2. Very little investment was being made in Jewish education to come up with new methods or curricula, or to teach great Jewish ideas, values, and texts.

3. National and regional communal organizations were simply not putting much money or energy into education alongside more traditional needs like alleviating poverty and supporting Israel.

4. Unlike in general education, almost no teachers in Jewish schools received formal training as teachers of Jewish subjects.

---

3 *A Time to Act: The Report of the Commission on Jewish Education in North America* (Lanham, Md.: University Press of America, 1990): 32, https://www.bjpa.org/content/upload/bjpa/c__w/Time%20to%20act.pdf.

5. Almost nobody was collecting reliable data on Jewish education, and there were no standardized tests for achievement or other measurements for what kids were actually learning in these schools.

These conclusions were pretty much in line with what I, and many others, had long suspected. And they added up to a startling conclusion: The Jewish community was not taking Jewish education seriously. And it had been this way for a long time.

Since the 1950s, Jewish schools had been mainly run by synagogues. But synagogues had no expertise in schooling. Jews just assumed good rabbis were also good pedagogues, but that's not the case, just like they're not always the best marriage counselors or public speakers or managers.

The same is true for synagogue lay leaders: Few of them are trained as school administrators or educators. Having them run your schools is like hiring a bus driver to fly a plane.

Over the decades, little had changed in the practice of Jewish education. Meanwhile, the modern field of education had advanced dramatically. Schoolteachers in public schools all had professional training, and many had master's degrees. In Jewish schools, they hired whoever was willing and had minimal knowledge of the subject matter, and the pay was poor. There was very little infrastructure for developing new methods, only a small number of specialized teacher training programs, no national networks, no viable career paths, no serious research or data about what the kids were learning. In fact, there was no way of even knowing the quality of a school, other than by how many kids showed up.

This failure was vast and systemic, and I had no doubt that it was a major source of the problems ailing the community as a whole. If we can't teach our kids to love, know about, and find joy in

Jewish subjects, if the memory of Hebrew school fills people with loathing, then we shouldn't be surprised if a generation later, they don't bother raising their own kids as Jews.

YITZ GREENBERG IS A TALL, lanky, clean-shaven Orthodox rabbi from the Bronx who has a passing resemblance to the actor Steve McQueen. I was impressed with his intellect from the first time I met him in the late 1980s. Like me, he was an inveterate contrarian who got himself into trouble on a regular basis for violating the accepted norms of the Orthodox world. Yitz was exceptionally well connected and respected among non-Orthodox Jews. And as I discovered through many long conversations, despite his dark suit and large *kippah*, he seemed to sympathize with my atheism to such a degree that I sometimes wondered whether he himself didn't share it, at least a little.

Yitz believed firmly, and for a time had me convinced, that full-time Jewish day schools held the key. As a founder of the SAR school in Riverdale, an excellent Orthodox institution, he had considerable experience with day schools. In his view, only day schools offered the kind of total immersive environment that would get kids to commit to Jewish identity amid the ocean of alternatives that modern America offered them. Instead of sending kids to dull and arduous afternoon schools, parents should put their kids' whole education in the hands of top-notch Jewish schools for the whole day. Orthodox day schools like Maimonides in the Boston area and Ramaz on the Upper East Side were among the best private schools in the country. Graduates often went on to attend Ivy League colleges and built committed Jewish lives.

Could the success of the day school model be replicated outside the Orthodox world? There were a few good non-Orthodox day schools, and the Solomon Schechter schools had done pretty well. But as part of the Conservative movement, they were still based heavily on religion. I already knew that traditional religious schooling was a nonstarter for the majority of Jews. Moreover, no matter how good the day schools were, fewer than 3 percent of non-Orthodox kids attended them. The largest denomination, Reform, never had more than around twenty day schools in the country. For most non-Orthodox parents, sending their kids to a day school was not a real option.

I was eager to explore something that could be the basis of a proud Jewish identity outside of the denominational framework. Could we imagine an American Jewish world in which Jewish kids enrolled in non-Orthodox day schools in very large numbers, comparable to the Orthodox world? To answer this question, in 1997 we launched, together with a group of eleven like-minded donors, the Partnership for Excellence in Jewish Education, or PEJE.

THE IDEA OF PEJE WAS straightforward. We offered seed money to start new day schools or to expand existing ones to more grades (an elementary school that wanted to add on a middle school, for example). The aim was to dramatically expand the world of non-Orthodox day schools. We launched programs to help train school administrators and school boards, but the most important thing we offered was a matching grant. Any group across America that put together a serious proposal to start a new school, and fit the criteria, could get a matching grant of up to $300,000 over five years. Although $120,000 a year (including the match) might not sound like enough to run a school, it's a significant core commitment around which to build out a local fundraising effort. Combine that with tuition, and it seemed like more than enough to get a bunch of schools off the ground.

The biggest force behind PEJE was Yitz. He was deeply impassioned and wanted to go big with it. To head up the project he brought in Joshua Elkin, who had run a Solomon Schechter school in Boston for twenty years and had an impressive record of expansion. A soft-spoken, straight-shooting Conservative rabbi, Josh threw himself into it with everything he had.

In advance of the 1997–1998 school year, Josh sent out his first Request for Proposals to communities around the country. Although we avoided saying outright what kind of schools we would support, we were clear that we were offering money for new programs only.

Immediately, we were criticized by leaders of existing day schools who saw this as money that could have been going to them. This was a little odd: It *wasn't* money that could be going to them. I had no interest in passively funding existing day schools, and the assumption that the creation of new schools would threaten the old ones misunderstood the nature of both the problem and the solution we were investing in.

Meanwhile, PEJE immediately received a lot of high-quality applications. Many of these were existing schools asking for money to pay for things they were already doing. But the number of serious proposals was encouraging.

Thus began a period of rapid expansion of day schools. For the first five years or so, we were launching new schools left and right. In 1997, we launched four schools as a pilot program. In 1998, ten more. In 1999, another eleven, including two high schools, and in 2000, another nine. In 2001, we launched an additional fifteen.

By 2003, a total of sixty schools had gotten off the ground at the elementary, middle, or high school levels. And not just in the New York area. We had schools going up in Albuquerque, in Palo Alto and the San Francisco Bay Area, in Los Angeles and Miami Beach, in Toronto and Toledo and Texas, in Nashville and Las Vegas and St. Louis. All over North America, it seemed, Jewish communities were emerging that really wanted and needed Jewish day schools.

I visited many of these schools and absolutely loved the experience of seeing all these kids enjoying, for the first time, an immersive Jewish educational environment. It felt like we were Zionist pioneers, draining the swamps of assimilation and building a whole new world of American Jewish identity.

We also hosted biannual gatherings of day school donors from around the country—which eventually also included administrators and educators. This apparently hadn't been done before, bringing everybody together to educate and energize the field. The conferences grew, and within a few years, we had more than a thousand people in attendance. Judy and I hosted the first one in 2000 at our home in Bedford, where some 250 donors attended, each of whom had given more than $100,000. I remember them getting off the buses that brought them in from New York City, looking around, and seeing our animals and the beautiful scenery. Stunned and bewildered, one of them said, "Wow! It's like the day schools are having a bar mitzvah!"

The excitement was palpable. Things were going great.

Until they weren't.

SOMETIME AROUND 2003, WE STARTED finding it much harder to get new schools off the ground. I used to meet with Josh every few months, and for the first few years, these meetings were exciting—fifteen new schools, twenty new programs, pilot grants, conferences, all sorts of things happening. Then the numbers just became much smaller. Eventually, it was clear: Though we hadn't changed anything we were doing, our efforts had simply run aground.

To be fair, Josh had warned us from the beginning that this might happen. Part of what impressed me about him was his no-nonsense approach. One risk for a philanthropist is being bombarded with people who are trying, usually in a pretty transparent way, to tell him things they think he wants to hear. (Note to future fundraisers: Nobody likes to feel like they are being sucked up to by strangers looking for money. Distinguish yourself through honesty and straight talk, and you'll get a lot farther.)

Josh wasn't like that at all. He wanted, more than anything else, for the project to succeed. But he also didn't want to overpromise, and he saw it as part of his job to manage our expectations. He had warned us that at some point we might "saturate the market"—that we would run out of groups and communities, especially in the non-Orthodox world, where new schools could be launched.

So we knew that there might be a limit. The problem was, when we started PEJE, neither Josh nor Yitz nor anybody else had any idea what that limit was. Would we end up launching six, sixty, or six hundred schools? Nobody knew.

Turns out the number was sixty.

We hired a consultant to review our operations and to help us put together a strategic plan for what to do next. By this point, we were giving out millions of dollars to the schools we had launched. The consultant recommended that PEJE shift its focus from launching new schools to working with existing schools to develop their programs and build their fundraising capacity.

So that's what we did. In the years that followed, we continued to host conferences and work with our schools to help them build stable fundraising operations. At the same time, we also started extending the program to existing schools. If day schools all needed help with fundraising and cash flow, why not help all of them?

The reasoning was sound, except for one problem: This wasn't anything like what I had in mind when we launched PEJE. I had long embraced Yitz's argument that a dramatic scaling up of day schools was a key to strengthening Jewish identity among non-Orthodox Jews. Capacity building for the ones that already existed, without launching new ones, was not for me.

Sixty new schools, some of them covering only a few grades at a time, would not be anywhere near the scale required to fundamentally change American Jewish life. It was good and important—but not what I had gotten into philanthropy for. "The ultimate measure of success of PEJE's efforts," the organization had declared in its three-year report in 2000, "will be the attendance of hundreds of thousands of Jewish children in day schools." By that measure, PEJE was clearly heading for failure.

That was the beginning of the end of my involvement in PEJE. The major partners agreed to a second round of five-year funding commitments, through 2007, but at a certain point, we let the schools know that would be it. If after ten years of funding from us they couldn't stand on their own, then they'd need to be prepared for a significant reduction.

IN 2009, MORE THAN A decade after launching PEJE, the Avi Chai Foundation (one of our philanthropic partners) published its census of Jewish day schools. They did this every five years, so this was the third census since we started. The aim was to understand and monitor the progress of day school enrollment, something nobody had bothered doing before.

The report showed that over a ten-year period, Jewish day school enrollment had gone up by 25 percent. Impressive, right?

Wrong. Almost all that growth was in the Orthodox and ultra-Orthodox schools—which, you'll recall, constitute the vast majority of Jewish day schools in America. When you consider the core demographics of communities that have lots of kids, especially among the ultra-Orthodox, ten years of natural growth explains a lot of that 25 percent.

Although we didn't discriminate based on denomination, it wasn't exactly the kind of value-add I had been looking to create. Meanwhile, among the non-Orthodox schools, we saw an increase in enrollment of only 5 percent.

Five percent. After all the efforts, all the money, and especially all the time, enrollment had grown by just a small fraction.

And that wasn't the worst of it. Apparently, there had been more growth in the first five years and then a *decline* of 2.5 percent in the second five. Part of this decline was due to the 2008 financial crisis, which hit the schools hard and led some of them to close. But the bottom line was clear: After thirteen years of PEJE, non-Orthodox day schools were actually moving in the wrong direction.

Why was this happening? Yitz had been convinced that the entire problem with low day school attendance among non-Orthodox Jews was one of supply. There weren't enough schools, the reasoning went. So let's build a lot more, and let's subsidize tuition so Jewish parents could afford them.

This added up to an enormous amount of money. And it might have been worth doing if the diagnosis were correct.

But I don't think it is. The real problem is one of *demand*—specifically, the low demand for Jewish-only schools. And it won't be solved by building more schools. Again, in the Orthodox world, day schools are part of an entire ecosystem of identity that includes families, synagogues, extracurriculars, and distinctive values. Outside of Orthodoxy, there is little appetite for insularity. Jews today no longer want their kids to grow up cut off from the non-Jewish world. Having made it in America, they want their kids to make it too.

That means integration with non-Jews from the earliest age. The whole idea of surrounding yourself only with Jews strikes many of them as part of a dead past.

Think about it: If money were the only problem, wouldn't the wealthiest non-Orthodox Jews *all* be sending their kids to day schools? Wouldn't a lot of schools in wealthier communities already have been built, and wouldn't they be packed with Jewish kids?

Perhaps it was a quality issue. Maybe if you could make better schools, with more engaging teachers and superior content, and with high standards and high acceptance rates to top colleges, you could reinvent the brand of Jewish day schools. That's a lot of ifs, and it was the motivation behind changes we made within PEJE during its later years. It also lay behind our two aborted attempts at creating an elite, nondenominational high school in Manhattan, to which we will return.

But I suspect there is a deeper problem. What if it turns out that, beyond a small number of already-committed families, most non-Orthodox Jews do not *want* their kids to study in an all-Jewish environment? What if most Jewish kids don't want to go to an all-Jewish school at all, no matter how good it is?

This was the real reason behind PEJE's failure. The number of non-Orthodox Jews who would jump at the chance to send their kids to an all-Jewish day school was, apparently, much smaller than we had hoped. We had picked all the low-hanging fruit, the small number of communities that wanted day schools but couldn't afford them. It didn't take long to run out of apples.

I DON'T THINK THIS WAS the only reason that Yitz and I parted ways in 2007, but it was high on the list. Increasingly, we could no longer agree on the main educational project or a vision for the future of non-Orthodox Jewish America. Yitz wasn't willing to support formal Jewish education in which non-Jewish students might be allowed to participate—whereas, I thought it might be the only way to convince larger numbers of Jewish parents to send their kids to Jewish schools. He also wasn't bothered that the model could never be scaled up. From his perspective, launching even a few dozen schools was infinitely better than not doing it at all. The option of moving away from the model of exclusively Jewish schools was never something he could contemplate.

I realized that at his core, Yitz was still an Orthodox rabbi. And Orthodoxy is hardwired to socially insulate Jews from non-Jews.

In December 2009, after the Avi Chai report came out and I had made clear that PEJE had, from my perspective, reached a dead end, Yitz apparently sensed that there was now a serious threat to the goal he had long been fighting for. So he published an op-ed in the *Forward* called "There Is No Alternative to Day Schools," in which he spelled out his views:

> *It is time for heroic increases in support for Jewish education [...].*
> *The community must muster its will to live and step up to pay the*
> *price—whatever it costs—for the highest level of Jewish education*

for its young. The Jewish mega-foundations and our community federations—even with depleted resources—remain best positioned to help. They should raid their reserves and spend down for the next few years if necessary. This is like the cost of a war for survival.[4]

What I admired most about Yitz was his courage. Here was a man willing to take unconventional positions and publicly fight for them. He didn't care if the whole Orthodox world thought he was too liberal. He cared deeply, had bold opinions, and went to the mat for them. This heroic quality attracted me.

There's just one problem. It's true that you can't fix big problems without dedicating yourself to bold ideas. But it's also true that not every bold idea is a good one. Despite the findings of the Avi Chai report, despite what he had seen with his own eyes, Yitz still believed that the only reason day schools weren't being embraced by non-Orthodox American Jews was a lack of money.

As for me, after a decade of putting my own money behind this particular solution, with limited results, I could not agree with an argument that I should "raid my reserves" to underwrite more of the same.

This was not the only unsustainable idea Yitz had pushed for. Over many years, he also argued for the creation of retreat centers across the country. Like Birthright, brief retreats offer fully immersive, intense educational experiences that can change people's lives. Why not have a dozen beautiful retreat centers of our own, in stunning locations around the country, and use them for intensive pride-building Jewish programs for different age groups from high school through college and beyond?

---

4 Irving Greenberg, "There Is No Alternative to Day Schools," Forward (December 2, 2009), https://forward.com/opinion/120123/there-is-no-alternative-to-day-schools/.

It was not, at first glance, a terrible idea. I'd been involved in student leadership retreats in the summer run by the Hillel organization, which I'd supported earlier in the 1990s. I'd seen how powerful it can be to bring people together, even for just a few days, in a luxurious rural setting, for an experience that is at once educational and spiritual. Done right, it changes people.

Yitz and I went pretty far with the concept, scouting actual locations for a retreat center that would serve as a pilot, drawing up plans for renovations and programming, and looking for potential funding partners. Yitz took me on tours of proposed sites, and I especially remember one of them, in Dutchess County, N.Y. It had stunning views, a pristine lake, and some delightfully quaint old houses on-site. Just inspiring.

What Yitz did not do was come up with a business plan that could make it financially viable. The costs would be immense, and at a certain point, it became clear that even if we covered the start-up costs, the only way we could hope to keep running these centers would be to also rent them out for general use by corporations and other groups for *three quarters of the calendar year*. In other words, we would need to launch a whole separate business that would subsidize the retreats. Other ideas included building luxury residences on the properties and selling them—again, an additional business operation.

I absolutely love the idea of retreats and the powerful experiences they can bring. But I didn't want to be in the corporate-retreat or residential-development business, and I didn't see how Yitz's plan was workable financially. Eventually, I shut it down.

For many years, I took Yitz's advice very seriously. And I continue to be grateful for the time we spent together and the Jewish wisdom he shared. He was the closest thing I ever had to a mentor in my Jewish activism. But at a certain point, our respective conceptions of the foundation's aims and methods were no longer aligned, and it became clear that we would have to part ways.

THROUGHOUT MY CAREER IN PHILANTHROPIC activism, almost every project I launched followed a similar pattern. The goal was always to instill a sense of pride in non-Orthodox Jews in an area that wasn't being covered by existing programs. I preferred launching programs that insisted on excellence, using the newest methods and top-quality production values; focused on younger, less-engaged Jews; could be measured in their effect; and could be scaled up to cover a large portion of the non-Orthodox community. In short, I looked for ways to make a big, lasting impact.

But even when a concept proved successful, I wasn't satisfied unless it could be sustained financially, at scale, over time. As wealthy as I was, my resources were severely limited given the size of the mountain I had chosen to climb. Consider the size of the Jewish philanthropic world, which covers federations, JCCs, JCRCs, community foundations, synagogues, schools, "defense" organizations like the American Jewish Committee and the Anti-Defamation League, Israel-focused organizations, and on and on—we're talking about billions of dollars each year. A single philanthropist swimming against the tide can do very little. I felt that my unique contribution, where I could add the most value to Jewish life, was to identify and launch, together with a few partners, new programs in areas not being well served. And if I hit upon something that worked, to find other sources of funding to keep it going.

Usually, the last part proved the hardest. Change and innovation are difficult for Jewish institutions. It took the double earthquake of the 1990 education report and the 1990 National Jewish Population Survey to get federations to put *anything* significant into Jewish education, or into Jewish identity more broadly. Before that, they had been funding programs for the poor and supporting Israel. They assumed education was being taken care of by the synagogues. It wasn't.

But even when you find something that works, it's extremely difficult to get philanthropists to pick up the ball and run with it. There's a whole system of accolades and honors and galas and plaques that numbs most donors into believing that they are already doing their part. Their public status is commensurate with the size of their gifts, not with their effectiveness.

There's a huge disconnect between Jewish donations and their real-world impact. One of the most glaring examples is the trees people continue to plant in Israel through the Jewish National Fund. For over a hundred years, Jews have been planting trees through the JNF in Israel's north and central regions, with forests covering no more than about five hundred square miles of land—less than half the size of Rhode Island. Hundreds of millions, if not billions, of dollars have been spent on those trees.

But if you ask any Israeli: Over the generations, what were the most acute needs facing the Zionist enterprise in the Land of Israel? You'll discover that the absence of trees was always very low on the list. Urgent defense needs, economic development, immigrant absorption, water resources, agriculture, the list goes on and on. But trees?

For much of the Jewish philanthropic world, it's all about the donor's feelings, not actually solving our people's problems. I cannot tell you how few major donors I've met are truly committed to the impact of their gifts.

This wasn't always the case. In the early twentieth century, organizations like the American Joint Distribution Committee were built to help Jews around the world facing persecution and dislocation. The Hebrew Immigrant Aid Society (HIAS) helped take care of millions of Jewish refugees and immigrants who came to the United States over a period of decades. (Today, having become fully universalized under the rubric of *Tikkun Olam*, it now describes itself as a Jewish organization that helps refugees around the world.)

When it comes to relatively simple problems with relatively clear solutions—dislocation, poverty, healthcare, and so on—there have always been people who could be moved to act. But the material problems facing Jews in the Diaspora are much less than they were a century ago, and now our most burning problem is spiritual: The strengthening of Jewish identity through the inculcation of pride, which I firmly believe is the keystone of survival for secular Diaspora communities. This is a much harder challenge, and it requires new thinking and a lot of trial and error.

When you point out how bad the Jewish schools are, most Jewish philanthropists just roll their eyes and point to other priorities. This kind of complacency is utterly misplaced. Our identity crisis is a slow-motion brush fire raging through millions of acres, and we're just chatting about the weather.

THOUGH PEJE FAILED TO ACHIEVE its central goal, some good came out of it. First of all, a lot of the schools we started are still around. Over the last two decades, thousands of American Jews have received a day school education that they wouldn't have gotten otherwise. It's not the scale I wanted, but it's something. PEJE ended up folding into a new organization called Prizmah ("prism" in Hebrew), which acts as a clearinghouse for resources for Jewish day schools of all stripes.

But a completely different project, potentially much more successful, emerged from the conversations we had at PEJE. The issue of early childhood education became something our board members talked about a lot. This was a huge, if little understood, hole in the system of Jewish education—and a potential new area of big impact.

Early childhood is a critical time. Three- and four-year-olds are developing their personalities at a deep, emotional level. Powerful associations are formed. Love is kindled. At this age, education is mainly about developing knowledge and commitment through experiences, connections, curiosity, and relationships. According to research, the human brain develops in crucial ways during this period, and if you make preschool into a carefully planned educational experience rather than just a form of babysitting, the positive effects are immense, and may continue to resonate over the course of a child's whole life—even spreading to their siblings, parents, and ultimately their own children. We become what we learn during this incredibly sensitive time.

Jewish early education, however, did not exist as a distinct profession. Sure, there were thousands of preschools associated with JCCs, synagogues, and day schools. But these were more like day care centers than powerful shapers of identity. For many, their main goal was to free up parents to go to work.

At the same time, the field of early childhood education had developed greatly outside the Jewish context. As the 1990 education report put it, "Early childhood programs under Jewish auspices have been growing in number because increasingly both parents work. However, many of these programs have not made

Jewish education their primary focus because of a severe shortage of trained personnel." For the Jewish community, building a generation of effective, professional Jewish educators was, simply, not a priority.

There is a vast cognitive dissonance among Jews when it comes to education. We think we are smart people whose commitment to education gives us advantages in life. But in practice, our excellence happens despite, not because of, the schools we build. It's like we are spending down the intellectual capital we got from our parents and grandparents and doing little to renew it.

For some years, I had been concerned about preschools and even worked with a number of partners, including the Coalition for the Advancement of Jewish Education (CAJE) to look for solutions. In 2004, my foundation hosted a daylong meeting with philanthropists and educational experts at the Brandeis House, an old mansion close to Central Park on Manhattan's Upper East Side.

It was on that day that I first learned about Reggio Emilia, a city in Italy that has become one of the most important stories in the field of early childhood education.

LOCATED ON A BROAD PLAIN straddling the Crostolo river in Central-Northern Italy, the city of Reggio Emilia is quite ancient—so old, in fact, that when the Jewish Temple in Jerusalem was destroyed by the Romans in the year 70 C.E., this town had already been a center of Roman administration for more than two centuries. Until the Holocaust, Reggio Emilia hosted a thriving Jewish community for hundreds of years.

It was just a few months after the town's Jews were all but wiped out and the city was partially destroyed during the Second World

War that a young schoolteacher named Loris Malaguzzi came across a group of women in a nearby village. Using water from the nearby river, they were cleaning off bricks they had found lying around. The women told him that they were salvaging the ruins for the purpose of building a school for their young children. In the shadow of the war, these women passionately wanted a different kind of school—one that would teach their children to be good human beings, to prevent the injustice and horrors that Fascism had brought. Their school would end up being financed, in part, through the sale of nine horses, two abandoned military trucks, and a captured German tank.

Malaguzzi came to teach at their school, and he became fascinated by new educational theories that had emerged around the Western world. He developed a new approach to early childhood education and began implementing it in the city and the surrounding villages. Within a decade and a half, it had become the official approach to early education, supported by municipalities across the region. In the early 1980s, the approach started to be exported to other countries, and in 2002, the North American Reggio Emilia Alliance was launched. Today, thousands of preschools across the U.S. and Canada use this model.

The central idea is that young children learn through a process of spontaneous, curiosity- and relationship-driven experiences. Every child has, in Malaguzzi's words, "a hundred languages" they develop and deploy to engage with their world. The job of the educator isn't just to transfer information but to work together with the parents in developing a unique and powerful experience of discovery for each child.

It's a hard thing to fully internalize because it's so different from how traditional preschools are run. When they're not just day care centers, preschools sometimes add an educational component meant to prepare small children for the challenges of elementary school. But day care is for parents, while elementary school children are in a completely different place from preschoolers. Reggio reinvented the preschool, tailoring an educational experience to match the specific kind of lovable eccentricity that three- and four-year-olds embody.

DIANA GANGER WAS BORN IN Argentina and moved to Israel, where she first encountered the idea of multigenerational education. In 1985, she became director of the Moriah Early Childhood Center in Deerfield, Illinois. There she developed the first real attempt to fuse the Reggio approach with Judaism. By the time I met her at the Brandeis House in 2004, she had been working on it for almost twenty years.

The idea of using Reggio Emilia to instill Jewish commitment spoke to me deeply. In every project I've launched, there was an assumption that knowledge and experience went hand in hand. Learning isn't just something of the mind—it's something you live. Our values and wisdom come from a combination of the things we study, the human examples we meet, and our experiences. Just as I wasn't willing to provide experiences that didn't also include educational content, I didn't believe in providing education that didn't come with powerful experiences.

Reggio Emilia was originally meant as a humanistic, secular approach to education that begins with the individual child but extends to his or her relationships with other students and includes the families and staff into a single community. Learning is achieved by following a child's curiosity, putting together projects, some of them developing spontaneously, and getting the parents involved.

It's not easy, and it requires teachers who are properly trained. Reggio-inspired schools see educators as lifelong learners who engage in an ongoing process of "documentation," in which teachers constantly identify and collect the markers of children's creative development.

This should not be hard to adapt to a Jewish context, injecting Jewish values and ideas like mutual responsibility, the sanctity of life, self-propelled curiosity, family, and more concrete Jewish symbols like holidays and rituals. A child who enters kindergarten already possessing a powerful association of love for Jewish things will carry it for many years to come.

What I loved about it was that it also involved the parents actively. Preschool may be just a few hours a day, but under Diana's method, parents would get together for learning that ran parallel to what the kids were doing, and there were also programs for families and whole communities. Parents discovered new ways to do Jewish things both for and with their children and to involve themselves in the community. The result was that it wasn't just a school for kids but also for parenting, for fashioning Jewish homes. "In the end," Diana later wrote,

> what emerges is a complete child who embodies many Jewish funda-
> mentals: inquisitiveness, creativity, a relational stance, curiosity,
> emotional self-regulation, thinking, friendship, a budding morality,
> an identity within the greater Jewish community, and a family that
> looks to start or continue their life journey through a Jewish lens.[5]

The biggest result of that day at the Brandeis House was the decision to launch the Jewish Early Childhood Education Initiative,

---

5 Diana Ganger, "The Importance of Vision in Early Childhood Jewish Education," Prizmah (2010), https://prizmah.org/hayidion/educated-jew/importance-vision-early-childhood-jewish-education.

or JECEI (pronounced "Jesse"). We eventually hired Diana to be director of programs and made the Moriah Early Childhood Center one of our first pilot projects. We put together a group of about a dozen philanthropic partners, most notably Harold Grinspoon, the Jim Joseph Foundation, and the UJA-Federation of New York.

Within a few years, JECEI spread the word about the Reggio Emilia approach, engaged thirty-two schools, trained more than a thousand teachers, and launched seven formally accredited JECEI schools, each in a different metropolitan area, which act as a showcase for Jewish educators across their respective regions. We also built a system for the collection and analysis of data—something we insisted on with almost every project we launched. All told, more than six thousand families, with eight thousand children, participated in JECEI educational programs.

OF COURSE, NOTHING IS SIMPLE. One of the best things about JECEI was that we weren't trying to build new schools from the ground up. Instead, we were offering a way to inject Jewish content into the thousands of JCC and synagogue early childhood centers that already existed. Parents and children alike came away inspired, committed, and possessed of a deepened sense of Jewish pride. We had commissioned studies that proved it worked. Who wouldn't want that?

And yet, there was opposition. We expected our biggest struggle to be against inertia: Communities, schools, and teachers who didn't fully understand what was wrong with the old system and how hard they'd have to work to change it. What we didn't expect was the sharp pushback we got from national organizations. "Why do you have to do your own thing?" we were asked more than once by the then head of the Jewish Community Center Association (JCCA), the umbrella organization that networks all the JCCs. "Just give us money to pay for the schools we already have."

We were working successfully with a number of JCCs, but for the JCCA, the question of impact and identity didn't matter. Just like with the day schools, some of the people running early childhood centers assumed that because we had decided to put money into early childhood education, our money was somehow already rightfully theirs, and they couldn't understand why we wouldn't just give it to them. They didn't want new approaches complicating their jobs. They didn't want competition or disruption. That was it.

This was the kind of pushback we routinely got from the Jewish establishment—especially "umbrella organizations" like JCCA, which seemed to be locked in a permanent battle to justify their existence. (The JCCs themselves made their own money through memberships, so they didn't really need the JCCA; what exactly would happen if one day their umbrella organization disappeared, nobody actually knew.)

We felt we were tackling the gravest threat to Jewish life in America. But they felt we were competing, stepping on toes, somehow threatening their ability to raise money and carry out their ambiguous and transparently unsuccessful missions. Instead of acting like a mission-driven organization that tried to achieve impact and raised money to do it, they seemed more like a big marketing operation that also happened to run programs. Instead of being better at their own jobs, or at least getting out of the way, they were trying to stop us from embarrassing them in front of their donors.

I'm always amazed at the lengths Jewish institutions will go to protect their turf at the expense of their mission. This is an ugly truth about Jewish communal life, a truth I've had to confront with almost every project we've launched. It just proves how little they really care about the things they say they care about. When your principal concern is keeping your job and raising money, you'll be extremely sensitive to anything that might make you look bad.

The number of amazing innovations and fantastic initiatives that have been preemptively crushed by this Jewish Turf Machine is scary. A few years ago, a group of Israeli-American families lobbied their state legislature to allocate funding for Holocaust education in public schools where their children attended. The measure was sharply opposed, lobbied against, and ultimately crushed, by key people associated with the local Jewish federation. Why? Because, you see, the federation raises money for Holocaust education. These people saw it as *their* turf. Public funding would make their efforts unnecessary and make them look impotent.

So instead of being thrilled that something so important would become a permanent part of the state-funded public school system, focusing on impact as their primary goal, or putting their weight behind supporting a measure that would actually solve the problem they said they were working to solve, they focused only on what it meant for their own brand and cash flow and took action to stop any potential competition.

But where there is demand for something like high-quality Jewish early childhood education, there's only so much the Jewish Turf Machine can do to stop it. JECEI's thirty-two schools and eight thousand students were a strong start. We could easily envision it scaling up dramatically if we could find a way to fund it.

But even the excellent group of philanthropists we had assembled would not be able to continue JECEI forever. As with my other projects, our goal was to get it off the ground, prove the concept, then bring in new and bigger sources of funding to help it scale up and run indefinitely. And this we failed to do.

At a certain point in 2010, Bob Aronson, who had replaced Yitz as president of our foundation, said to me, "Give me a year." We agreed on the number of major philanthropic partners he needed to recruit in that time in order to keep JECEI going. "If I don't meet that goal," he said, "we'll shut it down."

A year later, he and my staff came back to me. "We got about 70 percent of the goal," they said. "Let's shut it down." I reluctantly agreed, and that was the end of JECEI.

LOOKING BACK, I'M NOT SURE it was the right decision. On the one hand, it's important to have discipline in your investments, to follow your own decisions, and to resist the temptation to throw good money after bad. On the other hand, JECEI *worked*. If you ask anyone in the field of Jewish preschools, they will tell you that the impact of JECEI went far beyond the specific schools and teachers we supported. The schools we supported are still mostly using the method, and many others have adopted it. The Reggio Emilia approach continues to ripple across the Jewish preschool world.

In 2010, a study was conducted to assess JECEI's impact. I was impressed by its findings. Obviously, you can't really tell what the lifelong impact of an early education program on small children will be until they become adults. But you can see certain indicators that suggest an immensely powerful tool.

Most evident was the impact on the lives of the parents. According to the report's conclusions, "the vast majority of Jewish and interfaith parents [who participate in JECEI...] are more positive about Jewish life, more engaged in Jewish living and learning, and anticipate increased engagement in the future."

So these programs, it turned out, weren't just injecting pride into young Jewish children—they were having a big impact on their families and communities as well. According to the research, 81 percent of previously nonengaged Jewish families that participated in JECEI reported that they were now "doing Jewish things with other families" more than before—and 30 percent said they were doing "a lot" more. Moreover, 97 percent were celebrating Jewish holidays more than before (56 percent "a lot more"), and 92 percent were spending more time talking to their kids about Jewish values and ideas (41 percent "a lot more"). Finally, 43 percent said they were more likely to send their kids to Jewish camps, and 39 percent said they were more likely to send them to Hebrew school.[6]

These numbers were taken from surveys of both inmarried and intermarried parents—but only from families that hadn't been Jewishly engaged before sending their kids to JECEI schools.

In other words, JECEI was changing lives. Young families that weren't previously engaged in Jewish life had chosen to send their children to a Jewish preschool, and the result was that the parents themselves were becoming much more committed to leading Jewish lives, having Jewish friends, and raising Jewish children. It was scalable, too. Because the schools already existed, we didn't have to build a whole infrastructure from the ground up, but we did have to carefully redirect the culture of the schools and mentor and train everyone involved. This was the kind of added value I had gone into philanthropy to achieve.

---

6 Pat Bidol Padva and Roberta Louis Goodman, "Pursuing Excellence in Jewish Early Childhood Education: A Case Study of JECEI's Transformative Change Model," *JECEI* (June 2011), http://www.jecei.org/PDF/17%20JECEI%20Presentation%20 Paper-Int%20Conference.pdf.

Because of the importance of what we had done and the possibility that someone would want to invest in it in the future, we decided to preserve all the research and curricular resources on a website, jecei.org. To this day, it's seen as one of the most influential initiatives in the field, with hundreds of "Reggio-inspired" Jewish preschools flourishing around the country.

I'm not a big fan of regrets and don't believe in ever looking back on a trade. But in this case, I do wonder whether I pulled the plug on JECEI too early. One of the report's findings was that the longer the teachers were exposed to the JECEI model, the better they got at it, and the better the results. It takes time for a school to change its approach—and the more time went by, the more these schools were embracing it. Part of me wonders whether another couple of years might have positioned us better to convince the federations and major donor communities to get on board.

Once again, I saw the limits of what I could accomplish on my own. If the Jewish community as a whole can't see the value of a project, no matter how successful, there's not a lot I can do about it.

As Yogi Berra once said, "If people don't want to come out to the ballpark, nobody's going to stop them."

PEJE, TOO, REACHED THE END of its day. But again, the problem with PEJE wasn't just funding. Unlike JECEI, which I still believe is the right solution to a serious problem, PEJE was based on flawed assumptions about the scalability of day schools.

Why is it that so few Jews have any interest in sending their kids to an exclusively Jewish school? To many people, the question itself may seem outdated. Over the last two or three generations, the world has opened up for American Jews. The genie is out of the bottle. They want their kids to see and know the diversity of the world. To have Jewish and non-Jewish teachers and friends. The biggest dream of their immigrant grandparents was to *make it in America*—and there's nothing that says "musty, old-world, gefilte-fish parochialism" like sending your kids to an all-Jewish school. At a deep level, I think the idea represented a step backward in their American story.

This was a point of an intractable dispute between me and many of the professionals I worked with who came from a traditional background. The issue turned into a heated debate during our efforts to build an elite, secular Jewish high school in Manhattan, which I mentioned earlier. Those efforts got pretty far, including extensive research and focus groups. We pulled together a topflight group of individuals committed to building a flagship school, including Leon Botstein, president of Bard College, as well as the veteran Jewish educator Rabbi Michael Paley, and others. But it never got off the ground, in large part because all of our world-class Jewish educators and thinkers and philanthropists couldn't agree on what a superior Jewish education actually looked like.

Leon, who is also a renowned musicologist and a proud secular Jew, helped put together a detailed proposal. He felt strongly that to succeed, the school had to allow some non-Jews to attend, or you'd turn off the most important Jewish constituency we wanted to reach.

For Yitz and others, this was a nonstarter. The idea of encouraging Jewish kids to go to school with non-Jewish kids—and potentially date and even marry them—was crossing some kind of unthinkable red line.

I get it. Jews are a small people, embattled and threatened, and we have a very long history of insularity. It's a big part of what has preserved us. But I am not willing to write off the vast majority of non-Orthodox Jews in America who have no interest in all-Jewish schools or Jewish insularity. If we are going to use schools to build a vibrant, proud secular Jewish identity in America, they will have to be open to non-Jewish students as well.

As with so many other projects I launched, I wanted an answer that could be scaled up to reach a very significant portion of Jews. Otherwise, what was the point?

AROUND 2007, I STARTED LOOKING for a new approach to formal education. I found it in the concept of the Hebrew-language charter schools—publicly funded schools that offer Hebrew language and Israeli culture to children of all backgrounds, Jewish and non-Jewish. To understand this move, however, we need to talk a little about the importance of the Hebrew language itself.

Can you imagine how different things would be if a significant portion of non-Orthodox American Jews were fluent in Modern Hebrew? Not necessarily all, nor even a majority. But if even 10 percent—more than half a million non-Orthodox, non-Israeli American Jews—were fluent, it would change the entire character of the community.

Language is the portal to a larger world. Anyone who's ever learned a second language to an advanced level knows it. Suddenly you see everything in three dimensions. It changes how you see the world you live in and how you move through it.

Not long ago, studying Hebrew didn't give you much more than the ability to read the Bible and the traditional prayer book. True, that's nothing to sneeze at. But today, if you know Modern Hebrew, you have access to the vibrant Jewish civilization that has been built over the last century in Israel. Even if you move there, you can't really be Israeli until you know Hebrew. And now that Yiddish is pretty much gone, Jews don't have a widely spoken, living language of their own other than Hebrew.

There was a time, not long ago, when almost all Jews were multilingual. If they lived in Europe or had recently immigrated to the U.S., they knew Yiddish or German as well as English. Others spoke Russian, Lithuanian, Polish, Ladino, Arabic, or Persian. They also learned Hebrew, to be able to read the Torah and other holy books. Rabbinic scholars needed a working knowledge of ancient Aramaic as well.

Learning languages was always seen by Jews as a smart investment. You never knew when you might need it. But the benefits were cumulative, giving you access to countries, cultures, and books that would otherwise be closed to you.

The case for Hebrew as a gateway to Jewish identity has always been obvious to me—even if it took me a long time to translate that insight into an actual project. There is an entire country of Hebrew-speaking Jews that have spent the last century developing a unique, secular Jewish culture—in Hebrew.

Knowing Hebrew not only creates access to Israeli culture. It also lets you take part in the conversation with Israelis about Israel. So many American Jews have been frustrated in the last few years by developments in the Jewish state—with respect to the Palestinians, the settlements, the religious and political movements—and they feel Israelis don't listen to or understand their concerns. But how hard have they tried to understand Israelis? The first step is learning their language.

I say this as a Jew who, regrettably, never mastered Hebrew. I know it may sound funny coming from me, and whatever personal reasons I offer will probably ring hollow. But the truth is that language is the access key to any culture, and ever since my first trip to Israel, whenever I hear Israelis speaking the language, I can immediately sense the essence of their vitality and humanity. It is not something I can prove, but I am convinced that the specific sounds of modern Israeli Hebrew are woven into the very fabric of the new Israeli Jewish reality.

We owe the early Zionists a great debt for their successful resurrection of Hebrew. Today it's the Israeli language, to the point that there are probably more non-Jewish Arab-Israelis fluent in Hebrew than American Jews. But that can change: We can imagine Hebrew becoming a living language for Jews everywhere, in which we as a global people can talk and create and develop together.

Perhaps the most important reason for learning Modern Hebrew, however, is that the spirit of Zionism is hard to translate into English. I spent my life as an outsider, looking at the products of that spirit—the incredible achievements in Israeli industry, defense, immigrant absorption, the start-up nation. A century's worth of serious thinking, arguments, hopes and dreams and pep talks—all in Hebrew. But I never had direct access to that culture or the conversations taking place every single day among millions of Israelis.

Today, the percentage of non-Orthodox, non-Israeli American Jews who know Hebrew is astonishingly small. Most don't even know the alphabet. According to the Pew Research Center, only 12 percent of American Jews can carry on a simple conversation in Hebrew, and almost all of these are either Orthodox (very few of whom are fluent), the children of Israelis, or graduates of a non-Orthodox day school. Among Reform Jews and "Jews of no religion," it's more like 2 percent—and those presumably include a fair number of Israeli-Americans. So the real percentage of non-Orthodox, non-Israeli American Jews who can hold a simple conversation in Hebrew today is precariously close to zero.

When our foundation started looking into the issue around 2007, the first thing that struck us was how little infrastructure there was for proper Hebrew language education in America. Part of it had to do with a lack of teachers. While America is now home to more than a hundred thousand native Israelis, very few were trained to teach Hebrew as a second language. Almost no textbooks existed in English for courses in Modern Hebrew—though there were plenty for biblical Hebrew. Almost no programs existed for training teachers, either.

Instead, educational programs relied on inexperienced Israelis looking for work or Americans who studied Hebrew using traditional methods that never made them really fluent or only gave them the tools for studying the Bible and Talmud. But because most non-Orthodox kids have little use for these classical texts, they weren't interested. The poor supply and the lack of demand went hand in hand.

Today, most young Jews know that Israel has a fascinating culture, and they catch glimpses of it when they watch TV shows like *Fauda* or *Tehran*, hear the music of Static & Ben El or Balkan Beat Box, or watch Gal Gadot playing Wonder Woman. They are amazed to discover the vitality of the country when they go to Israel through programs like Birthright. But the bandwidth of cultural exposure to Israel among American Jews is still extremely narrow. They can barely hear the music; they sure can't understand the words.

Of course, Modern Hebrew language study suffered from the same poverty of educational infrastructure as the rest of Jewish education. But the question that nagged at me was this: What if American Jews, in very large numbers, could study Hebrew using professionally trained teachers and cutting-edge methods? What if high-quality Hebrew classes were available in public high schools and colleges just like French and Spanish? What if American Jews embraced Hebrew as a living part of their Jewish lives, even writing Hebrew songs and producing Hebrew-language movies?

What could that mean for Jewish pride? Was such a thing possible?

I ASKED MY FOUNDATION'S EXECUTIVE director, Rabbi David Gedzelman, to explore the question of promoting Hebrew language study in America. He reported back that in every conversation he had with experts around the Jewish world, a single name kept coming up: Vardit Ringvald.

I first met Vardit in our office in New York and was immediately taken by her sharp mind, her energy, her creativity, and her determination. She was an Israeli of the classic type, the type that had so deeply inspired me on my first trip to Israel in 1962 and kept me coming back.

Vardit's parents had come from Czechoslovakia around the time of the Holocaust. Her mother had survived some of the most horrific aspects of the Nazi genocide and rarely talked about it. Her father had come from a religious-Zionist family in Prague, and as a boy, he had watched, with his own eyes, as Adolf Hitler marched into the city in 1939. He managed to get out a few months later and made his way to Palestine, in spite of the British blockade. In 1948, he fought in Israel's War of Independence, surviving the horrific battle of Gush Etzion where many of his closest friends were killed. He was active in the politics of the early state, and members of the Knesset routinely visited the family home in the coastal city of Netanya.

Vardit served in the IDF Intelligence Corps during the Yom Kippur War in 1973. At Jerusalem's Hebrew University, she studied art and Hebrew language. She wanted to be an artist and started teaching Hebrew the same way many other Israelis do— by accident. She spent a few years with her husband in his native Uruguay. She was bored. One day, Vardit went to the local Jewish school in Montevideo and asked the principal, who was Israeli, if there was anything she could do to help. He said, "Uh, yeah, you can start teaching Hebrew, tomorrow."

She soon discovered something very troubling. Vardit had been trained in the classical method of language teaching: structures, grammar, vocabulary lists. Language as a logical construct. But after a year of teaching kids Hebrew, she realized that they still didn't know anything. By contrast, she herself had come to Uruguay without knowing a word of Spanish, and within three months, she was functionally fluent. But the kids in her school *were not actually learning Hebrew as a functional language.*

She and her husband then went to Boston, where he enrolled in university. Vardit looked for a job and soon discovered that the Hebrew language department at Brandeis University was hiring.

This was around the time, in the mid-1980s, when a revolution in language instruction was taking place. The new method was called the "proficiency approach." The idea was that language isn't an abstract, logical construct. It is, rather, a tool for interacting with other people. It is the medium in which human interactions, transactions, and relationships take place. It is, in other words, functional in its essence. The best way to learn, therefore, is to teach students how to *do things* with language, in a manner similar to the way children naturally learn it—first orally, then through literacy with an emphasis on functionality.

American kids don't learn English by first studying the grammatical structures and verb conjugations, and there's no reason they should learn Hebrew that way either. Rather, they learn language through the things they can do with it, and not just how to order in a restaurant but how to have important conversations, and eventually to read Israeli books in the original, and to explore Israel's cultural offerings on their own.

It was at Brandeis that her department chair suggested to her the idea of applying the proficiency approach to Hebrew. Vardit discovered that all across America, Hebrew was taught using old methods—a mixture of Eastern European *haskala*, Orthodox *heder*, and old-fashioned Western methods. The bottom line was that kids were going through many years of day school or Hebrew school and still couldn't read an Israeli newspaper or carry on a conversation. She decided to do something about it.

At Brandeis, she began advocating for adapting the proficiency approach to teaching Hebrew. She began publishing papers and giving talks around the country on the subject. She began training Hebrew teachers as well through a master's degree program. In 1990, she published the first guidelines for teaching Hebrew in the proficiency approach, and, in 2005, she published *Brandeis Modern Hebrew*, the first-ever textbook for teaching Modern Hebrew to English speakers using the proficiency approach.

When I first met her in 2008, she had just gotten an offer to build an entire program at Middlebury College in Vermont, a famous center for proficiency-based language study. For her, it was a dream come true. Suddenly, she could train dozens of teachers each year in a master's degree program instead of one or two. I eventually decided to support her efforts in a significant way.

"Language is an art," Vardit once said to me. "It addresses every level of our consciousness. You can't teach it just through logic and memorization. It has to be lived."

Together with David Gedzelman, I spent a few days visiting her at Middlebury in 2017. Here, suddenly, was the Israeli spirit, the instinctive Jewish pride that I admired, being channeled into the context of language study—there was culture, there was singing and dancing, there was an immersive experience. I questioned the students about the program, to find out what they were learning and also what they felt. It was powerful. It reminded me of the pioneering spirit I had felt on every trip I had taken to Israel. I found in Middlebury something that should be found in every Jewish educational experience in America, but in practice is still very rare: The joy of being Jewish.

Vardit was also a central force in our project to build Hebrew charter schools across America.

Though the specific laws vary from state to state, the idea of charter schools is simple: They are state-funded public schools, but they are run independently and specialize their focus on certain kinds of subject matter above and beyond the core curriculum. In some (more liberal) places, the idea is to offer an opportunity for disadvantaged kids to excel. In more conservative places, the aim is to offer parents a greater degree of educational choice without having to pay for private school.

As oddball as it seemed at first, the idea of Hebrew charters kills several birds with one stone. Because it's a public school, they can't teach religious subjects. So instead of teaching Jewish texts and prayers, these schools offer Hebrew language and secular Israeli culture. There is, therefore, no temptation to make it religious, which automatically would trigger turf wars among the denominations and turn off the most religiously unengaged Jewish families.

Further, because it mixes Jewish with non-Jewish students, it appeals to a much broader swath of Jewish parents and kids who don't want to be in a Jewish-only environment. The schools are open to all, but the subject matter will naturally draw Jewish families. And while there are plenty of wealthy Jews, there is a much larger number who can't afford private schooling.

The result is that Hebrew language and Israeli culture can potentially become mainstreamed in American life as a big piece in the puzzle of secular Jewish identity. Unlike day schools, as long as the education is of high quality, most Jewish parents will happily send their kids, and the system can be sustained from a financial standpoint.

But it wouldn't have been possible without the work we were doing with Vardit to develop a professional Hebrew-language curriculum and to train teachers who know what they're doing.

Charter schools have given us another building block in the construction of a proud, secular Jewish culture in America. It's unfortunate that so many Jews require non-Jewish validation, seeing non-Jewish kids singing Hebrew songs and learning about Israel with them, in order to be proud of their own culture—but that's the reality today.

The project was complicated, as anything involving the government inevitably is. To be clear, we weren't the first to jump into the pool. In 2007, the Ben Gamla Charter School was launched in Hollywood, Florida—a Hebrew-English public charter school with a very different model from what we ended up pursuing. As we explored it, we learned how each state has its own specific regulatory approval process and oversight, and there are also both grants and bureaucratic hurdles at the federal level.

In 2009, we launched our first Hebrew charter school in Flatbush in Brooklyn, called the Hebrew Language Academy Charter School. My daughter Sara took the lead representing the school, putting together a team under David Gedzelman's leadership that designed the curriculum and educational model for the school, and also met with city officials to make sure we met all the requirements. The Areivim Philanthropic Group, a partnership I began with Bill Davidson in 2005, which pulled together partners to provide initial funding, got behind it as well, helping secure the location and other start-up costs.

Once the school opened, the *New York Times* ran a feature about the school, filled with both Jewish and non-Jewish, mostly minority, kids—"a broad range of students, all seeming confident enough to jabber away as if they were elbowing their way down Ben Yehuda Street in Jerusalem." Word began to spread.

The following year, with the help of our foundation, the Hatikvah school opened in New Jersey, as did the Kavod Charter School in San Diego. By 2013, two more had opened, in Harlem and Washington, D.C., and the following year we supported the launch of the Lashon Academy in Los Angeles, one of our most successful schools. Today there are fourteen schools on ten campuses, mainly in the New York area and Philadelphia but also two in Los Angeles. There are more on the way.

Again, these are not "Jewish" schools in the traditional sense of the word. There is no reference to religious holidays, religious practices, or religious texts. They are much more Israeli in the same way that a French charter school will immerse students in the experiences, the people, the culture, and the language of France. Because of the content, they will disproportionately attract Jewish students—but not always even a majority.

It turns out that such dual-language charter schools attract kids of many different backgrounds, often from disadvantaged and minority urban centers, whose parents see them—both because of their superior educational standards and their commitment to learning a second language—as a way of getting a leg up in life.

I've been thrilled by the progress—and also by the fact that Sara has taken the leading role, as chair of the Hebrew Public organization, along with Jon Rosenberg, its President and CEO. Together they've done a tremendous job navigating an exceptionally complicated challenge and making sure that Hebrew charter schools keep growing and succeeding.

As the schools have grown, new programs have been added, including trips to Israel for eighth-graders, and trips for teachers who are brought to Israel, where they spend some time teaching English to Israeli kids through a program we support called TALMA. In addition to any benefit we gain for Jewish identity, we are also bringing non-Jews to a country whose language and culture they've been studying and with whom they will have a deep sentimental attachment they otherwise might never have had.

I need to be crystal clear on this, because the point is confusing to many, including critics. My personal interest in Hebrew charter schools is in the consequences they deliver from a standpoint of secular Jewish pride. That purpose, however, is not shared by the Hebrew Public organization or the individual schools.

From their perspective, promoting Hebrew language and Israeli culture are ends in themselves. "Jewish pride" is not on their radar. From my end, both the promotion of Hebrew in the world—for Jews and non-Jews alike—and the benefits to Jewish pride in the Diaspora, which I understand is a totally unintended but nonetheless inevitable consequence, are worthy. That's why I will continue to support the project.

When the Hebrew charter schools first launched, I visited the school in Flatbush, and as I always do, I spoke not just to teachers and administrators but also to individual pupils, getting a sense of what they felt about the experience. Each year, they would host an annual Broadway Benefit event at a theater. Before the show, they brought the Hebrew Language Academy's choir to perform outside.

Just imagine, elementary school kids from all walks of life—Jewish and non-Jewish—singing popular Israeli songs, their Hebrew seemingly fluent and effortless. It brought me close to tears. The experience of seeing American kids from completely diverse racial and social backgrounds singing Hebrew songs—the vision of Hebrew spreading through the world—was deeply moving.

On some level, I knew that the Zionist pioneers, who could barely imagine a viable Jewish state, much less one successful enough to be spreading its language and culture through the world, would have been proud.

AS WITH ALL OUR PROJECTS, there has been pushback. But with Hebrew charter schools, the reaction was wide, public, and furious. The AJC's New York branch, egged on presumably by supporters of existing Jewish schools, came out against them, claiming they violated church and state separation. (They didn't.) And their lay leader actually wrote to the chancellor of New York City's schools, asking him to put a stop to it. (He didn't.)

Jewish day schools, for their part, were miffed that we were being successful with the charter schools in places where they would have loved to attract day school students but had failed to do so. Once again, they felt that any money being put into schools should have gone to them instead. When the New York State Board of Regents voted to approve our first school in January 2009, the only member who voted against it was Saul Cohen, a secular Jew.

The issue of church-and-state separation in charter schools is an important question, though, because it gets to the heart not just of a complicated constitutional controversy but also of Jewish identity. If Judaism is mainly a religion, as a lot of Jews still seem to believe, then it's hard to talk about Hebrew language and culture in a way that's divorced from theology, prayer, and religious practice. In fact, the Ben Gamla schools in Florida got into trouble for crossing that line more than once.

But for more than a century, Israelis have been developing a spirited, powerful, vibrant, entirely secular identity, based in the Hebrew language, detached from religious commitments, involving now millions of people. It includes not just music, art, food, literature, and film, but new holidays like Yom Ha'atzmaut, Yom Hashoah, and Yom Hazikaron that, for most Israelis, have nothing to do with religion. It also includes more than a million Hebrew-speaking non-Jews, most of them Muslim or Christian Arabs who participate in, and contribute to, Israeli culture.

Outside the Orthodox world, Hebrew as a national and ethnic language has become a lot more vital and viable than Hebrew as a classical language of religion. For that reason, it's not hard to create a curriculum based on Modern Hebrew and Israeli culture without having to cross the line—just as you can have Greek, Spanish, and French charter schools without invoking the Catholic or Orthodox Christian traditions.

Of course, a lot of American Jews have a hard time understanding it. Nothing we've done draws a sharper line between Jewish religious and secular identities than this. From the very beginning, we've had to make clear (and not just because of the legal issues) that this is about Israel and Hebrew language and not Judaism. Because of the confusion it causes, we don't describe it as a "Jewish" project at all. But Israel and Modern Hebrew are, to me, Jewish achievements, and there will be many unengaged

Jews for whom this can be a point of entry into a more powerful Jewish identity.

It is exactly this kind of proud secular Jewish identity that my foundation and our allies have been trying to build with all our projects, overturning the applecart of failed Jewish institutional and religious strategies to foster a new, vibrant non-Orthodox Jewish world in the Diaspora.

This is also why so many people are trying to stop the Hebrew charter schools. In one major city, we got a grant for a feasibility study to launch a school in the downtown area, where there was barely any Jewish institutional presence but a growing population of unaffiliated Jews. The local federation leader was thrilled about it. But when one of the main donors of an area day school—way out in the suburbs—found out about it, he threatened to stop giving to the federation if they supported the charter school. The federation turned on a dime and suddenly said they wouldn't work with us.

This was crazy: Remember, only a tiny percentage of non-Orthodox parents send their kids to day school, and the whole point of charters, from my end, is to reach the 97 percent who don't. I, for one, wouldn't ever have gotten involved in charter schools if it weren't for the colossal, structural failure of the day school model to reach a broader non-Orthodox audience. Our target market was radically different from theirs: I don't know if a single student would have switched from their school to ours.

Instead of trying to stop us, these donors should have joined us. And instead of giving in to threats, the federation should have called their bluff. But when the Jewish Turf Machine gets fired up, there's little you can do to reason with it. We put that project on hold.

Although charter schools ultimately become self-sustaining mainly through public funding, launching them requires significant philanthropic support, and here, too, we encounter a great deal of resistance. Jewish donors often have difficulty putting money into programs that build Jewish pride but aren't exclusively Jewish. Foundations and federations have officers who are given clear guidelines for giving away other people's money, and this usually doesn't fall into any of their preexisting categories. So we need to cultivate a philanthropic awareness of a totally new category, which is itself a heavy lift.

Unbelievably, there has even been opposition to efforts to reform the way the Hebrew language is taught. Vardit was warned that she would become *persona non grata* in the existing world of Hebrew educators. These teachers have spent decades teaching the old methods and were predictably upset about having their failures made so abundantly clear.

An increasing number, however, are starting to admit the need for change. Vardit once got a call from the principal of the Joseph Kushner Hebrew Academy, a well-regarded Orthodox day school in Livingston, New Jersey. He was fuming.

"How dare you?" he said.

"How dare I what?"

"You have students who graduated my school, after *twelve* years of Hebrew study, and you won't exempt them from Hebrew?"

Vardit took a minute to track down the files. "I'm seeing that they tested at the 'Novice High' level," she told him. "You can't expect me to exempt them if they don't even have Intermediate-level Hebrew."

It's moments like these that show what a Jewish educator is made of. The principal could have easily dismissed her as an imperious freak causing him an entirely unnecessary headache among parents and faculty. Instead, he responded by inviting Vardit to meet with the heads of an entire network of Jewish schools for an in-depth discussion of what can be done to dramatically improve their results.

Deep down, the leaders of Jewish schools know that there's something critically wrong with the way they've been teaching Hebrew for generations. They know that Hebrew, like any language, can be taught poorly or well depending on the training of the teacher and methodology used. Just because someone is Israeli or fluent doesn't mean they can teach Hebrew—after all, who among us native English speakers would know how to teach English well? Vardit's program was, and continues to be, the key to our goal to change American Jewish life through the Hebrew language.

Although the issue of long-term funding for Hebrew public charter schools can potentially be taken care of through the charter system, the same cannot be said for the huge amount of work we still have to do in turning Modern Hebrew into a more widely spoken language. Large numbers of teachers need to be trained, curricula developed, colleges and high schools convinced, online programs launched, and on and on. To do this is in a sustained way requires a large amount of capital.

In addition to the charter schools, a much bigger potential market can be found in regular public and private schools and colleges across America. The biggest reason Modern Hebrew isn't offered universally is that we don't have nearly enough accredited teachers. So far, Vardit's program at Middlebury has trained about 150 Hebrew teachers earning a master's degree in the proficiency approach. But we will need thousands.

Training them will cost a lot of money and will require the creation of teaching centers, run by Vardit's students, across the country. A few are in the process of launching, five or six in the first stage under the auspices of Brandeis University, to be followed by additional centers across the country. The goal is to leverage what has been built into a much larger operation producing potentially hundreds of teachers with MAs each year. Meanwhile, Vardit's approach is already having a significant impact on the way Hebrew is taught in some day schools. Boston's Jewish Community Day School, which Vardit also helped found together with Arnee Winshall (with a seed grant from PEJE), is built around teaching Hebrew with her method. Washington, D.C.'s elite Jewish day school JPDS has switched to the proficiency approach for teaching Hebrew and is staffed with Vardit's graduates. Other schools are following suit.

The most obvious place to begin the revolution is, of course, where students are already learning Hebrew. But there is so much more to do.

I want to believe that it's something the Israeli government will take upon itself. Other governments do this all the time. France has been funding French language and cultural studies around the world for a century. Qatar has been secretly behind a lot of Arabic-language programs in America. Even Greece—a country perpetually on the brink of default—somehow manages to find a budget for Greek language studies around the world. The Italian government spent at least a million dollars so that the College Board could create a new Advanced Placement exam in Italian.

From the perspective of Zionism, the rationale seems even more obvious. Hebrew language and literature were a central pillar of building the new Jewish state. The whole idea was to create an identity based on a living Hebrew language that would have a life of its own, like that of any proud and modern nation. Today there is probably no greater single tool for building under-standing and sympathy for Israel—among Jews and non-Jews alike—than fostering widespread fluency in Modern Hebrew. There's probably no greater barrier for Western Jews to move to Israel, or to invest in Israeli companies, than their lack of Hebrew proficiency.

But every time we've tried to get the Israeli government involved, we have come up empty. In 2013, Naftali Bennett, then Diaspora Affairs minister and today the prime minister, visited the Hebrew Language Academy, our first charter school in Brooklyn. With tears in his eyes, he watched Jewish and Caribbean and African American kids singing Israeli songs in Hebrew—a sight that was unimaginable just a few years before.

I could see that he was moved—as were then-Finance Minister Yair Lapid and the then-consul general in New York, Dani Dayan, who both visited several times. But political leaders come and go and so do the bureaucrats. We got a little funding at first, but the director general of the ministry was replaced two years later and the new one had no interest in funding Hebrew language education for non-Orthodox Jews in the Diaspora.

Why? We can only speculate. One possibility is the petty politics of it. A lot of Israelis see liberal American Jews as anti-Zionist—it's really not true, but that's the perception. Or maybe they don't think Americans will ever learn another language at all. But whatever the reasoning, the idea that you want to build Israel into a magnet for investments, for diplomatic support, for tourists, for Birthright participants, and ultimately for millions of new immigrants—but you aren't willing to pick up the tab for spreading the Hebrew language around the world—just doesn't make sense to me. I'm pretty sure that at some point, the bureaucrats will see it, too.

CAN WE HAVE BETTER JEWISH SCHOOLS? You bet we can. There is nothing written in stone that says they have to be boring, ineffective, or outlandishly expensive.

What is required, however, is that we reinvent the idea of Jewish education from the ground up, in a way that thoroughly takes into account the lived reality of non-Orthodox Jews in the Diaspora, as well as advances in the field of education, and offers both experiences and content that keep them coming back.

The first step is to dramatically expand the accreditation and training of teachers, using the most cutting-edge methodologies, at every level. Without high-quality teachers, you are sunk before you even begin.

In our efforts over the last twenty-five years, we built two models of Jewish schooling that were unlike anything that had been tried before. For preschoolers, we created a new kind of Jewish education that connected young children with parents, staff, and the community, infusing their lives with Jewish values and content. We created training and certification programs in the Reggio Emilia method. Although we stopped supporting JECEI, its impact continues to be felt across the Jewish world. And because it doesn't require building new schools, the long-term cost is much less than it would have been, say, for the vision of day schools.

In Hebrew charter schools, we found a scalable, fundable method to engage Jewish families with little interest in traditional Jewish schools. Here, too, the key is training excellent teachers at scale. In our work with Vardit at Brandeis and Middlebury, we built the necessary infrastructure to turn the Modern Hebrew language into a viable, accessible course of study for school-age kids, college students, and adults. In 2013, together with our partners in the Areivim Philanthropic Group, we also launched a new program called Kayitz Kef ("Summer of Fun"), which creates immersive Hebrew language experiences in Jewish day camps across America. By the summer of 2020, despite the disruptions of the Covid-19 pandemic, the program engaged over two thousand children in the

Hebrew language online and in person; and in the summer of 2021, we piloted it in four overnight camps as well. All told, thousands of kids each year, Jewish and non-Jewish, are learning to function in the Modern Hebrew language and enjoying everything that goes with it. And our studies show that it works, with participants in Kayitz Kef consistently demonstrating a deeper connection to Israel than nonparticipants at the same camps.

Needless to say, this doesn't cover all the bases. After-school programs like the one I attended as a youth are desperately in need of an overhaul. Sleepaway camps and youth movements hold enormous potential, but the number of Jewish kids participating in them is still a small fraction of what it could be. Scholarly research needs to be supported as well. In 2000, I committed $20 million to endow the NYU Steinhardt School of Culture, Education, and Human Development, which included a doctoral program in Education and Jewish Studies, and later another $5 million to pay for scholarships at the school.

The mission of creating a pride-filled, secular Jewish identity in America requires a lot of trial and error, and for that reason, I'm not troubled by the mistakes we may have made along the way as long as we learned something from them. In business, we call this "failing forward." PEJE taught us that all-Jewish day schools are not, ultimately, the answer. JECEI gave us a scalable model, and a proof of concept, for the community to implement through its existing preschool and day care infrastructure. And the Hebrew charter schools, coupled with Hebrew language study through the proficiency approach, are one of the most promising ways to enlist unengaged Jewish families into the beauty and richness of the Hebrew language and Israeli culture.

Formal education has its limits, of course. So much of our lives are defined by things that happen outside of classrooms. A totally different kind of project, one that focused on singular, immersive experiences, would ultimately turn our foundation into the hottest name in Jewish communal life.

Interlude:
A Philanthropic Revolution

THERE ARE TWO IMPORTANT FEATURES of cutting-edge Jewish philanthropy that are noticeable today but did not exist when I was starting out in the 1990s. I don't know how much credit I can take for them.

The first has to do with the rigorous use of statistical data in evaluating impact. Obviously, I had come from a financial world where success and failure were easy to quantify. Your clients' return on investment was measurable in percentages and dollars.

In the world of Jewish nonprofits, nothing like that existed. People gave to synagogues, schools, programs in Israel, or summer camps—but the only way they could measure the results of that gift was by how many people chose to participate. But very rarely did anyone decide whether or not to donate based on measurable impact, rather than activity.

Of course, identity is harder to measure than profits. But from the very beginning of the Steinhardt Foundation, we were adamant about collecting data and analyzing results. PEJE would never have gotten off the ground without Avi Chai sponsoring the census of day schools. Birthright Israel—the subject of the next chapter— became the first large-scale Jewish initiative that included rigorous data collection and analysis. We engaged some of the top demographers and social scientists to give us a much more granular sense of what works and what doesn't than has ever been seen. In 2005, I made a gift of $12 million to endow the Steinhardt Social Research Institute at Brandeis University to dramatically increase the amount and quality of data available about Jewish life in America.

Today, one often hears philanthropists talking about data and "metrics of impact." This is new and suggests a crucial shift in Jewish philanthropy, but it needs to go much farther. We need federations and other major bodies to be held accountable for the good, or lack of it, that is done with donors' money.

The second major shift has to do with philanthropic partnerships. Before the 1990s, the federation system, the synagogues, and mission-specific organizations raised money from individual donors large and small. If you were wealthy, you picked whom you gave to and didn't really involve yourself much beyond the check you wrote and the gala dinners you attended. You certainly didn't work together with other major donors to help set standards of performance or hold organizations accountable.

My attitude was different: Why not get together with a small number of like-minded people of means and launch or support specific projects that we thought could really make a difference? This way, we could make sure programs were done right: The right staff, the right data, the right incentive structures, the right methodology, the right proof of impact.

Almost all of our projects started with a small number of highly committed philanthropic brothers and sisters in arms. My best-known partnership was with Charles Bronfman—a remarkable man who understood the depth of the change that was needed and was willing to take action but who also was much better than I was at working together with the Jewish establishment. He and I started Birthright Israel, pulling together more than a dozen additional major donors who would, alongside the Israeli government and the federations, take on its immense financial burden. In the early years, I also participated in the Mega Group, the first effort of its kind to create a standing body of major philanthropists who together studied the landscape, and which spawned partnerships that got behind new initiatives. Later on, we launched the Areivim Philanthropic Group with a similar aim. This combination of standing and ad hoc partnerships, alongside the dramatic rise of private and family foundations, has changed the face of Jewish philanthropy in the last generation, breaking the establishment's monopoly in a variety of fields.

There is a deep connection between these two innovations. The failure of the establishment to preserve Jewish pride from one generation to the next was rooted in an unaccountable system that behaves just like any other unaccountable system does—ineffectively, protecting its turf and glorifying its false success. Data and partnerships addressed this problem from two different angles.

This philanthropic revolution is still in its early phases. There are not nearly enough donors who understand the change and have internalized it. The truth is, it's a lot harder to put time and energy into building a successful nonprofit project than just to send a check to the local federation. And the partnership model is limited: You can launch projects that cost millions, even tens of millions, of dollars a year this way. But once you get into hundreds of millions or billions—the kind of scale needed to address our biggest problems—even the richest individual Jews on earth aren't that rich. To sustain large-scale projects over time, you need to win over the establishment, and, hopefully, governments as well.

Of everything I've launched, only one program has gotten the kind of funding required to build it up to full scale and keep it running: Birthright Israel. It embodied these philanthropic revolutions, and it has, in a modest way at least, changed the face of Jewish life in the Diaspora.

CHAPTER 3

Why Birthright Worked

Depending on how old you are, you might not remember a time when Birthright didn't exist.[7] Since launching at the end of 1999, more than six hundred thousand young Jews from America and across the Diaspora have taken advantage of an intense, free ten-day trip to Israel. If you're under forty and Jewish, you almost certainly either went on Birthright or know someone who did.

Before Birthright, about two-thirds of the Jews in America had never set foot in Israel. They might have followed the news, read books, and heard stories about the country the Zionists built, but they had never walked its cities, deserts, or forests. They had never breathed in its acute human energy, ridden its public transportation, haggled at its markets, or eaten falafel on a Jerusalem sidewalk.

---

7 When we started Birthright, we discovered that the name conflicted with that of a political organization in Canada. As a result, its formal name in English became "birthright Israel" with a lower-case "b." The need for a lower-case "b," which caused endless heartache for proofreaders around the world, was subsequently resolved. The Israeli organization later on needed a Hebrew name for domestic purposes, so they called it Taglit, which means "discovery." So now its official name in Israel is "Taglit-Birthright Israel," whereas the foundation that raises money for it in the U.S. is called the Birthright Israel Foundation. Because most people just call it "Birthright," and because that's the name that I've always felt captures its essence, I'm using that as shorthand.

They had never rounded a bend on a mountain pass and suddenly been dazzled by the sunlight glinting off the Sea of Galilee in the valley below. They'd never seen young Jews wearing the olive drab of the Jewish army, colored berets pinned to their epaulets and rifles dangling from their shoulders. They had never tasted the gritty, determined, creative mettle of the country—an intensity that hits you from the moment you touch down at the airport. They had never laid their hand on the Western Wall, closed their eyes, and directly confronted the timeless spirit of our people.

And while there had been a variety of organized programs in Israel of varying lengths, only a small percentage of young, non-Orthodox Jews took advantage of them. Those who did were typically from the most engaged parts of the community: Youth groups, synagogue missions, leadership programs, study abroad.

At the same time, I knew very well from my own experience that a trip to Israel at a relatively young age can have a powerful impact on the trajectory of one's entire life. And I knew it wasn't just me. I had heard many similar stories.

In her 2005 book, *Stars of David*, Abigail Pogrebin interviews dozens of prominent American Jews about their Jewish feelings. Many of them looked back on a youthful trip to Israel as having changed their lives. Here's fashion designer Kenneth Cole, whose first visit included a few weeks on a kibbutz at the age of seventeen: "When I search back for one experience in my life where I learned and came away with the most, I think it might have been that summer." Here's Ron Perelman, the CEO of Revlon: "My turning point came when I was eighteen years old; we took a family trip to Israel. It was the first and only time I've been there. It just had this strong impact on me. I felt not only this enormous pride at being a Jew; I felt this enormous void at not being a better Jew." The renowned TV journalist Mike Wallace visited Israel at the end of the Six-Day War in 1967: "The sun was just beginning to rise, and people were just out there in their chairs waiting for the parade that was going to take place, and I just broke down. In that moment I was very Jewish, I was very Israeli, very proud." And here's Jason Alexander, best known for his role in the TV show *Seinfeld*: "When I was twenty-nine, I had a life-changing experience by going to Israel. Not the religious Judaism, but the cultural connection. It became important to me."

Everybody who's ever been to Israel vividly remembers his or her first trip. Even today, in the age of virtual reality, video calls, and live streaming, the great majority of first-time visitors are still overwhelmed by how different it is from what they imagined.

For a few years after the publication of the 1990 National Jewish Publication Survey, nothing much changed in American Jewish life. There was a lot of hand-wringing, finger-pointing, and impassioned sermonizing about assimilation. Rabbi Ephraim Buchwald, head of the National Jewish Outreach Program, an Orthodox group, wrote a widely circulated, somewhat overheated column in the *Los Angeles Times* describing assimilation as a "Silent Holocaust" that was destroying American Jewry.[8]

On the margins, new programs were being launched, especially from the Orthodox community, looking for creative ways to get Jews to become more observant. Outreach groups like Aish HaTorah expanded their efforts dramatically, and Chabad emerged as a global movement that continued to grow despite the death in 1994 of Menachem Mendel Schneerson, the last Lubavitcher Rebbe.

But in the non-Orthodox world, an acute crisis requiring bold new initiatives was instead met with...more of the same. It was

---

8 Ephraim Z. Buchwald, "The Holocaust Is Killing American Jews," *Los Angeles Times* (April 28, 1992).

almost as if they were deliberately trying to prove the Orthodox right, that *kiruv*, or religious outreach, was the only effective path to sustaining Diaspora Jewish identity. Sure, the federations—whose main purpose is to raise local Jewish funds and direct them to projects and organizations that they control or strongly influence—started allocating funds to education and community-building programs like Hillel. But there was no reckoning. A system that had spent generations reinforcing and protecting itself seemed incapable of taking real risks and making profound change.

IN JUNE 1997, I ATTENDED a gala dinner for the Israel Museum in Jerusalem and was seated at the same table as Charles Bronfman. Charles's family had built the Seagram's corporation out of Montreal during the Prohibition era, and he had become an extremely important Jewish philanthropist, an insider-outsider who knew how to work with the Jewish establishment but also shared some of my criticisms of it. Also, like me, he saw Israel as both a blessing and an opportunity for Diaspora Jews.

Though I've never considered myself a "right-winger," Charles was to the left of me politically. He had asked me to meet with Yossi Beilin, an acolyte of Shimon Peres and one of the architects of the ill-fated Oslo Accords. Yossi, a Labor Zionist whose belief in Jewish peoplehood was just as strong as his belief in peacemaking, had presented us with the idea of issuing vouchers to help pay for Jewish teens to come to Israel as a bar mitzvah gift. It wasn't a particularly developed idea, in part because other than a plane ticket, it didn't do much to guarantee a meaningful experience. And it wasn't a new idea, either, as the suggestion of free trips to Israel had been floated on and off since the 1970s.

But his proposal got me thinking. I asked Charles to take a walk with me outside.

In Jerusalem, the dry heat of a summer day gives way in the evenings to a cool breeze. The Israel Museum is built on a broad hill not far from Hebrew University's Givat Ram campus, and the museum has a wide, terraced campus of its own. We felt the wind sweep across the veranda as we looked out over the Valley of the Cross at the ancient-modern city and sensed the heartbeat of our people. The moment felt heavy.

I broached the subject. "What do you think about Yossi's idea?"

Charles took a deep breath. "I think it's a scheme to bankrupt the Jewish world," he said.

I pressed him. If we thought it through properly and figured out the funding, I said, including support from the Israeli government, it could potentially change the entire relationship between the Diaspora and Israel. We could create a trip that wasn't just a free plane ticket but something more intense—even life-changing. Something like the "Israel Experience" programs Charles had launched in the past, which had brought kids of different ages on high-quality trips of varying lengths, but to do it at a far greater scale. "We need to do something big," I said. "Much bigger than anything before."

"Well," he said, "this is an audacious scheme."

I looked him in the eye. "If it's audacious," I said, "why don't we try to figure it out?"

Both of us knew the potential power of a trip to Israel. I had been supporting a wonderful program called Livnot U'Lehibanot ("To Build and Be Built"), based in the ancient, artistic city of Safed in the north, which combined religious learning for beginners with community service. Charles had been far more involved, having launched elite fellowships in Israel as well as the Israel Experience.

But what kind of trip would it be? Who would run it, and how would we get participants to come? How would we make it so flexible that it could hit a home run for a wide variety of young people and could scale up to reach much bigger numbers than all the existing programs combined? Most critically, how could we make sure it remained funded in the future no matter how large it got?

We spent about a year in the design phase. Charles and I put our best people on it and also enlisted a broad range of experts in various fields. Charles brought in Laurie Blitzer, a consultant at McKinsey, whose team helped put order and credibility into the process. He also brought Jeff Solomon, who led his foundation, and Mark Charendoff, a professional with experience in Jewish philanthropic projects, to help lead the design process. Barry Chazan, a veteran scholar of informal Jewish education, was charged with leading curriculum development.

On the Israeli side, a team was set up to explore the logistics and regulatory issues we would face on the ground. Shimshon Shoshani, a former director general of both the education ministry and the Jewish Agency, would become Birthright's legendary CEO for many years. He was joined by Gidi Mark, who headed Birthright's brilliant marketing division and later replaced Shimshon as CEO. And of course, we had Yitz as my foundation's president as well as his son, J.J. Greenberg, a charming and effective leader who did a remarkable job as the foundation's executive director before he was tragically killed while cycling in Tel Aviv in September 2002.

It was a powerful team. But we still had a million questions that needed answering.

BIRTHRIGHT WAS NOT MY FIRST venture into developing a sense of Jewish pride among American college students.

Years before, I was introduced to Richard Joel, the CEO of Hillel International. Joel was an unusual figure. An Orthodox Jew who had somehow become the head of the nation's largest campus organization for non-Orthodox Jews, as well as a former law professor and assistant district attorney in New York, Richard had turned Hillel from a lackluster branch of B'nai B'rith into a strong, vibrant, independent movement with chapters all over the world.

I may have mentioned it before, but I have a soft spot for certain Orthodox leaders. People like Shlomo Carlebach, Yitz Greenberg, and the Lubavitcher Rebbe. There's something about the confidence of their approach, their profound knowledge of Jewish history and texts and obvious commitment to Jews everywhere, and the successful growth of their communities, that impresses me deeply. But most importantly, I sense in them an unabashed pride and joy in being Jewish that resonate strongly with me. Although I don't see it nearly as often as I'd like outside of Orthodoxy, I believe it is the key to a successful Jewish future.

Richard brought that spirit into Hillel from the moment he took over in 1988. One of his first moves was to throw the organization's weight behind the Soviet Jewry movement, and when the USSR fell a year later, he expanded into the former Soviet Union as well as Latin America. In 1994—before I had even started the foundation—I worked with him to launch the Jewish Campus Service Corps (JCSC), a program that each year brought seventy to one hundred recent college graduates to Hillels on specific campuses across America, with the aim of having them reach out to unaffiliated Jewish students and get them involved. They would commit to at least a year of full-time work and invest all their time in what Richard called "engagement." (I'm not sure if he coined the term in the Jewish world, but he may have. He saw it as a much better word than "outreach.")

Over the course of its fourteen-year run, more than nine hundred JCSC Fellows went through the program, many of them staying for two or more years. And though we don't have precise numbers, it probably brought in upwards of one hundred thousand students to engage in Jewish activities who otherwise wouldn't have. The program was headed by Rhoda Weisman, a charismatic figure who inspired the fellows and who really was the secret to its success. Recent studies have shown that, in addition to the students who were affected by these fellows, a great many went on to assume leadership roles within the Jewish community.

Each summer, Richard would invite me to a leadership assembly at Camp Moshava in the Poconos, where hundreds of Hillel student leaders, staff, and outside professionals came together. That was when I saw him fully in his element, energizing young Jews, playing the accordion as he led them in singing and dancing, and giving inspirational speeches.

I made a point of including Richard in the early stages of Birthright. Partly because I saw Hillel as a crucial partner in jump-starting recruitment—which it in fact became, sending fleets of buses from campuses across America each year. But on a deeper level, I saw him as a brother-in-arms. He understood not only the roots of that proud and joyful Jewish spirit but had successfully brought it to hundreds of thousands of previously unengaged Jewish students— exactly the audience that we would have to reach.

For years, we benefited greatly from Richard's insight, spirit, and hard work as Birthright grew and Hillel continued to be a central partner. Then suddenly, in 2003, Richard accepted a job offer as president of Yeshiva University, the citadel of Modern Orthodoxy. Just like that, we non-Orthodox Jews were left without one of our most important lights. A few years later, sadly, JCSC was disbanded at Hillel's initiative.

Hillel hosted a farewell dinner in Richard's honor at the Marriott Marquis hotel in New York, and I wanted to share my mixed feelings in a comical sort of way. I dressed up as a Hasid, with a *shtreimel* and long frock coat, and stood up to speak, affecting a thick Yiddish accent:

> *It is my honor, my joy, baruch hashem, baruch hashamayim, baruch hayom, baruch halayla, to welcome to the world of the righteous Reb Richard Joel…. Mazel tov on your rebirth as a tzaddik. As your former colleagues burn in the everlasting fires of gehenom—oy vey!—you will taste the succulent fruits of Talmud with Moshe Rabbeinu, tzaddik hatzaddikim, baruch hashem…*
>
> *As many of you know, I used to be a mamzer myself, a leader in the world of atheism and moral philandering. I spit on my old self! When I learned that Reb Richard had seen the light, I realized that the days of Mashiach must be near and made haste to change my ways. Bimheira v'yameinu, amen, yasher koach!*

This, of course, was highly inappropriate. It was offensive to ultra-Orthodox leaders, who attacked me publicly afterward. David Zwiebel, executive vice president of the Agudath Israel of America, accused me of "publicly mock[ing] the dress, language, lifestyle and beliefs of a sector of the American Jewish community that has faithfully and successfully transmitted authoritative Jewish identity and pride to future generations." Richard certainly wasn't thrilled that I had thrown a wrench into his evening of honor.

But I wasn't trying to be offensive to ultra-Orthodox Jews. I was trying to make a point, in the time-honored spirit of Jewish self-mockery. The world of secular Jewish identity was, and continues to be, desperate for extremely talented leaders, and Richard was one of the best we ever had. Yeshiva University, as far as I could tell, didn't need him nearly as much as we did. My affectionate clowning wasn't meant to belittle other Jews but to call Richard's choice into question. Something needed to be said, and I was willing to handle the consequences.

Anyway, inappropriate or not, I thought my performance was funny. And so did much of the audience, as far as I could tell. As uncomfortable as it may have been for some, I do believe I got my point across.

WHAT WE PRODUCED, BY THE end of the Birthright design process, was a complete reinvention of the introductory group trip to Israel.

Programmed trips to Israel had been around for decades, ranging from two weeks to a full year. But Birthright was something else entirely. Not everything we did was original. But by bringing together best practices, adding major innovations of our own, and investing in top-level marketing, we created something that was leagues beyond anything that had been done before. It was a revolution on multiple fronts.

First: the length. After consulting with educators and tour operators, we decided that a ten-day trip was perfect. It was long enough to include at least one Shabbat and gave participants a chance to get over jet lag, encounter a variety of people and experiences, build relationships, and digest what they had seen. With something so intense and brief, we believed that every additional day could make a big difference in its long-term impact.

On the other hand, it was shorter than Israel trips had traditionally been—short enough to fit easily into a university schedule or in the summer alongside other plans for work, internship, or study. For graduates who had already entered the job market, it was minimally disruptive since people could use their vacation days.

Longer trips also cost a lot more. We knew we needed a program that could be financially sustainable at a high level of quality, so it needed to be brief. For participants who wanted to stay an extra few days, we allowed flexibility on the return date and, later on, supplementary programming through something called Birthright Israel Plus.

Second: the program. We understood that unengaged American Jews had a huge variety of tastes and desires. Years of experience with organized trips taught us that instead of running a single, "ultimate" Israel trip ourselves, we should harness the creative energies of other—existing or potential—organizations to design and run their own programs according to standards and specifications that we would supply.

This approach was Shimshon's brainchild. He knew that other people would probably be better than us at hiring the best tour guides, arranging for housing, and finding reliable bus companies. If we could outsource the execution—effectively creating a competitive marketplace for tour providers—combined with strict quality and content control, we could expand quickly without building a huge organization or straying from our core competencies.

Compared to a lot of bloated Jewish organizations that replicated what others were already doing, outsourcing allowed us to run a lean operation. We knew money would always be an issue, and even though we would ultimately raise more than a hundred million dollars a year, we wanted most of it to go to the trips themselves.

Our standards were rigorous. Some involved obvious things like restrictions on alcohol, drugs, or illegal activity, avoidance of political or religious bias (we did not allow trips to the West Bank at first or explicit efforts to get people to become observant, for example). But the more interesting rules, as far as I was concerned, had to do with the content itself.

Each Birthright trip had to offer a wide range of experiences covering Jewish and Zionist history, the Holocaust, a celebration of Shabbat, modern Israeli culture, and more. Experiences and travel were combined with conversations and presentations. The pace was intense. But there was also flexibility: For each requirement, we offered different options. When providers had suggestions, we listened carefully and got many of our best ideas from them.

One provider called Shorashim ("Roots") believed strongly in having participants spend meaningful time with Israelis of a similar age, many of them serving in the IDF. This was something we had talked about a lot, but Shorashim implemented it. They called it *mifgash* ("encounter"), and it really changed the way a trip to Israel was experienced. Instead of meeting each other in canned, formal contexts, these Israelis went through the trip with our participants, joined their buses, and opened themselves up. Shorashim's Birthright participants ended up building real relationships not only with each other but with their new Israeli friends.

This was brilliant. For me, the most important part of my own first trips to Israel—the thing that first attracted me and brought me back again and again—wasn't the landscape or the country's historical sites but the qualities of the Israelis I met. The spirit of the people who had built the country and continued to drive its unique, seemingly miraculous success.

Finding a way to overcome the language barrier and to give young American Jews a direct human connection with their Israeli peers was critical. This had been largely missing from many other Israel trips, which felt either too choreographed and mediated or kept its participants in a bubble, showing them the historic sites but feeling more like a theme park or museum tour than a real introduction to Israeliness. Once Shorashim proved it could be done, we built a permanent relationship with the IDF's education division to provide the soldiers and adopted *mifgash* as a central part of all Birthright trips.

Outsourcing proved useful for recruitment as well. Many of the Israeli organizations had their own networks abroad or could partner with groups in the U.S. One of the most important was Mayanot ("Wellsprings"), a provider affiliated with Chabad. Their network of Chabad emissaries on campuses and around the world, combined with their soft-pedal approach to religious outreach, made them a natural partner.

Third: Who got to go? Eligibility was an extremely sensitive issue. On the one hand, we didn't want to spend money on young people who were already engaged with Israel. We, therefore, decided that if you had gone to day school, had already participated in an organized educational peer-group trip, or had spent three months in Israel after the age of twelve, you wouldn't qualify.

On the other hand, the classic question of "Who is a Jew?" suddenly became urgent for us. Every denomination had its own definition, and the question of how to make sure non-Jews didn't take advantage of the program also came up. But we didn't want to be in the business of adjudicating people's Jewishness. So we decided that anybody who either had at least one Jewish grandparent and hadn't converted to another religion or had converted to Judaism through one of the major denominations could come.

We had to limit the age range as well. Again, the goal was to help young people build a uniquely personal connection to Israel, Jewish identity, and the Jewish community. But how young? Charles wanted teenagers: It was an accepted belief at the time that the younger you reached people, the bigger the impact. But I knew that wasn't always true. My own transformative Israel experience happened at age twenty-one after I'd finished college and had some work experience under my belt. There's something about early adulthood, with its newfound freedom and responsibility, which made me feel it might have an even greater impact than bringing teenagers.

Ultimately, we settled on a range of eighteen to twenty-six years old. This is what sociologists call "emerging adulthood," the period when people are on their own for the first time, exploring and discovering and redefining themselves. For a number of reasons, we also wanted Birthright to be dealing with legal adults. For one thing, it was meant as a gift to them, an opportunity to help them shape their own destinies, not a subsidy for their parents. We also wanted the luxury of being able to ignore the wishes of tens of thousands of worried or disgruntled parents. As for the top of the age range, we knew we needed to cut it off somewhere; the point was to maximize the impact on a person's life. In recent years, we have begun experimenting with supplementary programs for older participants.

Fourth: data. I didn't want Birthright to turn into another Jewish institutional monstrosity that lacked accountability and ultimately existed mainly to perpetuate itself by making donors happy. I wanted Birthright to prove its impact. If it turned out that it didn't really change people's lives, then I didn't want to spend time or money on it. Turns out, a lot of the other philanthropists we brought on board agreed.

Never has a Jewish educational program been so meticulously recorded or subjected to such rigorous evaluation. Today, data collection and analysis of Jewish educational and identity-building programs are quite common. Back then, they were unheard of.

Leonard Saxe, a social psychologist from Brandeis University, was given responsibility for building a data-gathering system. From the moment potential participants apply, they are answering questions that enter a database for later analysis. There are questionnaires before and after trips. There are follow-up calls to participants months and even years later to monitor impact. We have the ability to analyze how many are going on to a life of Jewish engagement as measured through their subsequent choices in marriage, observance, parenting, and institutional involvement.

Most importantly, we can study them in comparison to nonparticipants. Most programs suffer from selection bias: You're measuring only the people who chose to participate or whom you chose to accept. But with Birthright, we had an unusual circumstance. During the first few years, demand far outpaced our available slots. Many eligible young people had to be turned away—more or less at random. Yet we had their information and were able to survey them later, along with the participants. In other words, we have something almost no sociological study gets: something resembling a control group.

The value of this is hard to overstate. The control group is the difference between real and fake science, between hard facts and self-aggrandizing illusion. I'm not saying that all of our studies are perfectly reliable. What I am saying is that Birthright has better data, and can reach more confident conclusions about its impact on Jewish identity and commitment over time, than anything before or since.

THE BIGGEST CHALLENGE IN MY philanthropic career has been figuring out how to turn a proven pride-building program into something financially sustainable at scale. PEJE had been pretty good at that, seeding schools that would later raise their own funds. We simply misjudged the size of the potential market for all-Jewish day schools. But many of the schools we started are still thriving today without our help. When it came to JECEI, however, we couldn't find enough philanthropic partners to carry the ball down the field. Hebrew charter schools, on the other hand, have succeeded because we found a way to cover most of the costs with public funds. Training enough Hebrew teachers so that courses can be offered in hundreds of schools and colleges around the country is trickier.

Charles and I understood that if Birthright were to scale up, there was no way individual philanthropists could carry the load. We could probably make Birthright happen for as little as $3,000 per participant. The maximum desirable scale, we figured, was around fifty thousand participants a year. Above that, you ran into the limitations of what a small country like Israel could handle in terms of quality of accommodations and programming.

The total number of qualifying potential participants was around eighty-five thousand for every year of eligibility—meaning that there was around that number of Jewish eighteen-year-olds who hadn't been to Israel, plus a similar number of nineteen-year-olds, and so on up to age twenty-six. If we could bring in fifty thousand a year, and keep doing it for many years, this meant we could conceivably involve, over time, more than half of non-Orthodox Diaspora Jews. This would be an incredible achievement—but it would cost upwards of $150 million *every year*.

We decided it could work only if we got commitments from both the Israeli government and the institutions of the Jewish community, specifically the federations.

The State of Israel stood to gain tremendously from Birthright. At full capacity, the program would produce an infusion of billions of dollars in economic activity over time—especially if you factored in subsequent trips that participants wouldn't otherwise have taken, donations to Israel, investment in Israeli companies, and new immigration that could happen down the road. Over the years we would make exactly this case to government officials based on hard data, most recently in 2018. It turns out that even if you only take into account the total expenditures for the trips, the money that participants spent in Israel during and after them, and subsequent return visits—leaving aside the long-term financial contribution of donations and investments that might otherwise not have happened—the Israeli economy has already brought in more than $1.4 billion from Birthright, almost four times as much as the government has put into it.

But beyond that, it was clear to me that the last thing Israel needed was for the Jews of the Diaspora to lose interest in the Jewish state. Birthright wasn't just a sound financial investment for Israel. It was also a strategic imperative.

Getting the government on board began with a meeting I had with Prime Minister Benjamin Netanyahu in 1998. Say what you will about Bibi, he is a very smart man who understands the value of a big ambitious vision. We laid out the concept and made our pitch. Could the Israeli government cover a third of the cost?

"I can do that," Bibi said. And in November of that year, at the federations' General Assembly in Jerusalem, he announced the launch of Birthright Israel, with the first trips to begin a year later.

Keeping the government on board over the years proved less easy. It was the first time in Israeli history that the government was putting serious money into helping North American Jews—reversing the classic relationship between the two communities. By the time we launched our first trip, Netanyahu had been replaced by Ehud Barak, who fortunately agreed to push Birthright through an arduous budget allocation process.

The formula we agreed to involved splitting the cost three ways. One-third would be paid for by the Israeli government. Another third would be supported by the North American Jewish community, as represented by the federation system. The remaining third would be covered by a group of philanthropists, including Charles and me, which we took responsibility to cultivate and grow.

The last part turned out to be easier than expected. We started making calls with a hard ask of $5 million over a five-year period. I generally do not enjoy fundraising. I'd rather be *doing* than selling. But I had a superb pitch. This, I told them, was a one-time opportunity to do something really monumental to address the number one crisis facing our people, to do something important for both Israel and the Diaspora, and to bequeath a perpetual gift to future generations.

Our goal was to fund Birthright for five years. Within a few months, we had gotten commitments from no fewer than fifteen donors. (And fourteen of them actually paid up, which is rare in this business.)

This achievement—raising $75 million in pledges in just a few months—was breathtaking. Partnerships among big donors for specific projects were not very common in the 1990s. I believed in this approach, in part because that's how things worked in finance: You find partners, you start a firm together, some leave and others come in, you work together with talented individuals to make things happen. But we had no idea that such a dynamic could work with a large-scale philanthropic project like Birthright.

The hardest part would prove to be getting the Jewish communities on board. This was a potentially enormous source of funding. All across the American Jewish community, Jews were systematically solicited by local federations to give what was once known colloquially as a "Jewish tax," which paid for many of the community's most acute needs and was also the principal channel for donations to Israel, which were pooled together and sent to the

Jewish Agency. All told, the federations raised billions of dollars each year, a few hundred million of which were already going to Israel. There were a few specific federations—notably New York and Chicago—that raised more money each year than Birthright would ever cost. Surely, the system could spare twenty or fifty million a year to match what we and the Israeli government were doing—for the sake of their own children.

In theory, at least, the federations needed Birthright more than anybody else. Federations are permanently terrified about their future. They see older donors passing away each year and are constantly trying to figure out how to replace them. Over time, the growing disconnect between young Jews and Jewish engagement hits them directly in their bank account. Many of them have built "young leadership" divisions, for the sole purpose of getting younger people into the habit of giving them money. But that's not going to work. If you want people to donate generously and consistently, you have to get them excited about the cause, not just the giving. Birthright had the potential to supercharge an entire generation of Jews to throw themselves into Jewish life. Surely, if they played it right, this would potentially result in a lot of future donations for the federations themselves.

But the federations didn't see it that way. If anything, they were dragged into Birthright largely against their will. With some notable exceptions, most saw Birthright as an alien imposition that competed with their preexisting interests, something they had never asked for or initiated on their own. They barely had enough money for what they already wanted to do, they said, and didn't need the extra burden. They had already been involved in supporting different kinds of Israel trips, though such trips were neither free nor achieved any kind of scale. Critics dismissed the idea as "Bronfman's blunder and Steinhardt's stupidity." There were further complications that felt like excuses. They couldn't decide, for example, whether college students should be allocated based on their home federations or on the location where they were studying. And so on.

The real reason for their reluctance seemed pretty clear. The Jewish Turf Machine doesn't like threats to its control. As the people who saw themselves as the central representatives of Jewish philanthropic will, as the financial embodiment of "the Jewish community" itself, they were miffed that someone outside the system had started something new without their blessing and had even gotten the Israeli government on board.

This was, mind you, the first time in history that the Israeli government had undertaken a major public project directly with philanthropists instead of getting donations exclusively through communal organizations via the Jewish Agency. The Agency, for its part, opposed Birthright and initially refused to put in any money at all—and even launched its own program called Masa ("Journey"), which involved much longer trips. (Eventually, it became more of a complement than a competitor to Birthright.) Federations, for their part, couldn't stand the fact that we were embarrassing them into contributing. So while the Israelis and the donor group more or less kept their commitments—and even enlarged them—the American Jewish establishment never kept up its end, and still hasn't.

A lot of the effort to whip the federations fell to Charles, who was much more of an establishment insider and had even served as the first chairperson of the United Jewish Communities, as their umbrella organization was then called. At one meeting of the UJC, at the height of the second Palestinian intifada, one federation representative confronted him about how they had been "bull-dozed" into accepting the commitment. Charles apologized for having moved more quickly than they were used to, but then asked them bluntly: "In light of the intifada, would the program ever have been started if we had not done so?"[9] The room fell silent. They all knew the answer.

Even when Birthright became a runaway success, with many of the same Jewish leaders who initially opposed it now praising it and encouraging people to go, and tens of thousands of potential future federation donors flying to Israel each year—the amounts the federations provided were much less than what the other part-ners were putting in.

So while the annual budget of Birthright eventually ballooned to over one hundred million dollars, the entire federation system would throw us a few million a year. Combined with the Jewish Agency's share, it's now around $12 million out of an overall budget of more than $140 million.

To be honest, I was never surprised. The reason I got started in activist philanthropy was that I didn't believe the same people who had caused the problem of plummeting Jewish pride could be trusted to solve it.

OVER THE YEARS, WE HAVE been fairly lucky with the financing of Birthright. It helped that it was so clearly successful. Within a few years, participants were applying by the tens of thousands, driven mainly by word of mouth. For the first decade, we had a lot more demand than we could meet. So we always faced a shortfall and had to scramble for donations. The Birthright Israel Foundation, based

---

9 Leonard Saxe and Barry Chazan, *Ten Days of Birthright Israel: A Journey in Young Adult Identity* (Waltham, Mass.: Brandeis University Press, 2008), 124.

in New York, did an incredible job building an entire operation to make up, through private gifts, what the Jewish community failed to provide through official channels.

We also knew that the original commitments of the big donors were only good for five years. When we started, that commitment amounted to a total of fifteen million a year, which was fantastic at the beginning but, with our rapid growth, was nowhere near what we'd need to cover a third of what it would ultimately cost.

Enter Sheldon Adelson.

I first met Sheldon in the early 2000s at an event at Tel Aviv University, where we were both being honored. He had made billions in a variety of businesses, most famously the Las Vegas Sands Corporation that ran casinos in Nevada as well as Macau. Some people were put off by his brash demeanor, but I was instantly taken by his bluntness, his strong opinions, and his low tolerance for bullshit—and especially by the fact that he shared my feelings about the failures of the Jewish establishment. Judy and I, over the years, got to know Sheldon and his wife Miriam, who is Israeli. We had them over at our home in Bedford, where we gave them the gift of a serval, a kind of wildcat native to sub-Saharan Africa.

I know this won't make me the most popular guy in some circles, but I consider Sheldon Adelson, who passed away in early 2021, to have been one of the few real heroes of the American Jewish community.

Why? Because he cared, he acted, and he was fearless. He was his *own man*, to a degree I have rarely encountered. And he was willing to dedicate enormous resources for the benefit of the Jewish people. At a certain point, he fell in love with Birthright and would end up pouring more than $100 million into it, making him by far the largest individual donor. And he did it without being asked. When Charles first asked him whether he might join the donor group at the same level as the others, he scoffed. "I don't play for peanuts," he said. He didn't commit to a number, but then he showed up with a gift of $10 million the first year, in 2007, and it only grew in the years after that. Sure, he had the money, but so do Mark Zuckerberg, George Soros, Larry Page, Sergey Brin, and quite a few other super-rich Jews.

Of course, he got deeply involved in politics as well, both in Israel and the United States, mainly for conservative causes and politicians. He was known in America as one of the most prolific Republican donors of the last two decades. For this reason, critics of Birthright have added "right-wing" to their list of complaints.

This is nonsense. Sheldon gave a huge amount of money to many causes—it's really astonishing and impressive. Many of them had nothing to do with politics. He and Miri have donated heavily to medical research, both in Israel and the United States. Has anyone accused the Adelson Program in Neural Repair and Rehabilitation in Boston, or the Adelson Clinic for Drug Abuse Treatment and Research at Tel Aviv's Ichilov Hospital, of being "right-wing"?

True, Birthright is not a hospital. It affects the deepest passions and opinions of its participants. Yet at no point did Sheldon attempt to influence its politics or ideology.

Of course, some people think that Zionism itself is somehow inherently "right-wing." Despite the breadth of the Zionist tent, including both extreme socialists as well as extreme nationalists, despite the fact that Israel today is as politically diverse as America, you still get a sense that in certain places in American Jewish life, there's a belief that loving Israel is somehow a "right-wing" obsession.

I'm a lifelong Democrat, albeit a conservative one. At one point, I got deeply involved in something called the Democratic Leadership Council, which I believe had a decisive impact on Bill Clinton's election as president in 1992. Charles Bronfman, again, is to the left of me. But in our view—and in Sheldon's as well—there is nothing political about a concern for Jewish peoplehood, or about introducing young Jews to their homeland. This nonpartisan commitment has been shared by all our major donors and by Israeli governments of both right and left.

AFTER THE INITIAL ANNOUNCEMENT BY Netanyahu in 1998, a chorus of naysayers emerged. Some of them had vested interests that they may have felt were being threatened; others were politically motivated, opposing anything that Netanyahu supported; still, others merely lacked imagination.

At no point was I deterred. I was, however, nervous. Not because of the criticism, but because I knew that an awful lot could go wrong.

The first trips would be crucial. Much of the success of the program would depend on how the participants experienced it and the word of mouth, positive or negative, that would quickly spread.

Our first Birthright trip took place in December 1999. I decided I had to personally join—not just on the first trip but on many over the first few years. I needed to see it all with my own eyes. I would fly with the participants from New York and go from bus to bus and program to program, talking to them, experiencing it along with them, and getting their honest feedback.

I spent much of that first chartered El Al flight to Israel walking up and down the aisles, introducing myself to the participants and asking them how they felt. There was a palpable buzz—these kids understood they were not just embarking on a personal adventure but on an experiment that could change the future of Jewish life. When the plane landed, these groggy, flight-worn young adults were brought to a special hangar where they were greeted with food, music, and dancing. They loved it. We knew it was a good start.

I'm a pretty skeptical person. You don't succeed on Wall Street by being gullible or easily carried away. Or by seeing only what you want to see. Excessive optimism is a sure way to lose a lot of money.

So I hope it will mean something when I say that what I encountered during those first few trips was unlike anything I'd ever seen. To say it was "successful" is to completely miss the point. Somehow all the planning, the innovations, and the empowerment of the participants themselves came together to create something more powerful than I had thought possible.

Every day, participants were barraged with entirely new experiences—not just the vistas and historical sites but the food, the combination of cultures, the sounds and smells, and above all the special moments.

Moments like the visit to the Haas Promenade in the Armon Hanatziv neighborhood in Jerusalem—where, on a chilly, wet morning, buses unloaded participants into a beautiful stone path with a stunning view, across the Silwan Valley of the Old City and the Temple Mount, where the golden Dome of the Rock reflected the sun and the ancient site of Solomon's Temple sang to them of thousands of years of Jewish longing. Breathless, they started singing, too. Sore and exhausted from the grueling schedule, they started dancing.

Or the long drive south into the stark and sublime Negev Desert, where they soon found themselves clambering over a cliff and dangling from ropes a hundred feet off the ground. With the desert sun searing their skin, a sheer rock wall in front of them, and a Mediterranean moonscape all around, they gasped for their lives while being cheered on by their peers and reminded by the smart-ass Israeli guide down below that they were completely safe and capable of meeting the challenge.

Or the trip to Mount Herzl in Jerusalem, which is Israel's equivalent of Arlington National Cemetery. Jewish kids who had never held a weapon or seen an army barracks suddenly came face-to-face with the graves of Jewish soldiers, most of them kids their own age. On each grave was a photo of the young man or woman, taken at their peak of life and strength. A Jewish kid just like themselves. These Jews were not victims, like those seen at the Holocaust museum. They were heroes who had fought and died to build the Jewish future. You could see the impact on their faces, the questions it raised about their own lives and their personal stake in Jewish history.

Or the Mega Event, a huge celebration at the International Convention Center (Binyanei Ha'uma) in Jerusalem, where all the Birthright participants in Israel at the time, thousands of them from countries around the world, came together for an evening of performances, celebration, dancing, live music, great food, and speeches by major dignitaries. I will never forget one event I attended—and I have attended dozens—when Prime Minister Netanyahu spoke. As his motorcade pulled up, plainclothes security agents poured into the packed hall, an already giddy crowd started bubbling with expectation, and the prime minister took up a position at the podium. "Ladies and Gentlemen," he said, "participants in Birthright Israel from all over the world: Welcome Home!"

Yes—home. For these Jewish young adults, this was the real epiphany. Birthright represented something they had never had before and never even knew they needed: a Jewish homeland. All across the great hall, groups had organized according to their country of origin. One group waved Australian flags, another Canadian, another Argentinian. All were proud of their countries and loudly cheered when it was mentioned. But as they looked around at all the other groups, they became aware that they were also part of a *people*, scattered around the globe, who owed each other allegiance and love, and who had only one place on earth they could truly call home.

I could see it on their faces. Amid the joy and dancing and laughter, a lot of them were also crying.

ONE OF THE KEY DECISIONS we made early on was that we were going to treat these kids as adults. You can't expect them to feel empowered to choose their own fate while also infantilizing them. From their first visit to the Birthright website, they had to choose among dozens of options. There were specialized trips for foodies, outdoorsy types, artsy types, techies, LGBTQ, and more. And while on the trip, they were given time, especially in the evenings, to explore Jerusalem or Tel Aviv on their own.

In sum, they were given the freedom to make their own choices and time to process their reactions. Many of them took full advantage, walking up to young Israelis in the street and talking to them, exploring the cities, making connections, going to markets and bars. They pursued their own unique paths.

We also had guided discussions after dinner at several points on each trip. They split up into smaller groups and, led by their *madrich* or guide, opened up about what they were feeling and thinking.

This combination of intensive programming and the element of choice proved decisive. The experiences were made more powerful by the freedom with which they were chosen. For the first time in their young lives, they were making choices and confronting questions that could change their future. They were each given the tools, and the responsibility, to change themselves, to "build and be built."

Many of them were searching for meaning. Many came from comfortable homes, free of anti-Semitism. But now the facades of their well-ordered lives were cracking. For the first time, as newly minted adults, they were forced to rethink everything—a rethinking that, it seemed, they had secretly wanted all along. What did it mean to be Jewish now? What did each of them owe other Jews—those who came before, those who fought for them now, and those in generations to come? There were many conversations about peoplehood, about religion, about *aliyah*. Though we never explicitly encouraged it—the point of Birthright, after all, was to change the character of the Diaspora, not get people to leave it—moving to Israel suddenly became a real option in their minds. And they were going through it together.

One of the most important innovations in the design of Birthright was the idea of "the bus." This was the secret ingredient that made the experience so powerful.

What is the ideal size for a group trip to Israel? It's not a simple question. Programs in Israel can range from individual experiences to gap year programs like Young Judaea's Year Course or college programs like IDC, where you're just one of a couple hundred participants. Each program has a different purpose and, therefore, a different approach.

Our purpose was to change people's lives through an immersive ten-day experience. We realized that we needed carefully to curate not only the inputs they were getting but also the people around them. To create a sense of togetherness and intimacy. Our lives are defined not only by our seminal experiences but by the people we go through them with. These kids would potentially be making lifelong friendships on Birthright—and a few lasting romances, too.

And so we came up with "the bus." It's a simple idea: There would be a lot of traveling, a lot of programs that needed to be of a manageable size, from street tours to museums and historical sites. This could all be handled best if we assigned every participant to a bus, and those forty or fifty participants would experience the whole trip together. Before Birthright, a bus was just a way of moving people around. Now it would become something else: Like a cabin at sleepaway camp, it would turn something huge and overwhelming into something personal and intimate. All of Birthright, from recruitment to accommodations and programming, would be run in bus-sized units where everyone would live together, eat together, ride together, and work through their issues together.

Each bus would be assigned the same staff for the whole trip: an Israeli *madrich*, a security guard, and one or two staff members from organizers such as Hillel, who would fly with them to Israel. We built special programs in Israel and the U.S. to train the staff. Later on, when we added the Israelis in the *mifgash* framework, it would be the same group of Israelis in each bus for the whole trip. Staff would facilitate conversations, give guidance, enforce rules, offer a shoulder to cry on, and keep their finger on the pulse of the participants. The people on your bus were with you from start to finish. In many cases, it turned out, they'd be with you for life.

Again, this is one of those things that seem obvious in hindsight but was innovative at the time. It was through the idea of the bus that Birthright created the conditions for highly curated, consistently excellent, communal experiences. This was borne out by the data. A study conducted based on surveys of more than five thousand participants in trips in 2008 came to a clear conclusion:

"The bus groups that demonstrated stronger feelings of community produced greater connections to Jewish identity, Jewish community, and Israel, regardless of the varied Jewish backgrounds of the participants. In addition, individuals on buses with stronger feelings of community also expressed greater desire to date someone Jewish and raise Jewish children."[10]

With hundreds of buses organized by dozens of groups in different home countries and executed through dozens of providers, it is fair to expect some variation in the quality of the experience. What we discovered was that the quality of the bus group could make a huge difference not just in how they experienced the trip but in how their Jewish lives ended up looking years later. Which meant that we had to make the cohesion, quality, and internal dynamics of these groups a high priority.

Once again, this is what happens when you invest in planning, employ cutting-edge methodologies, are driven by results, and use accurate data to measure them. Unlike what decades of established Jewish life looked like, where institutions just kept doing the same thing over and over, at Birthright from day one we were constantly innovating, improving, iterating, learning, and perfecting the product.

FROM THE MOMENT CHARLES AND I started discussing this idea, I was adamant that this trip had to be free of charge. So adamant, apparently, that I somehow convinced him to accept this principle before we started approaching others, even though he totally

---

10 Shira Fishman, Michelle Shain, and Leonard Saxe, "What Happens on the Bus? How Community Impacts Jewish Engagement on *Taglit*-Birthright Israel," *Sociological Papers* 17 (2012–2013), https://sociology.biu.ac.il/en/node/1674.

disagreed. But it was my belief that this trip should be a gift—*had* to be a gift—in order to fulfill its goal. I wanted it to be called "Birthright" because it was exactly that. Every young Jew, I believed, had a right to visit his or her homeland. And it was our duty, that of the older generation of Jews, to make it possible.

It also struck me that if you want to really scale up, the trip had to be free—as counterintuitive as this may sound from a budgetary perspective. We needed to make the decision to participate as easy as possible.

I ran my Jewish activism much the way I had run my hedge fund: I gathered as much information as I could, then trusted my instincts to make a decision, while carefully monitoring the results. Every instinct I had told me that this trip could not be based on the same model as what had come before. It had to be free, it had to reach big numbers, and it had to be life-changing.

People made all kinds of arguments against a free trip. The most obvious was the immense cost. But there were others who claimed that it would be somehow bad, even self-defeating, to offer the trip for free. People only value what they pay for, it was said, and the experience would therefore be less valuable to the participants if they didn't pay for it.

In Israel, a lot of people couldn't understand why Israeli taxpayers should pay for trips taken by the children of wealthy American Jews. "It is not imaginable," said Member of Knesset Naomi Blumenthal, "that a youth from Kiryat Malachi can't go on a school trip because of a lack of money while Israel is willing to help finance a trip to Israel for a kid from Beverly Hills."[11] The Australian businessman and chairman of the World Jewish Congress Isi Leibler called the concept "bizarre." He wrote:

---

11 Saxe and Chazan, Ten Days of Birthright Israel, 122.

Providing vast sums of money for ten-day freebies to youngsters, including many from affluent homes, without requiring any form of commitment, is demeaning to Israel. In fact, it is counterproductive because it sends the wrong messages in relation to Jewish identity. It is also a sad and telling reflection on the pathetic state of Israel-Diaspora relations that nobody even bothers to challenge such an absurd project.[12]

For reasons I can only guess, *The New York Times* adopted a critical attitude toward Birthright as well and continued to do so for years. They have mostly chosen to ignore it, which is just as well because the few times they've written about Birthright, it wasn't very pretty.

In the early years, the *Times* gave a lot of space to critics like Leibler, quoting him and others at length. In 2008, they ran a smarmy piece called "Matchmaking, the Ultimate Government Service" that depicted Birthright as one of several programs around the world using taxpayer money to encourage couples to get together. I actually had no problem if Birthright resulted in couples getting together—on the contrary, I always believed that encouraging Jewish kids to marry one another was a crucial component in transmitting Jewish pride from one generation to the next. But the *Times* clearly saw it as something to criticize.

And there was more. In 2009, the *Times* went on for several paragraphs about Birthright's funding in an article that was supposed to be about the Bernie Madoff scandal. During the Gaza War in 2014, they unfavorably covered our decision to continue the trips, opening the article by quoting the misgivings of participants. And in 2019, when a dozen or so young anti-Zionist activists staged

---

12 Isi Leibler, "Birthright Israel—The Quick Fix," *Jewish World Review* (January 19, 2000), http://www.jewishworldreview.com/0100/birthright.html.

a theatrical walkout during their Birthright trip on the grounds that it (in their view) insufficiently showed the other side of the Israeli-Palestinian conflict, the *Times* blew it up into two lengthy articles, one of which appeared on the front page, along with a robust selection of letters to the editor.

One assumption in a lot of the early criticism we received was that we wouldn't be able to scale up because the demand wasn't there. In an article in *Salon* called "Why Birthright Israel Can't Work," the prominent Jewish journalist and longtime *New York Times* reporter Samuel G. Freedman summed up this conventional wisdom in an article that must in hindsight be embarrassing to its well-meaning author:

> *The Birthright venture [...] starts with a dubious premise: that lack of money is what stops American Jews from visiting Israel. In fact, American Jews are notably prosperous. [...] Even so, only one-third of American Jews have ever visited Israel. More of them, it has often been estimated, have been to Italy.*
>
> *Money, then, plainly is not the decisive factor. The causes of the breach between American Jewry and Israel can be found in both nations and across the religious and ideological spectrum, and they resist a mere financial solution.*[13]

Wrong. First, it assumes that people who earn more money struggle with it less. The truth is that no matter how "prosperous" American Jews may be on paper, most people are more likely to say yes to something of obvious value if it's free of charge without strings attached. This is especially true for younger people: Tell them you're giving them a fun ten-day trip somewhere they've never

---

13 Samuel G. Freedman, "Why Birthright Israel Can't Work," *Salon* (November 24, 1998), https://www.salon.com/1998/11/23/news_148/.

been, for free and with friends, and they'll jump at it—regardless of family income.

Second, this was not a "mere financial solution" to the problem of the Diaspora's waning attachment to Israel. It was a *powerful experiential solution*, made accessible to large numbers of Jews by removing the cost factor.

What Leibler and Freedman didn't grasp was that we weren't aiming for engaged Jews who already felt a serious interest in going to Israel. We were aiming for those—a much larger number—who had never really considered it at all. These were exactly the ones most likely to go *because* it was free.

Once the program got going, bringing tens of thousands of participants to Israel for the first time, we discovered something else that affirmed the importance of a free trip. It turned out that making the trip free of charge actually made it a *more* powerful experience, rather than less. The whole logic of you-only-value-what-you-pay-for, which does apply in many situations, does not apply to the great majority of participants who chose to come on Birthright—especially college students.

It's not hard to understand why. For many of them, this was one of their first big decisions made entirely on their own. Until they left home, most of their decisions were either made by their parents or at least were subject to parental veto. Once they get to college, they're making a lot of small decisions. What to wear and which fraternities and sororities to join. But since their parents are paying for college, big decisions—where to study, even what to major in—often are subject to heavy input.

Not so with Birthright. By removing the cost factor, we also removed the need for parental approval. These young adults were empowered to decide, entirely on their own, whether to go and how to structure their experience.

This proved critical within a year after our first trip. In September 2000, the Palestinians launched a huge wave of terror attacks that became known as the Second Intifada. Buses were blowing up in major cities. Coffee shops and restaurants, too. The carnage was horrific, and it was all over Western media. On June 1, 2001, a suicide bomber blew himself up at the entrance to the Dolphinarium discotheque on the Tel Aviv beachfront. Twenty-one Israelis were murdered, including sixteen teenagers, many of them new immigrants from the former Soviet Union.

Many parents didn't want their kids to come to Israel then. We got countless calls urging us to cancel the trips. We said no.

The following year was arguably worse. In the summer of 2002—after the Passover Seder night Park Hotel bombing in Netanya that murdered thirty Israelis, injured one hundred forty, and triggered the major incursion into Palestinian urban centers and refugee camps known as Operation Defensive Shield—American-organized trips to Israel plummeted. Youth groups and community-wide federation trips were canceled.

Most striking of all was the Reform movement, which was responsible for more than one thousand teens and young adults coming to Israel each summer. When I first heard that the movement had canceled its youth trips to Israel, I was furious. If a parent wanted to forbid their teenage kids from going to Israel, then that was one thing. But I could not understand a Jewish religious movement, which was meant to be the standard-bearer for what "being Jewish" means, canceling trips. What kind of Jewish identity, what kind of Jewish *religion*, includes abandoning other Jews in their hour of need? Why was this even a question?

I remembered very well the existential threat, the terrible fear of a second Holocaust that gripped us during the Six-Day War in 1967. My immediate response was the same as that of many other American Jews: Get on a plane and go. Maybe I could help a little. And if it ended in catastrophe, at least I'd know that I had done my part. Either way, the instinct was: *These are my people. I have to be with them.*

The Second Intifada, as horrible as it was, did not actually pose an existential threat to Israel. It was nothing like the Six-Day War. Yet here were thousands of Jewish parents trying to get their kids not to go and Jewish organizations canceling trips.

Yes, it was hard to blame parents for worrying about their children and hard to blame organizations for responding to these legitimate fears. Still, the wrong lesson was being taught. Instead of being encouraged to join their brethren at a moment of acute crisis, young Jews were very clearly being told, "Stay home." The essential solidarity of Jewish peoplehood that I had been taught since childhood was no longer a self-evident truth of American Jewish identity.

At Birthright, we decided—without any hesitation—that we were moving forward. Charles was as adamant as I was. We convened a call of the major donors, and Shimshon Shoshani, our CEO, told them that as long as the education ministry continued to allow school trips inside Israel, he had no qualms about running Birthright programs. The donors voted unanimously to continue.

Then something incredible happened. *The kids showed up.* Not all, but the great majority, and Birthright continued growing in numbers. A very large number of our participants during the intifada came in explicit defiance of their parents' wishes. This was confirmed both anecdotally and in the surveys we took after the trips.

This obviously couldn't have happened if the trip had not been free, because parents would have been able to veto their child's participation. There are few things as powerful in building a young person's confidence as making a big decision, overruling their parents, and turning out to have been right.

THERE WAS ONE POINT THE critics made that wasn't such a bad one. We were indeed gambling a huge amount of money on the unproven hypothesis that a short trip can really make a difference in a young person's life. And though it would be easy to gauge the excitement of participants during or immediately following the trip, we wouldn't have an inkling of the long-term impact for many years to come.

I'm still pretty surprised we were able to get enough serious donors on board as well as the Israeli government. Yet, we weren't flying blind. The evidence that a trip to Israel might change people's lives—especially those least engaged and most likely to assimilate—was plentiful, if purely anecdotal. Over time, however, we started to get a more scientific sense of the program's longitudinal impact. As we went back and surveyed people five, ten, and fifteen years out, the results were better than I, for one, thought possible.

The mastermind behind our data operation was, as I mentioned, Leonard Saxe. Charles and I first met him in the fall of 1999. He had just started a position at Brandeis in the field of social psychology—a relatively new discipline that studies how people behave in large groups. He also had a background in public policy at the national level, studying the impact of decisions in areas like mental health and substance abuse.

When he made his first presentation to us, he spoke a language that most Jewish philanthropists and communal professionals simply didn't understand. "This is an opportunity to conduct an incredible experiment for the Jewish world," he said. "To scientifically test the theory that the connection to Israel can create a path to engaging with their own identity as Jews."

Len Saxe was a big fellow, with the kind of dark beard and curly hair that exude scholarly preoccupation, and he spoke with the intensity of a man who loves numbers like a squirrel loves acorns. He got especially excited by the prospect of having a control group made up of those who had applied but didn't end up going.

At that, Charles jumped. "Sorry, Professor," he said, "but I'm not spending my money to study people who don't go on my program."

"Hang on, Charles," I said. "I know what this professor is trying to do. He wants a rigorous study of the impact of the program. And if rigorous studies are just going to say that the program doesn't work, I'm not sure if I'll really need to spend the money to find that out."

In truth, I really did believe in what Len was proposing, but it was so unusual in the Jewish context that I needed to see how he went about defending it.

"Mr. Steinhardt," he began. "I understand you're investing $5 million in this program over the next five years. And that you, Mr. Bronfman, are also putting in $5 million. Are you both telling me that you don't want to know whether this was a worthwhile investment?" Then he got louder. "What is it about stuff in the Jewish world that it shouldn't be evaluated with the same level of rigor that we evaluate all kinds of other social programs?"

I turned to Charles. "Maybe we should let him talk." He did, and we signed him up.

Within a few months, his team had reinvented the application process and had built a database for all applicants as well as for the post-trip questionnaires. Over the years, they constantly improved the questions in order to fine-tune our understanding of the impact the trips were having, not only on what people said about it but how their lives were changed as a result.

I'll confess I was a bit skeptical at first about Birthright's potential. Even though it had a good enough chance that I thought it worth investing in and bringing others on board, the fact that it *could* scale up didn't mean it necessarily would. We put in a sizable budget for marketing—but still, I was nervous.

That changed once Birthright launched its website. Before a single dollar had been spent on marketing, we had more applicants than we could handle, a trend that would accelerate once the trips started and word of mouth spread. It would take close to ten years before we were able to bring over the great majority of eligible applicants. In the meantime, Len had a very robust control group for his "experiment."

During the first few years, the data didn't tell us much I didn't already know from simply meeting with the participants. For them, it was a thrilling experience, and that was reflected in Len's research. In his 2006 report, he compared attitudes to Israel and Jewish identity for participants and nonparticipants one, two, and three years after they'd applied. In all cases, participants reported a significantly greater connection to Israel and the Jewish people than nonparticipants, and the effects didn't really seem to fade. About the trip itself, the vast majority of participants reported having a fun, educational, and meaningful experience.

These were lovely numbers, but from my standpoint, they weren't decisive. All they told me was that if you spend millions to build a top-quality program that brings young adults to Israel for free, they will have a wonderful time, and it might have a big impact on the things they *say*. But what about the things they *do*? What about the choices they make later in life about whom to marry and how they participate in Jewish life or raise their children? To see whether our gamble paid off in those terms, we would have to wait a few more years.

In 2009—ten years after Birthright's launch—Len and his team produced the first study evaluating its long-term effects. More than twelve hundred people were selected at random from among eligible applicants between 2001 and 2004, so we were looking at a five- to eight-year impact horizon. Again, because eligibility requirements excluded people who had gone to day school or previously participated in Israel trips or lived there, we felt confident that we were getting a pretty good read on how Birthright was affecting the lives and choices of relatively unengaged, secular American Jews.

Let's start with what they said about the trip. "Five to ten years after the trip," his team reported, "nearly half of all participants (45 percent) felt the trip was 'very much' a life-changing experience, and many more (28 percent) felt it was 'somewhat' of a life-changing experience. [...] Participants were 24 percent more likely than nonparticipants to 'strongly agree' with the statement, 'I have a strong sense of connection to the Jewish people.'"[14]

Even if you acknowledge that people often say things that don't translate into real-world decisions, these numbers were pretty impressive. People don't blithely call their experiences "life-changing."

When it came to important life choices, we began to see some real impact as well. "Among married respondents who were not raised Orthodox, participants were 57 percent more likely to be married to a Jew than nonparticipants. [...] Among unmarried respondents, participants were 46 percent more likely than nonparticipants to view marrying a Jewish person as 'very important.'"

---

14 Leonard Saxe et al., *Generation Birthright Israel: The Impact of an Israel Experience on Jewish Identity and Choices* (Waltham, MA: Maurice and Marilyn Cohen Center for Modern Jewish Studies, Brandeis University, 2009), 1–2.

Wow. By 2009, it began to look like Birthright was starting to make a dent in intermarriage.

And yet, five to ten years is still a pretty short timeline. What you really want to see is the impact over the course of someone's life, especially in how they raise their kids. Very few participants in the 2009 study had reached the point of building families—and most of them weren't even married.

Subsequent studies have confirmed the impact, however. The most recent one, published in October 2020, covered participants from 2001 to 2009. In the nearly two decades after applying, only 39 percent of married nonparticipants had married a Jewish partner—a figure that more or less matched what we knew about intermarriage rates in America. For participants, that number went up to 55 percent.

It seemed pretty clear: If you went on Birthright, you were about 40 percent more likely to end up marrying somebody Jewish.

Marriage is an important indicator of the impact on a participant's actual life. Because it combines instincts, beliefs, planning, and action, it's a pretty good proxy for how deeply a person's Jewish commitment is affected by the trip over a period of years.

It's important for another reason too. Our studies show that marrying a Jew has a huge *indirect* impact on overall Jewish engagement down the road—what Len's team called the "spillover effect":

Because Birthright participants are more likely to be partnered with other Jews, they are more likely than similar nonparticipants to raise their oldest child Jewish, to have brit milah for their oldest son, to be connected to Israel, to be synagogue members, to volunteer for Jewish or Israeli causes, to participate in events sponsored by Jewish organizations, to have Jewish friends, to celebrate

Shabbat, to attend Jewish religious services, and to celebrate Jewish holidays.[15]

Even among those who intermarried, Birthright participants were still "more likely to feel connected to Israel, to have Jewish friends, to attend Jewish religious services, and to celebrate Rosh Hashanah and Passover," the report concluded. So not only was Birthright reducing intermarriage quantitatively, and not only were those Jewish marriages resulting in higher Jewish engagement overall, but it was also mitigating the effects of intermarriage among those who married non-Jews. They were assimilating less.

Birthright's effects were also felt in the social circles that participants went on to develop. Ten to fifteen years after they submitted their applications, only 16 percent of nonparticipants reported that "most or all" of their friends were Jewish. For participants, that number rose to 26 percent.

This is, to me, a very important point. I've asked hundreds of people over the years how many of their ten closest friends, outside of family, are Jewish. In almost all cases, people who say "eight or nine" are also intensely committed Jews, while those who say "three or four" tend to be much less so. Perhaps it's not so scientific, but you're welcome to try it yourself. In my mind, social circles are a good proxy for Jewish pride. So if Birthright was seriously affecting that number, to me it signaled real impact.

All this, from a single ten-day trip to Israel, taken at the right point in one's life.

Relying too heavily on such impressive numbers goes against a lot of my instincts as a contrarian, a skeptic, and an inveterate

---

15 Graham Wright et al., *Birthright Israel's First Decade of Applicants: A Look at the Long-term Program Impact* (Waltham, MA: Maurice and Marilyn Cohen Center for Modern Jewish Studies, Brandeis University, 2020), 1.

pessimist. The numbers often strike me as too good to be true. I've tried to find the fatal methodological flaws. There are, it seems, areas where Birthright wasn't having any impact at all—such as the intermarriage rate for people who didn't marry until their mid-thirties or later, which was the same for both participants and nonparticipants. But the fact that the reports pointed these out only served to highlight the areas where the impact was clear. (As I write this in the spring of 2022, with the return of Birthright trips after more than a year-long hiatus because of the Covid-19 pandemic, we are already seeing the pent-up demand, a flood of applications, and hopefully a gradual return to the level of participation we have grown used to.)

Could a single program really be making such a difference? Could we have actually succeeded in altering the course, even a little, of non-Orthodox Jewry's journey to oblivion?

Because I am uncomfortable with excessive optimism, the most I will confidently say about these numbers is that they show Birthright has had *an effect*. Not a knockout punch against assimilation but one big enough to register. We've built a program that involves close to half of all young, non-Orthodox Jews. And it is, on the whole, affecting the trajectory of the Jewish community—probably more than any other single effort in the last half century.

Not a bad return on our investment.

AT THE END OF THE first Birthright trip in December 1999, I flew back with many of the participants to New York. The return flight felt very different from the flight there. On the way over, there had been the nervous excitement of American college students starting an adventure. It had felt like a crazy roll of the dice. On the way back, a deep silence blanketed the cabin from takeoff to landing. At first, I wasn't sure what to make of it. Was it awe at what they had been through? Shock at how much their sense of self had been challenged? Physical and mental exhaustion? Sadness at having to go home, like the last day of summer camp? Probably a combination.

I had been thrilled by the joy and the dancing, the tears and the profound spirit these kids had shown me in Israel. But nothing came close to the sublime satisfaction I felt from the silence on that flight.

In my mind, I have always preserved a posture of skepticism and wouldn't be satisfied until I saw real data showing real impact. But in my heart, I knew already that a profound change was taking place that would ripple across the Diaspora for years and maybe generations to come.

Interlude: The Envelope

NOT SO LONG AGO, JEWISH pride was, for most of us, the natural outcome of a comprehensive way of life that enveloped every Jew from the day she or he was born. You were born into a Jewish family, spoke a Jewish language, grew up in a Jewish neighborhood, attended a Jewish school, ate Jewish foods and listened to Jewish music, married a Jewish partner and raised Jewish children, married them off in a Jewish ceremony, worked for Jewish businesses, and eventually were buried in a Jewish cemetery. Being Jewish was the backdrop to every step in life.

Today things are different. While most Orthodox Jews continue to live within a reinforced Jewish envelope of schools, shuls, daily rituals, and close communities, non-Orthodox Jews mostly do not. Instead, we are overwhelmed by the possibilities, the freedom, the warm embrace of the liberal world around us, and the allure of competing claims to our sense of self. We have been unbound and, in our exuberance, many of us have come to see the question of Jewish identity as a choice between observance or oblivion, either constraining our lives through rituals and rules or gradually losing our Jewish sense of self.

But this is a false choice. In Israel, for example, a powerful, secular Jewish identity has emerged, sustaining millions of people in every aspect of culture. But there, too, you have the luxury of an immersive national identity. Being a secular Israeli Jew affects every hour of your day, from your language and schooling to your army experience and through adulthood.

Imagining a robust, secular Jewish pride in the Diaspora will require finding ways to similarly envelop ourselves in identity, but to do it without insulating ourselves from the modern world. Jewish schools, youth groups, summer camps, Hebrew language learning, and powerful experiences like Birthright can cover parts of it if they can be designed properly, scaled up, and sustained financially.

Alongside these, however, there's another aspect to our lives that is crucial for maintaining an ongoing Jewish commitment: We may call it "life habits." This is part of what makes the envelope of Orthodox identity so successful: the rhythms of prayer and synagogue, of Shabbat and holy days, of daily rituals and kashrut and life cycle events—all of it offers constant reminders and moments of engagement.

Today, however, non-Orthodox Jewish life lacks an encompassing system of engagement. We don't keep kosher, we don't keep Shabbat, and we don't pray every day. Synagogues tend to be lackluster affairs, often preserving outdated modes of worship and concerns of mid-twentieth century America. The largest non-Orthodox movements are at least a century old, in a world that has changed beyond recognition in that time. And while a variety of fascinating alternatives have emerged, their failure to scale up suggests that they are the exception that proves the rule. Most secular Jews see little reason to attend religious services.

We can take a lesson from secular Israeli Jews as to what the building blocks of such habits can be. In some cases, it means reengaging with classic Jewish rituals and texts, but on our own terms. We can reconceive Shabbat, holidays, and synagogue events in new, creative, relevant ways. We can adopt modern Israeli holidays like Yom Ha'atzmaut and Yom Hazikaron, but we can also create new holidays, new habits, and rituals of our own.

We will also need to find ways to reignite Jewish culture. We used to have a thick retinue of conspicuously Jewish comedians, literary figures, musicians, cuisine, and more to engage with and give us a sense of our collective selves. We used to have a language of our own, Yiddish, which let us conduct an internal conversation. If today we do not have Jewish walls blocking out the rest of the world, the way the Orthodox do, we will need Jewish cultural content that can successfully compete against non-Jewish culture for the attention of young Jews. This is entirely possible: As with the sciences and business, Jews excelled in the arts from the moment they left the shtetl. Some of our most powerful identity-building habits are in the cultural products we consume, from TV and film to books and magazines, art and music. This is an arena in which Jewish secular culture can be rebuilt.

Culture is one part of a whole life of habits that can engage the Jewish spirit. We can envision a rich secular-Jewish life that includes our weekly rhythms and especially Shabbat, but also the books we read, the music and films and food we consume, and the friends we make outside our immediate work and family lives.

Over the course of the last three decades, we've explored a variety of approaches to creating a new Jewish cultural envelope, one that competes favorably with, rather than cutting us off from, the non-Jewish world. It turns out, there's a lot that can be done, some of it to tremendous effect. There is, in fact, an enormous demand for the creative reinvention of secular Jewish life.

CHAPTER 4

The Formation of Jewish Habits

Culture gets to the heart of a people, distilling its unique spirit into a song, a poem, a meal, a film, a sculpture, or a novel. It is how we translate who we *are* into how we *live*. What we want from life, what inspires us, the interplay between individual experience and our collective lives are all touched on, in one way or another, in every romantic comedy, ethnic restaurant, or stand-up routine.

Although I wouldn't say I'm much of an expert, I've always been sensitive to how things of the spirit express themselves in cultural products. I built one of the world's largest collections of Judaica and have always loved great art. I've involved myself with the Israel Museum and am something of an aficionado of klezmer music. And I can say with certainty that the non-Orthodox world will never feel the depths of Jewish pride without having a rich secular cultural universe of our own. On a profound level, "Jewish" becomes meaningless outside of religion if there is no uniquely Jewish culture. And for that, you need Jewish institutions that are pouring new creations into the world.

The American Jewish experience over the last half century has involved the systemic erasure of a uniquely Jewish culture. Most of our greatest cultural creators have abandoned explicitly Jewish works in favor of Hollywood, mainstream record labels, and best-selling literature, with contents that are disconnected from any uniquely Jewish experience. We often forget that these very institutions were founded by Jewish artists, entrepreneurs, and cultural impresarios who forged a new identity for themselves and their fellow American Jews. It's gotten to the point that while America has benefited greatly from its Jewish creators, we, as a discrete community, have almost nothing of value that we call our own.

As a result, we have been spending down our cultural endowment and doing little to renew it. We have redefined our own values as "American," and as such we have done a lot to help Americans remain in touch with their own beliefs in equality, fairness, compassion, and the rule of law. But in the process, "Jewish" has stopped meaning something distinct and lofty on its own, a special system of ideas and values and feelings, and has instead come to mean little more than nostalgia, a few Yiddish words, Adam Sandler, corned beef and knishes.

I may be overstating things a bit. There are indeed pocke[ts] uniquely Jewish secular culture here and there. But they [are?] few, and engender so little interest among the mass of secula[r] that all they do is underscore how bad the situation is. Th[e] that the most successful American Jewish recording artist past twenty years—and I'm referring not just to a Jewish a[rtist?] to identifiably Jewish content—is probably the Orthodo[x] and reggae star Matisyahu (he has since become less O[rthodox] and, accordingly, less popular). The most famous Jewis[h] in North America overall is probably Drake, and there i[s] identifiably Jewish about his content; few people even know that he had a bar mitzvah.

How is culture created? We like to believe it just emerges organically from the talents and energies of artists. They create their work, and somehow it catches fire. But this is only part of the picture. There is also a big structural side to it, and a lot has to do with money.

Much of culture is popular culture and is funded by consumers. It's a business, and enough people are willing to pay for it that it makes sense for authors, musicians, and filmmakers to pitch themselves to agents and producers. But a lot of it needs to be subsidized, especially in the earliest phases, through grants from foundations and governments, without which these artists never get off the ground. These provide fellowships, seed money, workshops, networking opportunities, and more.

But no less important is the development of an audience through venues for performances and outlets for reviews, and through publishers and record labels willing to take risks on new voices. A careful eye, a gifted talent scout, marketing that can figure out how to connect with the audience, as well as contexts that encourage 'laboration among artists. All of this requires money, taste, and le chutzpah.

he of our first ideas when the foundation launched was to physical space in New York City where less-engaged Jewish dults, especially singles, would want to gather. Not a JCC, definition tries to appeal to people of all ages rather than lults specifically. Not a synagogue, either. (I was, despite sm, a member of B'nai Jeshurun, an incredibly creative and l house of worship on the Upper West Side.) What we stead was a secular cultural magnet, a hotspot. A club. ike that existed at the time.

At the age of three or four, growing up in 1940s Bensonhurst.

At the Coney Island pier, with my mother Claire, early 1940s.

My parents, Sol and Claire, took a day at the beach, late 1930s.

My Bar Mitzvah, in 1955, at the Bnai Isaac Congregation.

With Judy, the love of my life, on our wedding day, April 28, 1968.

Our children, David, Sara, and Daniel, at our Manhattan apartment in the mid-1970s.

A family vacation in Eilat, Israel, early 1980s, with Judy and the kids.

With Shula Navon, who led our family foundation in Israel in the 1990s and early 2000s.

SOLIDARITY SUNDAY FOR SOVIET JEWRY

I attended the UN Solidarity Sunday for Soviet Jewry rally, New York City, 1980s.

With former Refusenik Natan Sharansky at a rally in New York City, late 1980s.

With Judy at a Camp Moshava event in Pennsylvania, late 1990s.

With Jerusalem Mayor Teddy Kollek at an event of the Israel Museum.

A gift from an Orthodox friend with a sense of humor.

Deeply honored to be chosen, along with Rabbi Marvin Hier, as the first Diaspora representatives to light the torch at the national Yom Haatzmaut ceremony in Jerusalem in 2017.

Sharing my feelings with anti-Birthright protestors who had crashed a gala event honoring Sheldon Adelson in April 2018.

A new generation of proud Jews. With my grandson Eli, at the home of my son David in New York, 2015.

With my children, their spouses, and grandchildren at our home in Bedford in 2016.

Above: The whispered secrets of the camel. At my home in Bedford.

Left: The serval, one of my favorites, in Bedford.

Yitz Greenberg (left) and David Gedzelman (right) formed the leadership team of our foundation in 2004.

Participants in our Kayitz Kef summer Hebrew immersion program.

With Judy at an event of the New York Botannical Garden, 2016.

Vardit Rigvald is leading the revolution in Hebrew-language education in America.

Students learn about the language and culture of Israel at the Harlem Hebrew Language Academy Charter School.

Performance of the Hebrew Public students' choir before a broadway performance of Matilda, 2013.

My daughter Sara with kids from Hebrew charter schools at a gathering in Bedford.

With Andrea and Charles Bronfman at the Israel Museum event in 1997, when I first broached my "audacious" idea that became Birthright Israel.

With Charles Bronfman speaking at a Birthright Mega Event in Jerusalem, early 2000s.

Birthright participants from Canada at Ben-Gurion Airport, 2002.

Prime Minister Benjamin Netanyahu speaking at a Birthight Mega Event in Jerusalem, 2013.

The incredible vibe at the Birthright Israel Mega Event in Jerusalem.

Birthright participants hiking up the Snake Path at Masada.

Birthright participants dicovering the caves of Israel.

*Jared Waters,
a teacher at the
Harlem Hebrew
Language
Academy,
with pupils
in Jerusalem
as part of the
Talma program.*

The "Swiss House" at 35 West 67th Street in Manhattan, which became Makor.

Speaking to an excited group of future leaders in Israel with Excel.

Perry Farrell, frontman for Jane's Addiction, leads a raucous Purim party at Makor, 2001.

Aliza Kline, the founding CEO of OneTable.

David Gedzelman, who at the time was the head of Makor, with the actor Kevin Bacon at an event at Makor, early 2000s.

With Tamar Dayan, founder of the Steinhardt Museum of Natural History in Tel Aviv.

To date, more than a hundred thousand people have participated in OneTable Shabbat meals.

With Tova Dorfman, who heads our foundation in Israel, at a planning meeting for the Steinhardt Museum of Natural History.

Despite the pandemic, Birthright Excel kept going in 2021.

The men who made this book possible: At my home in Bedford with (l to r) David Gedzelman, President of the Steinhardt Foundation; David Hazony, my partner in writing; and Adam Bellow, founder of Wicked Son Books.

In 1995, Yitz hired a young man named David Gedzelman to take this on. An ordained rabbi who had previously directed a number of college Hillels in the Los Angeles area, David had proven himself to be an energetic and successful innovator. He had taken two lackluster Hillel branches he directed in the San Fernando Valley, rented out retail space in a strip mall on Ventura Boulevard, added a stage and sound system, and called it "Café Hillel." Each week, he booked high-level local musical acts performing original music. The thing took off, drawing hundreds of Jewish students from around the area.

David became the creative force behind an incredible, if short-lived, cultural center we launched on the Upper West Side of Manhattan that ended up engaging tens of thousands of Jewish young adults each year. (David would go on to replace Yitz's son J.J. as the foundation's executive director after J.J.'s death in 2002 and later on would become its president.)

Why did we believe this was needed? It might sound obvious today, but at the time, the idea of conducting focus groups to determine the needs of a given market was pretty much unheard of in the Jewish nonprofit world. Between the start of planning and the opening of the center, David conducted as many as sixty focus groups, and it became clear that young Jewish adults were mostly uninterested in participating in the programming that targeted them at the local JCCs and synagogues, or in the young leadership programs being run by federations and other institutions. They didn't want, in other words, what the community was offering them. They wanted something entirely different: a cultural space geared for people their age.

David, J.J., and Yitz settled on the name Makor, or "source" in Hebrew. This place would be a source for the Jewish cultural spirit, expressed through cutting-edge cultural experiences.

They found a beautiful building on West 67th Street. Built in 1905 by the Swiss Benevolent Society, the five-story, collegiate-Gothic brownstone housed poor immigrants from Switzerland and later served as a hostel for working women and, in its final years, Julliard dance students. The lower floors had generous public spaces, and the upper ones were dormitories that could easily be turned into classrooms.

We closed on the "Swiss House" in May 1996 for about $3.5 million and spent more than three years and $8 million renovating it. We hired the firm of Platt Byard Dovell, an elite designer of modern cultural and commercial buildings across Manhattan, to create a space that could serve as a vibrant cultural hub—with a café and bar, screening room, art gallery, classrooms, event and performance spaces, an outdoor area for parties, and more.

Makor was unlike anything that existed, before or since, in American Jewish life. A number of institutions have learned from it and attempted to capture its creative essence—particularly Sixth & I synagogue in Washington, D.C., and the 14th Street Y in the East Village. But nothing has come close to creating an immersive urban center that was both hip and unabashedly Jewish.

We knew that creating a genuinely unique cultural hub in the heart of New York City was no small undertaking and would demand getting everything right from early on. And so, rather than just open the center and see who showed up, we started hosting events around Manhattan during the planning phase, in part to help us understand the market but also to build awareness. By the time we opened our doors, we already had what we called a "core community" of about four thousand young adults.

Makor finally launched in October 1999—just weeks before the first Birthright trip took to the sky. Within weeks we had hundreds, if not thousands, of young people attending events, hanging out in the café, taking classes, and enjoying the exhibits.

David's official title was creative and rabbinic director, but, in practice, he was the aesthetic soul of the place. A significant part of the programming was brought straight from Israel, including some of the country's most important musical artists—performers included Ehud Banai, Corinne Allal, Aviv Geffen, and David Broza, all of whom filled arenas and amphitheaters back home. The neo-klezmer band Golem got its first major exposure through gigs at Makor. Perry Farrell, the Jewish front man for Jane's Addiction, the funk metal band recently inducted into the Rock & Roll Hall of Fame, hosted a Purim party in 2001 that packed the place and was covered in *Rolling Stone*.

At the same time, Makor offered a wealth of top-line cultural, entertainment, and literary events. In a given week you could "walk the Bible" with bestselling author Bruce Feiler, explore the creative process with our gallery artists, attend Shabbat dinner with a marquee speaker, explore Israel through its literature with the renowned critic Gadi Taub and Israeli fiction writer Ruby Namdar, discover career opportunities on Wall Street with Alliance Capital Vice-Chairman Roger Hertog, see a one-man show about King Solomon, join our young Jewish Poets' Circle, take classes in yoga or Krav Maga, hear a speech from mayoral candidate Michael Bloomberg, or join a twilight tour of Central Park ending with dinner at the Makor Café.

But Makor wasn't just a cultural showcase. It was about creating culture as well, at the highest levels. We had playwrights, screen-writers, filmmakers doing workshops, many with Jewish themes. We had musical artists being discovered. We had programs for visual artists, as well, and a carefully curated ongoing exhibit throughout the building. Theatrical productions, concerts, film screenings, book launches—all of it was happening alongside political discussions, Hebrew language education, new explorations of Jewish texts, and more. Hundreds of people passed through each night, thousands each week, taking classes, discussing a film, presenting new poetry, or attending the evening Makor Café with live music. As David told the *New York Times*:

> It was important to us [...] to offer a space that encourages artistic innovation. It's not just that it's an entry point—that people might come for the music and eventually go upstairs for something else. That's a piece of it. But it's also that if these things happen in the same place, they'll bleed into each other. The artistic innovation, the bubbling of creativity that happens downstairs in the cafe, is going to inform the intellectual, spiritual and religious exploration that's going on upstairs.[16]

We were, in essence, trying to create an entirely new kind of secular-Jewish institution for a new century.

Makor was not the only Jewish cultural center in Manhattan. The JCC of the Upper West Side, which was planning a big opening of their new center the following year, carried on the venerable traditions of Jewish Community Centers that combined events for all age groups, athletic facilities, and so on.

The JCC was deeply concerned about Makor's powerful potential appeal to young adults. So they tried to talk us out of it. They even offered to host Makor in their building.

How could we explain that to house Makor at the JCC would have been effectively the same as not doing it at all? "Young adults don't want to see strollers parked at the door as they walk in," David told them. "If you're going to reach them at all, it will be in a lounge

---

16 Allan Kozinn, "Many-Colored Coat of Arts," *The New York Times* (May 4, 2001): E, 1, https://www.nytimes.com/2001/05/04/movies/many-colored-coat-of-arts.html.

filled with other young people, with alcohol at the bar and live music, dimmed lights, and a nightclub atmosphere. That is where they are, and that is where their Jewish identity will be found, or it won't be found at all."

If you wanted to bring young, unengaged Jews into a place of Jewish connection, you had to prove to them first that you were attuned to their specific needs and weren't wasting their time. At Makor, we were not messing around.

PART OF WHAT MADE MAKOR so attractive to younger New York Jews was the fact that it didn't present itself as an exclusively Jewish venue. Significantly, we didn't put the word "Jewish" into Makor's name, and only about half the content was identifiably Jewish. Jewish culture might originate in Jewish sensibilities and artists, or express our people's experiences, but if you want to actually reach young Jews, it has to resonate with people attuned to the broader culture—and it has to appeal to non-Jews as well.

There's no reason why non-Jews can't get excited by Israeli popular music or the works of Jewish artists, and it was important to us—and to the clientele we wanted to reach—that Makor be welcoming to everyone. This proved to be a crucial edge, and we estimated that a sizable minority of people who came to Makor were not Jewish. Later on, this principle would repeat itself with Hebrew charter schools and other programs we launched. A great many Jews won't even look at something if it isn't good enough to compete in the broader world.

Ever heard of the pop vocalist Norah Jones? She launched her career at Makor. One evening our musical director, Brice Rosenbloom, brought her in for an unpaid gig. David heard her sing and brought a talent scout Brice knew from Blue Note Records to hear her. They offered her a contract, and her career took off.

Norah Jones isn't Jewish and doesn't count as Jewish culture. But her story says something about the league we were playing in and the power of the tool kit we developed. Brice forged a partnership with the Knitting Factory, the important chain of music venues that started in downtown Manhattan and went nationwide, and whose founder Michael Dorf is an active Jewish philanthropist. We also helped promote the artists of JDub Records, a nonprofit Jewish record label that made Matisyahu famous, and also injected the Israeli group Balkan Beat Box into the American music scene. At the same time, Makor created a relationship with WFUV, the mainstay radio station of folk and alternative rock in New York City. By putting Jewish and Israeli artists into the same context as the leaders of cultural creation in America, Makor sent a powerful message about the legitimacy and importance of Jewish culture.

It is possible, desirable, and absolutely necessary for our community to invest in the infrastructure of Jewish cultural creation.

Could Makor "scale up" to have an impact on American Jews as a whole? Could we see Makor branches all across America? Probably not. Few cities have the base of cultural creativity, the sizeable Jewish audience, and the local donor base that a venue on the Upper West Side enjoyed.

That said, there is no question that Makor could easily have had a nationwide impact if it could have been sustained over time. New York is the cultural center of American Jewry and, in many respects, of America as a whole. It is not hard to imagine Makor playing a central role in a rejuvenated national movement in the Jewish arts. By setting the standard for a secular Jewish cultural experience, we would find no shortage of imitators and collaborators around the country as well as consumers of the cultural products created within its walls.

MAKOR WAS NOT THE SAME as our other programs. We went into it very early in the foundation's history. We also didn't go in with major philanthropic partners lined up—a mistake which, looking back, proved fatal.

Moreover, the nature of the project made it impossible to collect and analyze data the way we did with Birthright and others. If your favorite nightclub made everyone fill out a questionnaire before letting you in the door, it would not be your favorite nightclub. We could track the numbers of participants, but there would be no way to prove impact in the long run. We can quantitatively measure how a trip to Israel affects people's lives over time. You can't really do that with a book, a film, a series of nights out with friends. The impact of culture is hard to measure, but it is certainly real and profound: If being Jewish is engaging, entertaining, and filled with new things, people will want it. If it's not, they won't.

So participation became the only concrete measure we had. And in this respect, we did very well. We had thousands coming through each week, participating in the full range of Jewish and non-Jewish cultural options. Nor were these participants exactly "the masses" of American Jewry: They included the leading Jewish influencers, culture makers, and connectors of New York City, alongside a growing crowd of local fans.

Yet despite these differences, Makor resonated deeply with our other projects. Like Birthright, we invested heavily in the planning phase in order to provide the best product possible for our audience, and we targeted young adults with a high-quality, immersive experience that offered educational opportunities and empowered them with choice. Like JECEI and Hebrew language teaching, it imported the most advanced available methodologies into a Jewish context for the first time. Like Hebrew charter schools, we offered a pathway to Jewish engagement that didn't exclude non-Jews. Like other programs we did, the aim was to innovate, to reinvent the habits of Jewish experience from scratch. Above all: It pointed to the possibility of a proudly Jewish secular culture that could help make Jewish identity into something attractive, vibrant, and viable.

But while I believed strongly in Makor, the financial model was not sustainable for me over time. I was spending more than I had intended for one local project. The operating budget was about $3 million a year, of which $1 million came out of my pocket. Another million came from whatever donations David could raise. The final million came from earned revenue—ticket sales, fees for courses, memberships, and so on.

This was something the big Jewish communal institutions could have, should have, but in the end did not have an interest in paying for, even after it had proved itself. We frequently had some very high-capacity philanthropists visit Makor. They were impressed, but I could see they didn't get it. They donated but never consistently or at scale. Federation leaders praised it but didn't take it on. Jewish cultural foundations—and there are a few—couldn't see the value in a vibrant cultural center like Makor.

I began to grow impatient. I wasn't worried about the sunk cost in the building, which goes in the ledger of real estate investments and can, in theory at least, later be recouped. But a million dollars a year for operations is roughly what I was giving to Birthright—a program that was going to scale up immensely and affect a large portion of the Diaspora. I started looking for an exit strategy.

In late 2000, we got an offer that seemed too good to turn down. The 92nd Street Y, a century-old elite cultural venue on the Upper East Side, was willing to completely take over my portion of the costs of Makor for a minimum of six years. As part of the deal, we also donated the building to them, and they added my name to the program, which would henceforth be known as the "92nd Street Y Makor/Steinhardt Center." We exchanged board members. They repeatedly made it clear that they loved Makor and promised they would never dream of changing it. They told us that Makor's vibrancy, creativity, and appeal to young adults were something they needed. It even seemed that they wanted our help in changing what they were doing on the Upper East Side.

Looking back, I can see my mistakes. When they put a lawyer from their board on the negotiating team with expertise in mergers and acquisitions, I should have paid attention. When my daughter Sara, who was made chair of the steering committee, begged me not to give them the building, I should have listened. When they made all the staff change the domain names for their email addresses to @92y.org, I should have seen it as a sign of their intent. Even changing the name to "The 92nd Street Y Makor/Steinhardt Center" should have given me pause. Instead of something original, creative, and fresh, it suddenly sounded like every other donor-endowed boondoggle in the Jewish institutional world.

For six years, Makor continued under their auspices. And then, in 2006, they announced that they were selling the building. Makor's programming would be relocated first to Hudson Street downtown and then later to their center on 92nd Street and Lexington Avenue.

The sale of the building hit me like a sucker punch. I now realized that I had been, for lack of a better word, snookered. The magnitude of the snookering only became clear, however, when I saw what they got for it. I had paid $11.5 million, including the renovation. They had put a total of $11 million into funding the programming over six years, more than they had committed to. Then they turned around and sold the building for $33.5 million—and poured the profits into a renovation for the 92nd Street Y. The Swiss House now became part of the City University of New York.

A lot of people were upset when the announcement was made that Makor was leaving West 67th Street. The journalist Liel Leibovitz wrote an extended lament in New York's *Jewish Week*, writing that Makor had been "the central address of young Jewish hipness [...] the crown jewel of the Upper West Side's young Jewish scene." Aimee Friedman, a bestselling young adult author, told Leibovitz that "Makor, in many ways, felt like the center of young Jewish activity, and [its departure] is going to change the neighborhood."[17]

This was the end of Makor as far as I was concerned. The name continued to be used for certain cultural programming of the 92nd Street Y for a few years. But the core idea of having a *place* with a certain strategy for attracting unengaged Jews and creatives into a Jewish environment, with a certain vibe, and a hub of Jewish creativity—all that was over.

To begin with, for those unfamiliar with Manhattan and its cultural divides at the time, the Upper East Side was not the Upper West Side. Upper East was wealth and all the sophistication

---

17 Liel Leibovitz, "Makor's Upper East Side Story," *The Jewish Week* (May 24, 2006), https://www.corcoran.com/nyc/PressMention/Display/3907.

that money could buy. Upper West was where you could find the writers, literary figures, and filmmakers, those unique creative souls who were on their way up. These were the people whom young, secular Jews wanted to be around. You could imagine a hip, intense magnet for young, single Jews around an edgy cultural hub on the Upper West Side. But not on the Upper East Side, where "culture" was more about classical music and literary readings. As Sara said to the *New York Sun* at the time, "I don't know anyone in their 20s and 30s who would look to go out and have a great time on 92nd and Lex."[18]

The whole idea of Makor was to exude youthful cultural excellence in every respect: The programming, the design, the curation, the food and drink, the atmosphere, and the location. To make people feel both privileged to be there and like they belonged—an utterly unique place full of promise.

But the moment you start compromising, the bubble bursts. You lose the integrity of the vision, and then you become just like everything else. A muddle. And that muddle inevitably serves the cause not only of Jewish mediocrity, but ultimately of the forces of waste, ego, and blurry goals that dominate the Jewish institutional world.

Did the Y see Makor as competition that needed to be co-opted? Did they see our success as a threat to their business model? Were they chagrined that we were attracting young Jewish adults and they weren't? Or was it purely about the real estate? We would never know.

---

18 A.L. Gordon, "92nd Street Y Using Makor Center To Help Fund Move," *The New York Sun* (May 18, 2006), https://www.nysun.com/new-york/92nd-street-y-using-makor-center-to-help-fund-move/32975/.

As with most projects that came to an end, Makor offered valuable lessons. First, it showed us that there's a demand, at least in New York, for an authentically Jewish, secular cultural hub. Second, it underscored the importance of partnerships. If Yitz and I had lined up the financial partners before going in, I would not have been so eager to get out. Makor was a magical place, but there's nothing that says the magic can't be found again. If you bring together the right people to fund and execute, you can make new magic. But for that, you have to be absolutely committed to the vision, recruit the right partners and staff, and have a clear path to financial sustainability.

We also shifted our focus away from bricks-and-mortar projects. Starting a new institution from the ground up is thrilling but incredibly costly. For example, with JECEI, we discovered it was much more cost-effective to inject the Reggio Emilia method of early childhood education programming into an existing infrastructure of Jewish preschools, without building new ones from scratch.

We began looking for ways to build on this insight by revamping existing institutions rather than founding new ones in helping create a new envelope of Jewish habits. And of those most desperately in need of reinvention, nothing stood out quite as starkly as the modern synagogue.

SYNAGOGUES IN THE NON-ORTHODOX WORLD were, generally speaking, in bad shape, suffering from dropping membership and attendance for decades. According to the National Jewish Population Survey of 2000, only 24 percent of Reform synagogue members reported attending at least once a month.[19] Later on, in 2013, the Pew study showed that only 16 percent of Reform Jews, and 26 percent of Jews overall, reported that religion was "very important" to their lives. In other words, the great majority of religiously affiliated, non-Orthodox Jews weren't particularly enthusiastic. On top of this, the number of Jews who had no synagogue affiliation rose from 16 percent in 1990 to 25 percent in 2000.

To me the reason was obvious. Synagogue was boring. A lot of Jews kept going, but there was nothing especially enriching about the experience. Those who showed up probably came because their friends did so or out of guilt. But this wasn't the 1950s anymore. Going to synagogue used to be a default: Membership and regular attendance were *de rigueur*. But by the turn of the twenty-first century, it was clear those days were gone. Jews went only if they wanted to, and most didn't. And except for outliers and marginal movements, most mainstream synagogues hadn't fundamentally upgraded their "services" in decades. This struck me as especially problematic in the Reform movement. The largest non-Orthodox denomination, whose very name signals a willingness to change with the times, had completely failed to adapt its synagogue experience in a way that would bring its own core constituents through the doors—much less offer something exciting enough to attract new people to attend frequently.

And so, not long after Birthright and Makor launched, we began to look into the question of how to reinvent the experience of Jewish worship.

In 2000, we helped launch a small organization called STAR, or "Synagogues: Transformation and Renewal." This was based on

---

19 Jack Wertheimer, "The American Synagogue: Recent Issues and Trends," *American Jewish Yearbook* (2005), https://www.bjpa.org/content/upload/bjpa/thea/TheAmericanSynagogueRecentTrendsAndIssues2005.pdf.

a partnership with Edgar Bronfman and above all Charles Schusterman, who had become wealthy in the oil business. We launched STAR with the aim of coming up with a new approach to the synagogue experience, something that would not only retain and inspire members but also attract unaffiliated Jews. A few months later, Charlie passed away, leaving his wife Lynn to carry the mantle.

Obviously for me, an atheist, this was a little unusual. Lynn, for her part, also wasn't a fan of religion in general. But Charlie had been, and she felt this was something he would have wanted. I was happy to follow her lead. Despite my rejection of religion, I know very well that it can be an important driver of Jewish identity. This was clear from my many encounters with the Orthodox and the rare occasions when I would attend Friday night services at B'nai Jeshurun. There I'd encounter an exceptionally moving prayer service, with liturgy arranged for instruments and vocals into a powerful spiritual experience that attracted thousands of people, many of them young.

It took a while for us to find the right person to head up STAR, however. At first, it was run by a consultant hired by the Schusterman Foundation. But we needed an insider-outsider, somebody who had not only great ideas and the drive to put them into practice but also a soft touch, who could actually bring along the leaders of an ossified synagogue culture that showed few signs of wanting to change.

Hayim Herring was an ordained Conservative rabbi in his forties who also happened to have a Ph.D. in organization and management and had spent a few years working for the local federation. On paper, he looked good. He had done some consulting for STAR and really believed fundamental change was possible, not just on the margins. He met me in 2002 at my office together with Yitz.

Often when I meet a potential hire or grantee for the first time, I start the conversation by coming down hard. I'll offer the most blistering critique of what they're doing—not in a personal way, but in a way that might take some people aback. But if I'm going to invest significant resources in someone, I want to see how they respond to the most obvious criticisms—not just to hear what they say, but to find out what they're made of.

Before Hayim had a chance to speak, I launched into a tirade about the state of American synagogues. "Rabbis and synagogues are hopeless," I said. "Within a generation or two, the Reform and Conservative movements will be dead. They are hemorrhaging members, and they deserve it. They have no desire to change, there isn't any point in trying." I went on like this for a while.

Then I looked at Hayim. "Why aren't you more nervous?" I asked.

Up till now, he hadn't said a word. "Well," he said, "you can't really see how I look on the inside, can you?"

I loved that answer. This guy wasn't easily intimidated.

Yitz turned to me. "Michael, would you like to give Hayim a minute to explain what his idea is?"

It was called Synaplex, a play on the Cineplex movie theaters that had become fashionable all over North America. It was bold, and possibly crazy. The idea was to change the nature of synagogues at their core by offering a multiplicity of Friday night programs, tailored for different age groups and interests, all happening in the synagogue at the same time, alongside traditional services.

Now, offering programming like yoga or performances or talks wasn't unusual—most synagogues were already doing that during the week or maybe after services. But only a relatively small number of people showed up to midweek programs—far fewer than on Friday nights. Hayim had clearly done his homework. For most Reform synagogues, the core of everything was Friday night services. For Conservative synagogues as well, Friday nights were at least as important as Saturday mornings.

If Friday nights could somehow be reinvented to draw a much bigger crowd, they could conceivably transform the entire community's relationship to being Jewish, by giving a lot more members a good reason to show up more than once or twice a year. Even more important, they could bring in a lot of new, previously unaffiliated people—and this was, again, my main objective.

Under Hayim's leadership, STAR would create a national network to help synagogues make Synaplex happen. We'd partially fund a synagogue's programming—not a lot, up to $12,000 a year, often less, for a maximum of three years—and they'd commit to run Synaplex at least one Friday evening every four to six weeks and to attend all the training sessions and other conference calls we did.

We'd provide a range of program ideas and material. We'd encourage and train them to upgrade the food they offered, to keep production values high, to recruit volunteers from the community to do most of the work, to get sponsors to cover costs above our grant, and to market and evaluate their programs. We required each participating congregation to develop a marketing plan, which was almost unheard of for houses of worship. Most important, we'd encourage them to constantly innovate. STAR would help them learn from each other, and us from them. We wanted to make it as easy as possible.

Here's a sample program from Temple Solel, a Reform Congregation along the shore north of San Diego, for a single Friday night in 2007:

5:30–6:45 p.m.: Yoga

5:30–7:30 p.m.: Building Blocks Workshop (Jewish History with LEGO), Ages 7+

5:30–7:30 p.m.: Create a Mural, for Parents and Kids 6 and Under

6:30–8:30 p.m.: Singles Only—Sushi and Sake, Ages 40+

6:30–9:00 p.m.: Wine, Cheese & Games in the Library

6:30–7:30 p.m.: Candlelight & Conversation—Adults-Only Dinner ($18 Plus Reservation)

6:30–8:30 p.m.: Youth Lounge & Social Action: Project & Pizza ($5 Plus Reservation), Grades 5–8

7:30–9:00 p.m.: Babysitting with Movie (Reservation), Ages 2–9

7:30–9:00 p.m.: Erev Shabbat Services with a Guest Speaker

7:30–10:00 p.m.: Beit Café with Live Music Beginning at 8:00 p.m.[20]

The events were staggered to allow some people to come straight from work and participate in more than one activity. Families could come together and break off to different events. It was almost like a little Shabbat festival for the whole community. It was, in short, a revolution. A completely different concept of what a synagogue was for.

Of course, as with every bold new idea, not everyone was happy.

The main opposition would come from the rabbis themselves. Every week, they'd prepare their sermon like it was a message from God himself. Friday nights were their moment on the stage, the only time they had a captive audience. What self-respecting rabbi

---

20 Program reprinted in Building Consensus for Joining STAR's Synaplex Initiative, revised May 2007.

would agree to run programs that competed with the service? We expected significant opposition. In most cases, we got it, especially since the benefit was as yet unproven.

But we knew that once a few synagogues saw success, a lot more would follow. Somewhere, there had to be rabbis and lay leaders with enough awareness of their own shortcomings, enough desire for greater impact, enough humility in the face of their movements' slow-rolling collapse, that they'd be willing to try a radical change—especially if we were defraying some of the costs. Hayim reached out to his rabbi friends and community leaders and was able to get almost a dozen to take the plunge during that first year, and this was apparently enough. Most were in the greater New York area, but there were a few in Los Angeles as well.

Rabbis weren't the only opponents. Hayim also got phone calls—a lot of them—from the movements' umbrella organizations, rabbinic associations, and synagogue associations. They told him he wouldn't have a future. That he was "destroying Judaism." That he should leave dealing with rabbis to them. He even got a call from his own rabbinical seminary, trying to get him to stop. "You have no business working with rabbis and synagogues," they told him.

I understand the resistance. People are very touchy about religious traditions—especially rituals. The whole point of them is preservation, not innovation. Right?

The results of Synaplex, however, were startling. We hired Hayim to lead STAR in 2002, and by 2003, there were eleven synagogues on board, representing about twenty-five thousand Jews. By 2008, the number of synagogues had jumped to two hundred fifty—including congregations from all denominations—potentially reaching over half a million people. Meanwhile, a few dozen other synagogues had taken the idea, including the name "Synaplex," and run similar programs of their own without us.

The rate of increase was incredible. Clearly, there was real demand and real potential to change the face of synagogue life in the twenty-first century. Participating synagogues reported doubling or even tripling the number of participants over a regular Friday evening service. They were overflowing.

As with Birthright, the keys to Synaplex's success were *quality* and *choice*. Much as Birthright had offered a platform for different providers to offer different experiences within a strict set of parameters and quality control, Synaplex let the synagogues themselves decide what to offer. But whatever the programs were, Hayim's small team worked extremely hard to make sure that they were implemented at a high level. The most important part was getting everybody thinking—taking risks, innovating, tweaking, evaluating, sharing. To turn every synagogue into a creative hub.

Also, as with Birthright providers, we learned from the synagogues themselves and shared successful programs with the network. Congregation Kol Ami of White Plains, N.Y., started offering candlelight dinners for older people called Candles and Conversation. It was a big hit, and soon many others were doing it.

AND THEN, JUST AS IT was reaching escape velocity, Synaplex ended. Just like that. On the face of it, the reason was simple: In 2008, as the program was quickly accelerating, the Schusterman Foundation decided to pull out. I never really understood why—it seemed arbitrary at the time. But they had been the lead funder, not us. Without them, it didn't make sense to go on. We told everyone that 2010 would be the last year.

Looking back, however, I now wonder whether I should have done something to save Synaplex. Ending it felt wrong at the time, and it feels just as wrong now. Like JECEI, Synaplex was *working*. It was scalable. It could be sustained because each synagogue's funding was capped at three years—which was enough time to prove its worth to the community and let them support it themselves. If you Google "Synaplex," all these years later, you'll find a lot of synagogues still doing it.

True, we didn't have enough staff to ensure the kind of hands-on involvement and quality control for two hundred fifty synagogues that we had at the beginning when it was just eleven. And we hadn't invested in the kind of data collection and analysis that our other programs enjoyed. To do it right would require more funding rather than less. Still, this model of impact had, in my mind at least, proven itself. We were engaging tens of thousands of Jews, a large number of them previously uninvolved. And we were reinventing the American concept of the synagogue in Jewish life.

Could I have launched an effort to sell Synaplex to other major donors, as I had with Birthright, in order to keep it going? It's not an easy pitch to put across—"the program is great but the main funder has pulled out, so will you take over?" Besides, like a lot of people, I don't particularly enjoy fundraising. But I still look back and wonder: Did I drop the ball? Could I have done more? The answer to both of these questions is probably yes.

The truth is, a lot of the programs that we launched worked. And it's not hard to imagine them working again. Synaplex would not be too difficult to relaunch with the right leadership and funding. Neither would JECEI. These are scalable, sustainable ideas that have already proven their impact.

Synaplex had all the makings of a winner. It could have dramatically changed the face of synagogue life, and of Jewish engagement, across America. Perhaps it still can.

SYNAPLEX DID PROVE ONE IMPORTANT thing to my satisfaction. As I had long suspected, Shabbat really is a key to the Jewish future.

Even before Birthright took off, before the first chartered flight brought a plane full of nervous young Jews to Israel on a portentous new adventure, I was nagged by the question of follow-up. Why bother creating high-impact, ten-day experiences if you're going to let the enthusiasm they generate dissipate over time?

For years, in almost every conversation I had with people in the Jewish world, I mined them for ideas about follow-up to Birthright. More trips to Israel? Local Shabbat programs? Reunions? Nobody seemed to have a firm sense of what an adequate "follow-up" might look like. We launched a new division called Birthright NEXT that was meant to figure out the answer. We launched some Shabbat programs and sponsored a series of TED-style public speeches called "The Birthright Monologues." But nothing really worked, and Birthright NEXT shut down in 2015.

There were efforts outside our organization, and some of them were pretty good. Working with Hillel, a project was launched by Barry Shrage at the Boston federation to place young college graduates on campuses to actively encourage Birthright alumni to participate in Jewish activities. Barry is one of the rare individuals of great quality in the Jewish institutional world. Another group called Bring Israel Home believed that the most important thing all Birthright participants shared was the bus-based group. So they created bus-based reunions for some carefully chosen groups and would fly over the Israelis from their bus, too, at retreats in the United States. But while it didn't cost as much as a Birthright trip, it was hard to imagine scaling that up and sustaining it, and it wasn't clear whether the value it added was worth it.

Still, my mind kept coming back to Shabbat. Why? Partly because of its frequency and regularity. Weekly engagement is real engagement. A central part of a new Jewish "envelope" will have to do with the frequency of doing overtly Jewish things. Some people pray three times a day, eat food that is strictly kosher, and follow a lot of rules that come out of our tradition. They are what we call "observant" Jews, and being Jewish is something they experience every day. Other Jews go to temple once or twice a year. They may be highly successful individuals, and "feel" Jewish, whatever that means, but they usually do very little to ensure that their kids share those feelings or have a base of knowledge to draw upon in formulating their own Jewish commitment.

In between these two categories, there is Shabbat. And since Shabbat happens to take place on the weekends, it's a great opportunity to fit something Jewish into people's busy lives. But there was a deeper reason for my fixation on Shabbat.

I had learned a lot about the power of Shabbat through my friendship with Harry Freund. I met Harry during my freshman year at Penn, and we quickly became best friends. Though he wasn't Orthodox, he had the most powerful Jewish identity of anyone I'd ever met. A child of the Upper East Side, he'd attended the modern-Orthodox Ramaz School. His mother Miriam was the national president of Hadassah. Penn was his first venture into the non-Jewish world. I kept accusing him of being "monomaniacally" Jewish, of seeing everything only through the prism of his Jewish priorities. "Those fucking Saudis," he would say late at night as we chatted in the dorm. "Why do they get all the oil and Israel gets nothing?"

Harry was especially bothered by the not-so-subtle anti-Semitism of the kid in the next dorm room over. His name was Sam, and among his other offenses, Sam insisted on blasting German marching music at all hours. Often he and his anti-Semitic friends would march up and down the hall to the music. This was barely a decade after the end of World War II and the Holocaust. (Sam's life became even more colorful after college. He went on to become a doctor and was ultimately convicted of murder after taking out a contract to have someone killed. He spent a decade behind bars, found religion in the Greek Orthodox Church, and then later wrote op-eds about the danger of drugs.)

Anyway, it was Harry who brought me to Hillel on Friday nights. Back then, there weren't many Jews at Penn. This was before Jews started attending Ivy League schools in large numbers and before Hillel became a global juggernaut under Richard Joel's direction. (In 2003, Richard asked me to give $2.5 million to dedicate a new, much larger, Hillel building on the Penn campus, called Steinhardt Hall.) Friday nights at Hillel were pretty much the only Jewish content you could get on campus. There were Jewish fraternities, but these were more like social clubs where Jews felt at home and didn't actually have Jewish content.

The Shabbat dinners I knew growing up were with my mother and grandmother, and we only had them about once a month. We didn't have guests and weren't invited to others. So when I first walked into a dining room with twenty-five other Jewish students, mostly male, I had never encountered Shabbat as something that could act as a powerful anchor of community and identity. But here we were, young Jews, most of us assimilated, yet drawn to an ancient Jewish practice, eating traditional foods, drinking the treacly Malaga wine, saying the blessings, and just being Jewish together. It was something I had no idea I needed, and it was something of a revelation about what Shabbat could mean for people my age.

Despite the simplicity of the dinners, there was something moving about them. For most of these kids, this was the only Jewish content they received on campus. But even for Harry and me, the dinners became a Jewish lifeline as we swam through unfamiliar WASPy waters—and I would continue to feel this way about Shabbat through my years at Calvin Bullock and during my time in the U.S. Army.

But there was another aspect of Shabbat that appealed to me as well—a spiritual aspect. This, too, came to me thanks to Harry. Halfway through my freshman year, I went to his parents' home on East 71st Street for a New Year's Eve party. The guest of honor was Rabbi Shlomo Carlebach, and it was my first encounter with that incredible bard of the Jewish spirit, the long-haired rabbi with his open white shirt, his acoustic guitar and driving voice wielding the eternal Jewish song like the twirling, fiery sword of the Garden of Eden.

Over the years, as I got married and raised a family in Manhattan, I stayed close with Harry, and we would often go to Shlomo's synagogue on West 79th Street. The singing rabbi wasn't always there. In addition to his synagogue, he had a center in the Haight-Ashbury neighborhood of San Francisco called the House of Love and Prayer, and in 1975, he set up a commune in Israel called Mevo Modi'im, informally known as "the *moshav*," which became a source of boundless Jewish creativity until it was destroyed by a forest fire in 2019. Shlomo spread his message around the world.

These two aspects of the Shabbat experience—community and spirituality—affected me deeply. Over the years, perhaps compensating for what I had not received in my own home growing up, Judy and I would turn our weekly Shabbat meals into a mandatory ritual. But more importantly, the power of this uniquely Jewish *collective spirituality* that doesn't actually need rabbis or halachic observance, and doesn't even need God—just a knowledge that we are a people doing something quintessentially Jewish together—has been a driving force throughout my personal and philanthropic life.

I have always seen this kind of spiritual experience as the key to the secular Jewish future. I know that every Jew has the potential to intuitively grasp it and to embrace it as a part of the cultural "envelope" of life habits that sustains our pride in being Jews.

ONE OF THE GROUPS THAT realized this years ago is Chabad, the official organization of the Lubavitcher Hasidic movement.

Chabad understood something that most Orthodox "outreach" programs did not: That young people want, more than anything else, to choose their experiences. They don't want to be told what to do. Chabad rabbis are trained to use their invitational Shabbat dinners as a showcase. By providing a (somewhat idealized) glimpse of Jewish life in a family setting, they present a powerful, if subtle, form of advertising for the Hasidic way of life. It's a home, it's kids running around, it's warmth and joy and song. It's very powerful and rings authentic to many Jews.

The problem for most secular Jews is that it is not really relevant to their lives. A nice place to visit, but you'd never want to live there. As such, it inadvertently perpetuates a sense that Shabbat and Jewish identity are fundamentally alien. It's a warm experience, educational, social, and fun. But unless you are planning on becoming an Orthodox Jew, Shabbat dinner at Chabad will never be your own.

It's also a very specific experience. Obviously not every Chabad house is the same, but what they offer is similar enough to create a sense—much like McDonald's—that everywhere on earth you'll be getting the same product. That has advantages, but if you don't like their version of Shabbat, you won't go very often.

For that reason, as big as Chabad has become, only a small minority of non-Orthodox Jews regularly participate, and even fewer actually become Orthodox.

I aimed for something broader. I wanted to change non-Orthodox Jewish life in America, which meant creating something that could potentially reach millions of people. Like Birthright, but for Friday nights. Something organic to secular Jews, that could become a *habit* for a significant number, and that could form the basis for meaningful Jewish engagement in a family setting.

That would necessitate an element of choice.

Part of what distinguishes non-Orthodox from Orthodox Judaism is the centrality of the individual's choices. The core secular-liberal belief is that everyone is unique, and there's something wonderful about finding your own path. This is both very modern and very ancient: The rabbis of the Talmud taught that each person needs to "choose their own Rabbi," to figure out on their own who is or isn't a mentor, to develop opinions of one's own and fight for them. But Orthodoxy today, it seems, is rarely like that. Instead, it's all about *following*: following rules, following rabbis.

We needed to reinvent the Shabbat experience for unengaged Jews the way we had reinvented the Israel trip with Birthright: from the ground up.

IN THE SUMMER OF 2013, Judy, Sara, and I had a meeting with the investor Paul Singer and his partner Terry Kassel to discuss our philanthropic interests. My foundation staff had been working for a while on an idea for how Shabbat could become the basis of a follow-up to Birthright. Birthright NEXT had created something called "NEXT Shabbat" under the leadership of Rabbi Daniel Brenner, but it hadn't grown. I had charged my staff with coming up with a model that could really grow, and I shared with Paul and Terry what they were thinking.

By this point, the internet had become a central tool in all our lives, not just for sharing information but also for conducting one's social life and organizing resonant events and experiences in a way that was, in theory, highly scalable. Though we had no idea at the time, specific websites and apps for putting people together with strangers for meals—known as "social dining" sites—were about to become a global phenomenon, especially for Jews. One of the biggest such platforms, eatwith.com, launched the following year for travelers looking for hosted meals.

Shabbat get-togethers—especially Friday night dinners—appealed to Terry and Paul. We agreed to work together as equal partners to see if we could develop the ultimate program to encourage Jewish young adults to start hosting and attending Shabbat dinners on a regular basis.

The result was something called OneTable, and aside from Birthright itself, it has become by far the most successful project our foundation has helped launch, reaching tens of thousands of people each year and growing rapidly.

OneTable has succeeded because it benefited from all the lessons we'd learned over the years. We had an excellent equal-stake partner in the Paul E. Singer Foundation. We put time into the concept and design, using best practices from the industry. We delved into the scholarly research and drilled down into the experience of young adults to understand their needs. We incorporated the idea of choice, allowing people to find the experience that best suited them, along with personalized support to maintain the brand and give people confidence in the experience. We established a relatable brand and messaging.

During the second half of 2013, we developed a plan for bringing Shabbat dinners to as many unengaged young American Jews as possible. For lack of a better name, we called it "the Shabbat Project," and the slogan I suggested for it was "Make Shabbat a Habit."

But most important—we found the right person to lead the project.

Aliza Kline brought a unique combination of experience when we hired her in January 2014. She had run a beautiful project in Boston called Mayyim Hayyim, which reimagined the Jewish ritual bath, or *mikveh*, in a modern, secular context. She therefore already understood the core concept of taking a Jewish tradition and making it accessible to the full diversity of the American Jewish community. She was a self-starter with a clear vision and experience under her belt. Aliza had a track record of getting things done.

The daughter of a rabbi, Aliza grew up surrounded by joyful Jewish celebrations. Her sister is a renowned Jewish musician and educator, and her husband is a rabbi. Aliza worked in Jewish organizations ranging from start-ups like the Jerusalem Open House to established mainstays like Hillel International, Aliza's familiarity with the organized Jewish world was an asset.

She spent most of 2014 applying a method known as "design thinking," which focuses principally on the needs of customers and the user experience. Aliza built on the vision we had and improved it immensely. She enlisted the help of experts in habit formation, often quoting the words of one of the field's leading scholars, an Israeli-American at Stanford named Nir Eyal. "Influencing behavior by reducing the effort required to perform an action," he wrote, "is more effective than increasing someone's desire to do it."

The goal was to learn about the barriers facing young adults when it came to Shabbat—and then systematically address each one to make the practice feel natural. Her small team learned as much as possible through observation and focus groups. They did a round of meetings with CEOs of a variety of web-based social platforms, ultimately enlisting Noah Karesh, founder of a social dining app called Feastly, who allowed Aliza to test the concept before starting to build a platform of their own.

Working closely with both foundations, Aliza also brought in a branding genius named Raphael Bemporad, who helped us understand the needs of the people who we were already engaging with to come up with the overall brand and value proposition of OneTable. This became about not just enjoying a Friday night Shabbat dinner but finding a sense of community. The project was rebranded and launched as OneTable in May of 2015.

I had always envisioned the Shabbat Project as a form of follow-up for Birthright. But OneTable, in the end, stood entirely on its own. It had its own separate brand, and while many Birthright alumni participated, it didn't use any Birthright resources.

Like most great ideas, the concept behind OneTable is incredibly simple. There are a lot of people who'd be willing to host Shabbat dinner, and lots more happy to attend, if they had the support they needed. Surprisingly, that included financial help, as well as hospitality coaching, Jewish resources (like audio recordings of blessings), and permission to make the ritual their own.

I had long understood that Shabbat dinner is an opportunity not only for great food and conversation but for meeting people who share your interests. If you can find a way to facilitate these dinners on a mass scale and create a mechanism and an incentive structure that offer consistently high-quality experiences—you will get a lot of Jews having Shabbat dinner who otherwise wouldn't have.

These are not professionally-led communal dinners in institutional settings. They almost always happen in a host's home, or restaurants, around an intimate table. The young adults themselves are the hosts and the guests, and they are forming Jewish habits that they can sustain once they have families.

The centerpiece of OneTable is a web-based platform similar to that of other consumer apps such as Airbnb—take a look for yourself if you haven't already. On any given Friday night, in any of seventeen major cities across America, you can choose from a wide array of hundreds of dinners based on different themes and styles. You can also host your own, anywhere in the United States, in 450 locales so far. Most dinners are free, some are potluck, and they usually have eight to twelve participants. It's incredibly intuitive and welcoming.

But behind the scenes, a lot is going on. In order to lower the financial barrier to hosting faced by many early-career, young adults, OneTable offers "nourishment credits" which can be redeemed through valued national and local vendors like Whole Foods, Safeway, and DoorDash. Regional field managers and ambassadors support and train hosts to provide the best experience possible and work hard to make sure that each region has a broad selection of dinners available. Educational materials and guides deepen the experience. The OneTable website is interactive so that participants can be matched with Jewish resources that meet their needs. Special efforts are made to turn participants into repeat guests and ultimately convert them into hosts themselves. And a whole range of partnerships have been built with suppliers and organizations that benefit from the platform.

Most recently, OneTable partners with Birthright Israel, training their trip leaders to elevate their Shabbat experiences during Birthright trips, and to lay the groundwork for a seamless transition into regular Shabbat experiences after the participants come back.

The goal from the moment OneTable launched was to achieve scale. And boy, did it.

AT THE END OF 2015, Aliza met with me in my office. She was thrilled to have reached her own ambitious goals of one thousand dinners and ten thousand "seats at the table," or meals served, in six months. It really was an impressive achievement in so short a time. I knew that she was proud of her accomplishment. But I also knew that everybody around her was probably telling her how amazing it was, and she didn't need me to add to the chorus of praise.

"This is bullshit," I said. "Our target audience is at least a million people. Why are you so excited?"

It may have sounded harsh. But frankly, I was wary of putting money into another limited Jewish program. The idea of scale is not well understood in the Jewish world. Very few new initiatives remain dedicated to the goal of changing the entire North American Jewish landscape. The most important thing I can convey in such a meeting is the goal and the absolute dedication everyone should have to it—if something works, scale it up, and if it's going well, scale it up more.

In Aliza's shoes, I would never have wanted to hear praise at having reached ten thousand people—just as I rarely celebrated my successes during my career in finance. I wanted people who shared with me the real goal: Having a tangible impact on the identity of American Jews. She got the message and immediately set to work figuring out how to reach one hundred thousand.

It is not easy to scale up. Even if you have money and flexible technology, you are still constrained by the fact that you're building relationships with current and potential participants, establishing a compelling brand, and needing to constantly improve the user experience to compete in the marketplace. To scale up, you need to staff up—and that takes time. You also need a strategy for expansion, and Aliza focused on twelve major urban centers with a high number of Jewish millennials, especially where the Jewish options were limited for a Friday night.

At some point in 2018, OneTable had reached around sixty thousand seats at the table. We had reached a tipping point, and suddenly the demand was spiraling out of control. Under the advice of David Gedzelman, who by this point had become president of our foundation, and his counterpart at the Singer Foundation, Debbie Hochberg, Aliza developed a plan—wisely—to limit growth until the organization could catch up. She did this in subtle ways (you can't exactly tell people you don't want them over for dinner), such as adding questions to the registration process that made it a little less easy to sign up.

Meanwhile, she invested time and effort into cultivating local and national donors, corporate sponsors, and white-label clients who pay to license and customize the tech platform, so that the growing cost wouldn't fall entirely on us. By 2021, the annual budget for OneTable had reached around $7 million—tiny compared to Birthright's—but less than a fifth of that fell on the Singer and Steinhardt foundations. The rest came from more than a thousand donors she had brought in from across the country.

WHY DID ONETABLE WORK? PART of the reason is that we helped young adults build a sense of community at a time when, according to studies, a lot of them were experiencing an acute sense of loneliness—more so than in my generation or even my children's. Something about our new world, social media, and the instant gratification and horrific distraction of our devices—it's all added up to what scholars have called an "epidemic of loneliness." People are hungry for other people.

Shabbat, and especially Friday night meals, can be a powerful antidote for loneliness. The grind through the workweek is hard. The Shabbat rituals—kiddush, blessings, the challah, the wine— create a framework for a powerful social moment. Participants report feeling more connected through this moment of joy and love, engaging with our traditions, and being a part of something bigger than themselves.

Jewish life used to be very different from what most of us have experienced. Families stayed in close proximity. Children usually didn't move away. In traditional Jewish communities, everyone had to live within walking distance of the synagogue, so your friends and neighbors were never far. Your world was built around close human contact.

But in the last century, industrial progress came with mobility and alienation. People started moving away from home and only coming back for holidays. Then came the internet, which eliminated distance entirely for parts of our interactions—first in writing (instant messaging and emails), then in speaking (web-based phone calls and voice notes), then seeing one another (video calls). But none of it, it turns out, is the same as having dinner at the same table. Nothing you do via phone can capture the same human warmth, the complete sense of togetherness.

Even biologically, you can't exchange pheromones over the internet. As we all discovered when the lockdowns of the Covid-19 pandemic came in 2020 and forced us into Zoom-based relationships, the easy yet limited access to other human beings can actually make you feel more lonely, not less, because you are reminded of what you are missing.

Aliza understood that this "epidemic of loneliness" had struck young adults, a generation often called "digital natives," powerfully indeed. OneTable was a way of bringing people together in a setting that met them where they were. "Millennials are the most stressed-out and lonely generation in America," Aliza said in an interview for the Jewish incubator UpStart. "Simply put, they need Shabbat—for the connections, the comfort of ritual, and the stress relief. [...] OneTable is designed to empower Jewish young adults to build micro-communities while creating their own authentic Friday night dinners, ultimately forming a lifelong Shabbat practice."[21]

Unlike Chabad, which offered a quick, bracing plunge into the pool of tradition, OneTable offered the possibility of making Shabbat dinner with others a permanent part of one's regular Jewish life.

As of mid-2021, more than 170,000 different people have participated in more than 65,000 separate Shabbat meals. The total number of meals served ("seats at the table") now exceeds 525,000. And the number of people who've been hosts—another key metric—has also been impressive, with more than 16,000

---

21 "Go Slow to Go Fast: An Upstart Interview with OneTable's Aliza Kline," *UpStart* (November 22, 2016), https://upstartlab.org/go-slow-go-fast-upstart-interview-onetables-aliza-kline/.

young people having hosted meals for their peers. Suddenly, almost out of nowhere and on a relatively small budget, OneTable has built a robust network of dinner hosts.

The growth rate has been far beyond our expectations. In addition, OneTable has improved its repeat rates, with more than 70 percent of 2020 attendees having participated in the past, up from 45 percent in 2016. This suggests that for tens of thousands of Jews in America, OneTable has helped them make Shabbat dinner a habit.

Naturally, with such a new program, and in the absence of a control group as Birthright had, we can't assess long-term impact to the same degree of certainty. Because it is based online, however, OneTable has collected extensive data to analyze. We can measure not just the number of participants and how many people are hosting meals but also, through surveys, their feelings and engagement both before and after.

It will be difficult to gauge exactly how much OneTable is affecting their Jewish engagement in other areas. Perhaps the data will still come down the road. But part of me says: Who cares? Birthright was an unbelievably expensive venture based on an untested theory that a short trip to Israel would have a long-term impact, and, therefore, the impact studies are central. OneTable is different. It's a tiny fraction of the cost, but participation is itself a form of impact. Shabbat meals are themselves Jewish engagement. The very fact that hundreds of thousands of non-Orthodox Jews have begun participating in Shabbat meals, the vast majority of whom would not have otherwise done so, is staggering in itself. It is a signal of massive untapped demand, coupled with a strategy for meeting it. If it continues to scale up, and we have no reason to doubt that it will, OneTable will make a meaningful contribution to the life habits of the secular Jewish world.

Of course, the success of One Table hasn't prevented critics from attacking it. In this case, most of the attacks come from certain educators, traditionalists, rabbis, and academic scholars who say it's somehow shallow, inauthentic, and fails to include advanced learning. This is the same thing they said about Birthright, that you couldn't get anything important out of a ten-day trip.

They were wrong then, and they're wrong now. First, because the kind of experiences they say should be provided hold no interest for the vast majority of unengaged Jews—it's a product without a market. It's also wrong because the difference between a life with no tangible Jewish activities and one with a Shabbat dinner every Friday night is enormous—for it is a habit of meaningful Jewish engagement.

Most importantly, it's wrong because it frequently comes from an irrational need to preserve things that are manifestly failing, a compulsion to bad-mouth efforts to do something new, and because too often it comes from people who never in their lives tried to create something better themselves and saw what kind of mountain we have chosen to climb.

ALL THREE OF THESE PROGRAMS, each in its own way, got the job done. Makor created a desperately needed Jewish cultural engine that combined compelling experiences with artistic creativity and the constant injection of new content into our world; it was magical, powerful, and expensive. Synaplex successfully reinvented Friday night services and was on the verge of a massive expansion when, for reasons I still do not fully understand, it was abruptly put on hold. Both of these proved their effectiveness and popularity, then failed because my own ability to fund them was limited and the broader Jewish community didn't see them as important.

This endemic communal failure to identify and support new initiatives with a proven ability to help solve the single greatest existential threat we face means that any program that does succeed must do so despite, not because of, the established Jewish community. OneTable, more than anything else I've supported other than Birthright, has managed to do exactly that. It has created a *new product*, a new piece of the secular Jewish "envelope" of the future. And it's figured out how to maintain its quality even as it expands to hundreds of thousands of participants.

But just like Birthright, OneTable is only one strategy. We will need many. And we will need a Jewish community that can recognize and develop radically new "products" to introduce into the Jewish marketplace. The responsibility for this problem lies squarely on the shoulders of major Jewish philanthropists: It is they who create the incentive structures, they who turn a blind eye to the turf wars, they who too often look for plaudits and plaques without insisting on transparency and impact. It is they who have enabled a sclerotic, self-preserving system to yawn at assimilation and punish or ignore the creative voices dedicated to addressing it.

There are many solutions, from creating an alternative set of philanthropic channels to a kind of independent watchdog group to act as a check on the Jewish philanthropic world. We will need a combination of approaches, which I'll discuss in more detail later on. But the most important first step is to understand just how badly the system is broken.

There are exceptions, of course. It is much more common now to encounter independent-minded philanthropists who care about impact and fighting assimilation than when I first started in 1995. But they are still a minority and are constantly thwarted by the

Jewish Turf Machine. The very fact that communal institutions still won't carry the burden of Birthright—after two decades and definitive proof of long-term impact that directly benefits their own communities—is all the evidence you need.

Interlude: The Jewish Future

OVER THE PAST TWO AND a half decades, I've dedicated the better part of my resources, including time, thought, and finances, to make a dent in reversing our eroding Jewish identity and to lay the groundwork for a proud, thriving, secular-Jewish community in the Diaspora. It has been, I think, a study in both how little and how much one man of means can do to change the face of Jewish life.

How little: Throughout the experience, I was constantly bumping up against the limits of my financial capacity. It took me time to understand that without partners of similar means and outlook, I would accomplish little—and that for any project to succeed, I would have to bring others in early and keep them committed. Many of our best programs shut down just as they were taking off because I couldn't sustain them myself and failed to convince others to keep them going. Some faced opposition from the Jewish Turf Machine, the entrenched institutional interests that interpreted our new approaches as a threat.

How much: In the case of Birthright and OneTable, we successfully launched and scaled up programs that are today having a direct and measurable impact on Jewish life. Birthright, in particular, also proved that the Israeli government can become a key partner in funding the infrastructure of pride in the Diaspora. In the case of a few other programs, we uncovered an enormous latent demand for high-quality pathways to Jewish engagement and found a formula for meeting that demand, even if we didn't have the resources to scale up at the time.

But beyond these achievements, we proved something more important: That the struggle to build Jewish engagement in the non-Orthodox Diaspora is not necessarily a lost cause. There are things we can do that really work, and they do not require giving up who we are. We can be proud Jews of the Diaspora, and we can pass that pride on from one generation to the next, without moving to Israel or becoming Orthodox.

The slow evaporation of the non-Orthodox Diaspora, in other words, is a problem with a solution. This is a huge statement, because the vast majority of the Jewish world has behaved as though there were either no problem or no solution—and there was, therefore, no need to change what they were already doing.

The moment one really understands this, one discovers that a true commitment to the future of the Jewish people confers upon us a responsibility to act. Yes, the challenge is immense, requiring that we pull together, reorganize ourselves, change our priorities and dedicate vast resources of time, creative thinking, and money into continuing down the path on which we've started. But once it's been proven that it can be done, nobody in the Jewish community has a right to abandon the fight.

Where does that leave us? There are still a few profound issues that have to be addressed in order to prepare us—conceptually, institutionally, and financially—for the coming battle. It's not enough to decide we want to fight for Jewish pride. We need to actually imagine what a better Jewish world looks like. We need to be honest with ourselves about the effectiveness of our existing institutions and the community resources they are currently absorbing. And we must be willing to part with a few long-cherished beliefs concerning Jewish philanthropy, our relationship with Israel, and the nature of Jewish identity itself.

But first, we need a clearer understanding of what Jewish pride really is and why building it is worth all the trouble I am calling for. We need to go deeper.

CHAPTER 5

The Three Pillars
of Jewish Pride

My philanthropic career hasn't followed a straight path. I was not driven toward a single project, genre, method, or institution. Instead, it has been more like painting a picture. I had a clear mental image of the finished product, an idea of what non-Orthodox Jewish life in the Diaspora could look like. Then I drew a line here, filled in some color there, usually going on intuition with the hope that the picture would eventually come into focus. The more successful projects, like Birthright and OneTable, appear as bold and colorful strokes. Others are little more than a dash here or a splash of color there, hinting at possibilities. One day, I hope, the picture that emerges will be clear, vivid, and beautiful.

I've tried to summarize this vision in two words: Jewish pride. A few more words: A proud, rich, creative secular Jewish identity that can be passed from one generation to the next.

But what do I really mean by pride? The word may seem self-explanatory, but it is not. To talk about all these different programs intended to foster pride and not go into some kind of discussion about what it really entails is a lot like only seeing the lines and dots on the canvas but never describing the whole picture.

Much of what I'm about to say has become clear only after the fact—the lessons I've learned from my efforts. I look back on the projects that instinctively resonated with me as signaling Jewish pride, and I try to understand them. What makes us proud Jews? What should?

What I'm looking for here is not the form of Jewish pride, in other words, so much as its deepest content. And what I've discovered is that there are three pillars to Jewish pride. Each stands on its own but is deeply interrelated with the other two.

They are peoplehood, excellence, and joy.

GROWING UP IN BENSONHURST, I was acutely aware that there were different kinds of Jews. When the refugees from the Holocaust came to our neighborhood with their tortured bodies and tattooed arms, I understood without having to be told that these were our people, and we had to care for them—even though they didn't speak English and had gone through something I would never understand.

But there were other Jews, too. Reform temples, built by Jews who came from Germany long before my family arrived from Eastern Europe, were a fixture of the Jewish landscape I grew up in. They had established an entire world of elite, secular Jewish culture of their own, which was very different from the gritty, traditional, Yiddish-speaking, working-class immigrant communities from Poland, Russia, Lithuania, and Ukraine.

Brooklyn was also home to a sizable community of Syrian Jews. They had come to America earlier in the twentieth century, establishing themselves many decades before other Sephardic communities, from North Africa and Iran, came to North America. This community saw itself as very different from the Ashkenazic Jews of New York, and they married almost exclusively among themselves. They had broad extended families and went into business, mostly in textiles and retail, among themselves.

One of my best friends, Jackie Marshall, had a Syrian mom and an Iraqi father, and he grew up speaking Arabic at home, attending Hebrew school at the Sephardic Magen David Synagogue, and eating the *kibbe* and baklava that his mom made. He later moved to California, became a noted poet, and even wrote a memoir, *From Baghdad to Brooklyn*, where you can read all about our neighborhood from his family's Jewish-Arabic perspective.

The Syrians were, and continue to be, a proud American Jewish community, mainly Orthodox-affiliated, which suffers no shortage of pride. They take care of their own, build their wealth through a limited number of professions, and curse at each other in Arabic instead of Yiddish.

The point is that I grew up understanding that being Jewish wasn't just about being an English-speaking American Jew who ate *kishke* and knew a few words of Yiddish. The range of what "Jewish" could mean was much wider. And it wasn't just a theoretical construct: I didn't think about "the Jewish people" in general. But I felt that Jews of all kinds, including those who led very different lives, were my people.

I later became fascinated with the diversity of the Jews. I traveled to the Jewish communities in Argentina, Uruguay, the United Kingdom, Russia and Ukraine, France, and South Africa. When many of us in America talk about "the Diaspora," we are really talking about the United States. And it's true that the seven-plus million Jews in the United States dwarf the rest of the Diaspora combined, who are probably about two million in total. But every one of these communities has its own story to tell and a unique Jewish experience.

Some of them suffer from challenges similar to those we face in the United States in terms of sustaining their Jewish identity. In the former Soviet Union, there are still hundreds of thousands of Jews, many of whom lack access to meaningful Jewish education and experiences, despite support from international organizations like the Joint Distribution Committee and Chabad.

The Jews of Great Britain, who number fewer than three hundred thousand, suffer both from internal division and a potent sense of ambient public anti-Semitism, which was especially acute during Jeremy Corbyn's brief reign over the Labour Party.

In France, the Jewish community (about half a million in total) is divided between a smaller, more established, secular-Ashkenazic elite and a much larger community of traditional immigrants from North Africa. They face a different form of anti-Semitism, at times quite violent, coming mostly from Arab-Muslim immigrants. Some have begun migrating to Israel in recent years.

The Canadian Jewish community, too, is different from America's in many ways. The two largest cities, Toronto and Montreal, still have identifiably Jewish neighborhoods, and Canadian Jews and communal leaders tend to have a more robust sense of their heritage and greater knowledge of Hebrew and Israel than their counterparts in the United States.

For family reasons, I've also gotten to know the Jewish community of South Africa. There, behind electrified fences built to ward off violent crime, and amid lingering tensions dating back to the apartheid era, the small Jewish community, now numbering around fifty thousand, manages to preserve a life built around synagogues and day schools and possesses a strong sense of who they are and a need to care for each other.

And of course, I have visited Israel dozens of times, getting to know this incredible culture where so many different Jewish traditions have fused together to build a society unlike anything in our long history. Most Diaspora Jews have little real sense of the multiracial, multicultural diversity of the Jewish people, but it's apparent to anyone who has spent significant time in Israel.

But even concerning other Jews within the United States, I'm amazed and disappointed when people within the non-Orthodox, Ashkenazic mainstream show ignorance about how other American Jewish communities—ultra-Orthodox Jews, Jews of color, Iranian Jews, Syrian Jews—live and think.

I do not pretend to be an expert in the unique histories of Jewish communities around the world. But I have seen enough to know that American Jews have an unfortunate tendency to be highly parochial when it comes to what counts, in their minds, as "Jewish."

Why does this matter? The truth is that such an approach is limiting when it comes to fostering an authentic Jewish identity. The last century saw massive relocations of Jews. If you are Ashkenazic in heritage, then most Jews around the world were, just a few generations ago, living in the same Yiddish-speaking lands as your own ancestors. They came from the same culture, lived similar lives, observed the same religion, even spoke the same language. With Sephardic Jews, you may need to go back a few hundred years more to find our common lived experience—but you'll still find we have a lot in common. To the untrained eye, the differences between Sephardic and Ashkenazic Orthodox religious practices are barely distinguishable.

In the Passover Seder, when we tell the story of the four sons, I've always been struck by the wicked son, who sets himself apart from the Jewish collective identity. The idea that a personal commitment to other Jews is foundational to who we are has always resonated with me, long after I had abandoned a belief in God or observance of the rituals.

There's something else to note about the wicked son. Yes, he has on some level alienated himself from the Jewish people. And yet he is *there*. He hasn't gone anywhere. He may ask questions in a way the rabbis don't approve of. But the very fact that he has shown up at all, and is asking a question, is a sign that he still cares about being Jewish, even if it must be on his own terms.

How many Jews today feel exactly as he does? Probably more than we like to admit.

Peoplehood has been central to Jewish identity since time immemorial. In the Bible, it was the entire people that were enslaved in Egypt; they gathered on Mount Sinai to receive the Ten Commandments and found their new home together in Canaan. It is also what allows any Jew, anywhere, to feel both proud of other Jews' achievements and responsible for their fate. "All Israelites are responsible for one another," the ancient rabbis taught. The Hasidic masters believed that every Jew carries a divine spark that sets them apart but also binds them together.

You don't need to be a person of faith to recognize the centrality of peoplehood to a proud Jewish identity. We have traditionally called ourselves *am Yisrael*, the "people of Israel." Being Jewish isn't the same kind of thing as being Christian, which is all about faith, or being an American, which is about citizenship, or belonging to an ethnic group, which is largely a matter of cultural heritage. It's an indelible brand that cannot be understood through any of these categories alone.

What I do know is this: I, and many others like me, feel a personal connection to every individual Jew. It is not one of automatic trust or friendship but more like a presumptive intimacy, a kinship, and above all a sense of responsibility. An attentiveness to their hardship, pride in their achievements, and a feeling that perhaps can be called love.

This long history of Jewish commonality is an indelible part of who we are, no matter how different we seem from each other today, or how far some of us may have drifted from a self-consciously Jewish life. Our instincts about how to live, the values we give our children, our cultural uniqueness, are not just a product of the choices we personally have made, or even those of our parents. They are also the product of centuries of cultural development. And they remain a part of us, influencing, whether we know it or not, how we respond to the world around us.

What this means is that we can never really know ourselves until we have discovered what we share with those Jews whose lives seem very different from our own.

I've therefore spent a good deal of time and effort helping Jews who do not share my background. The support I've given to underprivileged or distressed youth in Israel, or to educating ultra-Orthodox Jews, or to the Jews who were imprisoned in the Soviet Union in the 1970s, has not been part of my foundation's main objective to create pride-instilling programs like Birthright. Rather it has been a natural outcome of the bond I've felt with other Jews, whoever and wherever they are.

MANY OF THE PROJECTS OUR foundation in Israel has funded were under the direction of Shula Navon. Shula, a longtime aide to Teddy Kollek, launched our foundation in Israel in 1995. With her help, and with the help of Tova Dorfman who took over the foundation in Israel after Shula passed away in 2005, we have supported a range of programs helping youth at risk—clubs, youth villages, after-school programs, summer educational programs, shelters, and more. We've also supported some bigger projects focused on young adults, including the national Student Union and placing volunteers in underserved communities.

One of our most important programs is called TALMA, which we launched with the Schusterman Foundation and the Israeli education ministry in 2013. Many American Jews are under the misimpression that all Israelis have a good command of English, but it's really not true, and it depends a lot on socioeconomic factors. For disadvantaged Israeli kids, one of the best ways to close their gap of opportunity is through intensive English-language study.

In Israel, having good English is an important gateway to future employment, especially in the high tech and service sectors. So we've created a program to bring over teachers from the United States for a summer or a full year and place them in schools around the country, teaching English using the same "proficiency approach" we use to teach Hebrew in the United States. Many of these are drawn from teachers at our Hebrew charter schools, which means that we end up reaping two major benefits: Underprivileged Israeli kids get a top-quality, English-language education, and our own diverse cohort of teachers get to spend time in Israel, building their connection to the Israeli and Hebrew-language content at the schools to which they return.

More recently, the success of TALMA has opened the door for programs that focus on the ultra-Orthodox, or Haredi, community in Israel. There, too, the lack of English is a crucial barrier to building one's earning capacity, especially for women married to full-time Torah scholars. Although the Haredi lifestyle puts up endless religious barriers to integration into the broader society, the community's biggest problem is actually economic: Because they don't receive the same education as secular Israelis, they are at a huge disadvantage when entering the workforce. So even those who want to break out of the pattern of endemic poverty and reliance on handouts don't have the basic skills needed to make a decent living.

Through a Haredi group called KamaTech, an ultra-Orthodox, high-tech accelerator and incubator, we've gotten involved in programs that help train Haredi women in Israel to become well-paid computer engineers. This has opened the door for major high-tech corporations in Israel to hire significant numbers of Haredi women, working in conditions tailored to their religious needs.

In the United States as well, I have been a funder of Yaffed ("Young Advocates for Fair Education"), which tries to ensure that children in ultra-Orthodox yeshivas, mostly in New York, receive a basic education in English, math, social studies, and science. In New York State, where most American ultra-Orthodox Jews live, there are nearly one hundred thousand children in Hasidic yeshivas—a number that is sure to grow significantly—who do not learn to read and write in English, nor the other subjects I mentioned, and a great many of them are destined for a life of poverty as a result. I support Yaffed because I deeply care about these children's futures, and I don't want to see Jewish human capital go to waste.

Not all these programs are meant to promote "peoplehood" as such. But they do reflect an important part of my own sense of pride in being Jewish. I see peoplehood as less of an abstract concept and more about caring for other Jews, regardless of their background. It's about moving beyond the narrow concept of "Jewish" we may have grown up with, learning about the incredible diversity of our people—racial, religious, and cultural—and supporting Jewish life wherever I feel I can make a difference.

MY GENERATION WAS RAISED WITH the belief that Jews are not merely responsible for each other but also contribute something special to the world. So were many generations that came before me. And a great many still believe it today.

I will not belabor the absurdly disproportionate impact Jews have had on the world in so many different fields, from science and medicine to culture and the arts, to business and finance and law. The question that needs answering is what the sources are of that unique contribution and whether we are willing to do what is necessary to preserve them. I call this quality "excellence," and it is the second pillar of Jewish pride.

The more we Jews have merged into mainstream American life, building our professional and personal lives through interaction with non-Jews, the harder it has become for many of us to talk about this particular quality. We are increasingly uneasy about invoking the sort of casual Jewish "exceptionalism" that used to be commonplace in the days when we were seeking recognition and acceptance from the majority in society.

Today, calling attention to our achievements as a people, and the qualities that make them possible, may seem out of touch. Too often, success is now seen in many circles not as something positive but instead as reflecting an unfair advantage that certain people, including Jews, may have over others. In a recent issue of *Sapir*, Bret Stephens put his finger on the problem of talking about Jewish excellence in the current climate:

Success in America is coming to be seen as a function not of individual merit but of a deeply rigged system that calls itself a meritocracy but is actually a self-serving plutocracy. And just who, according to this view, has rigged this system? Precisely the people who have most benefited from it and now have the "privilege" of standing atop it. By any empirical metric, in nearly every major institution, a disproportionate percentage of the meritocracy is Jewish. And the goal of nearly every social justice movement in the United States today is to tear that system down.[22]

This is fairly new, but the truth is that even in the previous generation, it was difficult for many Jews to speak publicly about Jewish success. For them it was part of a broader problem of placing our universalism over our particularism—a feeling that there was something too tribal, too self-congratulatory, to take pride in our achievements or to look more deeply into the question of why we continued to excel.

But we have to talk about Jewish excellence. Because it is central to understanding and ultimately embracing Jewish pride.

Again: I do not believe we are a "chosen people" in the sense of being more worthy or better than others. I don't think God, if he exists, has granted us any special dispensation. This religious explanation offers too easy an answer to the difficult question of what has preserved the Jews as a people over the millennia and what has given them their special edge in the modern world.

That said, Jews have clearly carried with them something unusual over many centuries, passed from parents to children and from teachers to students; something that gave them an unmistakable edge when, after centuries of being largely confined

---

22 Bret Stephens, "Is There a Future for American Jews?" *Sapir Journal* (Autumn 2021), https://sapirjournal.org/continuity/2021/10/is-there-a-future-for-american-jews/.

to ghettos and shtetls, they were finally free to engage with the non-Jewish world.

We can hope to recreate the sort of qualities that lifted our achievements, on a per capita basis, far beyond those of any other ethnic or religious group in the United States, only if we first understand the nature of those qualities.

What creates Jewish excellence? Why were our achievements so far beyond our numbers across the twentieth century? Here it is important to pay attention to the specific fields in which we excelled: all of them required a certain excellence of the mind. We would not be leaders in the sports world or the military. Our achievements were and remain fairly narrow—but while narrow, their impact on America as a whole was radically disproportionate. Whether this has continued to the same degree in the early twenty-first century is unclear. But the historical impact of the Jews in America is not.

When we look back at the many contributions Jews have made to Western civilization, and to America in particular, we notice that the vast majority—whether in the arts or the sciences or business—involved a highly developed form of creative intelligence. We might call this special form of intelligence the *applied creative intellect*.

Yes, we were proud of our ballplayers and comedians and of Jewish children who grew up to be doctors and lawyers. We were proud of fellow Jews who built wealth when previous generations had to grapple with hardship. But the ones who really made us stand tall in our own eyes were those who made world-changing contributions in scientific and cultural fields. Those like Einstein and Sigmund Freud, who mastered a challenging discipline and overturned its assumptions—and in the process changed the world for the better. It was this unique contrarian genius, this intellectual humanitarian benevolence, which made our centuries of struggle worthwhile.

Every human culture has its own peculiar strength, a special quality that sets it apart. For Jews, that special trait was a focus on cultivating and training the creative intellect. This focus is reflected in the idea that when a child asks a question or challenges authority, it's an important moment, something to be encouraged and celebrated rather than punished.

If you've heard the expression *yiddishe kop*—a "Jewish head"—you'll know that Jews have always perceived themselves as being different from others not just in speech and dress and religious belief but in our way of *thinking*. It's a quality of mind that we connect with creativity, questioning, innovation, problem-solving, and restless exploration. It treats the new idea as inherently valuable and the question itself as in some way superior to the answer. It also connotes a certain impatience and quickness of mind. There is an urgency to this kind of thinking.

For Jews, these mental attributes are preferable to the Protestant ethos of hard work, discipline, and self-reliance that has traditionally been valued by America's majority culture. Not that these qualities aren't important—many Jews possess them as well. But they aren't reflective of the *yiddishe kop*.

I would argue that the *creative intellect, applied to the benefit of the world*, is our most distinctive trait and is central to what has made the Jews so special.

Don't get me wrong. There are plenty of Jews who do not reflect this special kind of excellence today. The process of assimilation includes a progressive dissipation of our unique cultural qualities from one generation to the next. There are also plenty of Jews who are exceptionally endowed with creative intellect but have unfortunately chosen to apply it to do bad things. We have no shortage of swindlers, con artists, and other miscreants among us, some of them quite infamous.

But if you look, even today, at the lists of top scientists, cultural figures, business executives, global philanthropists, tech gurus, and so on who make extraordinary contributions, Jews are still dramatically, almost absurdly overrepresented. Jewish excellence has always been central to who we are. We may no longer boast about it or even admit it to ourselves—but it's there.

The problem for Jews has often been when they find themselves in situations outside the Jewish context where their specific cultural qualities, so deeply valued at home and in their communities, are seen as problematic. We interrupt and talk over each other. We prefer spontaneity over careful planning, improvisation over following instructions, drive over discipline, social talk and even gossip over silence. At the office, we'd rather work late nights making large amounts of money in new, creative ways, as I did when I worked at the Jewish Wall Street firm of Loeb, Rhoades & Co., than leave every day at 5:30 knowing the clients' money was in good hands for a modest gain, as I did at the Protestant firm of Calvin Bullock. Whoever preached that "slow and steady wins the race" was certainly not a Jew.

If the Protestant leadership vision is that of steering a ship with a steady hand over rough waters, ours is careening across the ocean in a speedboat, sometimes getting swamped.

The excellence of Jews who emerged from the shtetl was not limited to cerebral efforts of science and commerce but also had a fiercely spiritual component. Across the twentieth century, for example, most of the world's greatest concert violinists were Jews—Jascha Heifetz, Isaac Stern, Itzhak Perlman; there were pianists as well, like Arthur Rubinstein and Daniel Barenboim; composers like Leonard Bernstein, or in the sphere of popular music, singer-songwriters like Bob Dylan, Paul Simon, Carole King, and Leonard Cohen; filmmakers like Steven Spielberg, Stanley Kubrick, and the Coen Brothers; poets like Allen Ginsberg, Philip Levine, and Stanley Kunitz; and in the visual arts, painters like Marc Chagall and Mark Rothko. Something about the combination of technical mastery, breaking the mold, and unleashing the fires of the human soul, fit especially well with the particular quality of the Jews.

But the creative intellect is not only an essential Jewish trait. It's also something Jews believe to be essential for humanity itself. And that is why it is a special source of Jewish pride.

Only human beings can progress. Only human beings can invent, change what they do, record those changes, and build on them over generations and centuries. Animals and plants adapt to change; human beings cause it.

But if what sets humanity apart is change, then humanity is at its best when we affirm the aspect of our nature that drives change. The Jewish form of human excellence, in other words, represents a creative, world-altering intellect that should be nurtured and celebrated.

We see this legacy across our tradition, beginning with our foundational texts. The Bible begins with God the Creator. This God rejects the void and fills the universe with beings of all kinds. But only mankind he creates in his image. And man's first act is to challenge God's authority and to eat from the forbidden tree of knowledge. The Bible is filled with characters who rebelled against those in power, and even God himself, and also with figures whose questioning led to failures and terrible consequences.

It is precisely this rebellious, creative Jewish intellect that makes our rabbinic tradition so fascinating, even for someone like me who is unreligious. For me, the essence of being Jewish is not so much a matter of laws, rituals, or religious beliefs. It's the arguing. The constant coming up with questions, theories, alternative explanations, and the belief that from an early age, Jewish children must develop this ability. The Nobel physics laureate I.I. Rabi once said that his mother made him into a scientist by asking him each day when he came home from school, "Izzy, did you ask a good question today?"

So if you ask: Why is it worth preserving Jewish peoplehood at all costs? I would say it is has something to do with our absolute commitment to the rebellious, questioning, humane creative intellect. Every Jew is a kind of emissary of this message.

How CAN WE MAINTAIN Jewish Excellence? Though I never quite put it this way, this has always been one of my central concerns as a philanthropic activist and entrepreneur.

There's one program that is very dear to my heart, even though so far I haven't said much about it. It's called Birthright Excel, and it is one of our only major projects that can be called "elite," designed to remain small without intending to ever scale it up.

Birthright Excel is a highly selective internship program for college students, mainly from the United States but also from many other countries. Each year, we take about forty-five out of an applicant pool of close to eight hundred. They spend ten weeks in Israel, interning for some of the top Israeli businesses. They meet Israeli CEOs, train under Israeli mentors, and build their networks—not just with Israelis but with each other as well.

Excel emerged out of a conversation I had with Tova Dorfman in 2010. Although raised in the U.S., Tova was born in Israel and reminds me of the best of the Israeli spirit—feisty, talkative, thorough, a doer. We were sitting together in Jerusalem, and somehow we found ourselves talking about two different subjects. One was that Israel lacked a culture of unpaid corporate internships so that Jewish students from the Diaspora looking for a summer internship abroad inevitably ended up going to Europe or elsewhere instead. The second had to do with future leadership, and how we might create a group of young elites who could be encouraged not just to connect with Israel but to dedicate their lives to building Jewish pride in the Diaspora.

Excel offered an answer to both problems. By bringing top American students to Israel for ten-week internships with top Israeli companies, we created a small but extremely talented cadre of energized Jewish young adults who, through a range of retreats and other programs, built a select professional network. We hired Vered Fishbein as Excel's director, and she worked tirelessly for several years to make it succeed. Today, there are more than a thousand Excel alumni in that network, many of whom went on to graduate from top universities and are now entering the workforce. These are people who will likely accrue wealth and influence. And if the current graduates are any measure, they will work together to contribute significantly to new, high-impact Jewish initiatives across America and beyond.

Because the program is small and has been placed under the umbrella of Birthright, and because an internship involves relatively few costs beyond lodging and limited programming, we can run it for a relatively modest cost: About $1.7 million a year, of which about a third is covered by the Israeli government. The rest is paid for by a partnership between my foundation in Israel, the Paul E. Singer Foundation, and the Schusterman Foundation. By limiting the program's size and involving the Israeli government to help fund it, we can keep Excel going for a long time.

Launching Excel wasn't easy. Because Israel didn't have a tradition of internships, there was no legal framework to allow for unpaid work. We had to overcome bureaucratic resistance, working with Israeli government ministries to help them understand why this was really an educational program. We also had to convince the corporations themselves of the value of having highly talented, unpaid but untrained, young workers join their teams for ten weeks at a time.

In the end, we were able to place interns at major international and Israeli firms like General Motors, Deloitte, Ernst and Young, and Check Point. Two or three interns at each, working in business development, marketing, and more. Each company assigned a mentor to act as their guide and manager. Excel interns got to know each other through weekend and evening programs as well as annual gatherings in New York after they returned.

Once it was up and running, Excel opened the door for newer internship organizations to emerge, especially Onward Israel, which today brings more than three thousand students a year for months-long stays and has recently been absorbed into the Birthright framework as well. In other words, Excel acted as a kind of vanguard for a much larger movement. We also expanded Excel to include Israeli interns, students from places like Tel Aviv University or Reichman University in Herzliya, many of whom previously served in the IDF's most elite units. The aim is to create a vibrant social network of Israelis and Diaspora Jews, future leaders of the Jewish people, developing what we call a "lifelong fellowship" that includes both a sharp camaraderie and a commitment to building our collective future.

I can think of few better ways to foster Jewish excellence than to place the most talented young people in the service of qualified

Israeli mentors and in programs where they meet each other, develop their skills, and build lasting relationships.

These are the conditions in which great changes are made. The potential for concerted transformation that can result from a broad network of extremely talented, like-minded Jews, emerging in successful positions across a variety of influential industries, is enormous. As we will see, infusing the Jewish world with a new approach to building Jewish pride will require a combination of collective will, recalibrated communal priorities, creative experimentation, and significant philanthropic resources. A key element in this change will be a network of committed, talented influencers enlisted in this cause. Excel alumni will, I believe, play a central role.

MAKE NO MISTAKE: IT IS entirely possible that Jewish excellence will, one day, come to an end.

How would you feel if twenty or thirty years from now, you discovered that this "Jewish edge" had somehow disappeared? If in a given year, you noticed that Jews were all but missing from the Nobel prizes, Oscars, Pulitzers, the Forbes 400, and the other world-ranking lists?

Jewish excellence emerged over centuries as a combination of educational values and experiences that began thousands of years ago with universal literacy (among boys only, at first) at a time when very few people on earth could read and write; continued with generations of creative Talmudic disputation; and eventually was channeled into intelligence-driven pursuits like finance, trade, medicine, and law. It resulted from thousands of years' worth of rabbis telling us that we should be studying continuously. Probing. Challenging. Expanding our knowledge. Struggling to understand.

And in every generation, it begins with habits and values instilled in the home.

Perhaps it was also the product of knowing that in the absence of armies of our own, of political power in the traditional sense, against a sea of at times violent hatred, it was only the quick, creative thought that could mean the difference between life and death.

It therefore stands to reason that a loss of Jewish identity over time will also risk losing that special Jewish edge, thus abandoning our deepest commitment to what it means to be Jewish.

Just as peoplehood carries with it the burden of caring about Jews who are different from yourself, Jewish excellence carries the burden of understanding and passing on the special qualities that have made us so successful. Preserving these two pillars has required a great deal of effort and sacrifice over many generations. Taken together, the commitment to both Jewish peoplehood and Jewish excellence sounds like a recipe for a challenging life.

Fortunately, there is a third pillar that makes it all worthwhile. I call it Jewish joy.

THERE IS A FAMOUS INTENSITY about Jewish life. It expresses itself in our drive for excellence, our entrepreneurship, our activism, and in our sense that life is precious and fleeting and urgent. It's felt in our anxiety and insecurity, parodied in countless movies and self-denigrating jokes. It's felt in the long memory, the constant fear of anti-Semitism, and our deep attachment and commitment to other Jews.

Underneath all this intensity, however, is an emotion that is hard to define and describe. But I have always experienced it as joyfulness. A simple, yet profoundly energizing joy in being Jewish, in having Jewish friends, a Jewish family, and leading a Jewish life.

I felt it growing up in Bensonhurst, whenever there was an engagement or a wedding, and young people would pour into the streets, with musicians playing, people singing and dancing in circles to celebrate. I felt it in Shlomo Carlebach's music—especially that incredible performance outside the U.N., during the 1967 war, as Israeli soldiers were dying and the fate of the young Jewish state seemed to hang in the balance. I feel it today whenever I hear live klezmer music, the lively clarinet playing in a minor key, a beam of joy reaching across our painful collective history. I have felt it in the circle dances of the *hakafot* in the synagogue on Simchat Torah, or at the very end of the Yom Kippur service, when an entire congregation, exhausted from a twenty-five-hour fast, breaks into dancing and song even if it means you'll have to wait a little longer for that glass of orange juice. I've felt it at Orthodox weddings, in which hundreds of younger people—many of whom are normally as inept at dancing as I am—suddenly fuse into a single moment of swirling, untempered joy.

But while traditional Jews may have more opportunities to feel and express this kind of joy, it is by no means restricted to them. I have had some incredible experiences at the non-Orthodox B'nai Jeshurun synagogue in Manhattan. In Israel, I have seen it in completely secular contexts. You feel it most acutely, for example, at the end of Remembrance Day, or Yom Hazikaron. One of the saddest days of the year, commemorating the IDF soldiers and others who lost their lives in the nation's wars, transitions abruptly with the setting sun into Yom Ha'atzmaut. Suddenly, grief gives way to parties and fireworks. On this day, during my visits in the late 1960s and 1970s, Israelis would flood the streets, celebrating and singing, armed with plastic toy hammers that squeaked when you hit someone with them on the head.

Another tradition among Israelis is *shira b'tzibur*, sing-along events where the lyrics of popular Israeli songs are shown on a screen and a professional singer leads the crowd. I've attended a number of these, led by Einat Sarouf, the most famous of these sing-along leaders. Sing-alongs may seem old-fashioned, but in Israel they keep going, offering opportunities for Jewish joy.

Perhaps the most surprising place I've felt this joyful spirit has been at Israeli political demonstrations. It seems like Israelis turn every protest into a festival. When Tel Avivians flooded the streets in 2011, demonstrating against the high cost of living, musicians performed, street food was sold, and people somehow channeled their anger into joy. And this is just as true on the Left and the Right sides of the political map: There's a need to show that, beneath the protest, there is a sense of lively, positive vitality.

And of course, I've encountered it repeatedly during my years in communal life. I've mentioned many of them: the Birthright Mega Events in Jerusalem, a moment of joy so powerful that I have flown to Israel just to attend; the Hillel summer leadership retreats, with Richard Joel playing the accordion as students sang and danced; the Middlebury College event with Vardit Ringvald's students, united in a quest for mastery of the Hebrew language; Israeli musical performances at the Makor Café; the daily morning dancing and Israeli music at camp Ramah in Nyack, N.Y.; the Hebrew charter school students' performance at a Broadway theater, singing Hebrew songs.

Such moments are fundamental to a sense of Jewish pride. I have searched for them all my life. And I don't think I'm alone.

What do these moments of joy, arising even in the midst of grief or anger, really mean? What they have in common, I believe, is that they point to something outside of ourselves. It's not just about being happy or about losing yourself in the music. In Jewish joy, you're not losing yourself at all. If anything, you are expanding yourself, embracing the real people around you, maybe even the Jewish people as a whole—present, past, and future.

In moments of Jewish joy, we join an ancient people that has traveled a long way. It is a kind of collective elation, a sense of our Jewish spirits forged in ancient times, driving us into the future. In that moment, we feel the other two pillars as well, both Jewish peoplehood and Jewish excellence, as part of a community of infinite importance to the fate of the world. But it is also concrete: We rejoice with each other, including with those we've never met and whose names we may not know. In that moment, nobody is a stranger.

Jewish joy is not an escape. We are not ignoring the hardship or tragedy or anger but rather maintaining a perspective that says no matter what we have to suffer, we celebrate the fact that we are together.

Having experienced this special kind of joy, we never stop looking for it. And not just among large groups of Jews. It affects, often unconsciously, the social circles we build. Earlier on, I mentioned the odd correlation I had noticed over the years between a strong Jewish identity and having a lot of Jewish friends. People for whom eight or more of their ten closest friends are Jewish also display a powerful sense of Jewish pride. But now we can begin to see where this comes from. As Jews, we long to be together. To put our feet, over and over, in the deep river of joy that runs beneath the tumultuous surface of Jewish life.

JEWISH JOY IS EXPRESSED IN our humor as well. Today, the phrase "Jewish humor" sounds a bit outdated. But for generations, it was obvious that Jews were funny, and their humor added something unique to American culture.

From Groucho Marx to Mel Brooks to Sid Caesar to Joan Rivers to Woody Allen and Carl Reiner and Lenny Bruce and Jackie Mason and Gene Wilder and Larry David—the list goes on and on. These comedians embodied a kind of Jewish irony inherited from centuries of Yiddish humor. An anxious, intelligent, self-deprecating humor that found comedy in even the most tragic moments. Jerry Seinfeld is perhaps the best example in the last generation. A few others continue this tradition as well, but it seems the ranks of great Jewish comic stars have been thinning of late.

Nor is this special Jewish humor limited to a professional class of entertainers. It was, and is, a part of each of us, including those who have otherwise abandoned their Jewish identity.

Over the generations, our humor gave us strength. It gave us a unique way of flouting our tragic fate. A way of joining together and sharing our troubles. We laugh as a way of not just protecting ourselves as individuals but also of circling our wagons against a threatening outside world. When we laugh, we aren't under any illusions. We just know that through the joke we may yet affirm ourselves, our Jewish pride, come what may.

MY LOVE OF JEWISH JOY, combined with my lifelong concern for Jewish peoplehood, and my desire to promote the kind of excellence that is imbued in Jewish children from an early age, have led me to think a great deal about the question of the Jewish home and family life. This naturally includes the promotion of Jewish marriages and the desirability of more Jewish homes filled with more Jewish children.

I was raised in a world in which promoting Jewish families and fertility had been a priority for the American Jewish community for many decades, especially after the Holocaust, when it was considered an urgent necessity to replenish our ranks. Every Jewish parent and grandparent in those days thought nothing of speaking bluntly to their children about it, despite the risk of being overbearing. Indeed, the idea of having and raising children was considered a communal priority by all the major Jewish institutions.

Today, this "pronatalist" approach, calling for increased Jewish fertility, is not without controversy. Jewish feminists have rightly pointed out that male communal leaders and scholars often speak blithely about increased fertility without due regard for the unequal burden this places on Jewish women. Some see any discussion of Jewish fertility as inherently sexist. Others, like Mijal Bitton of the Shalom Hartman Institute, look for ways to combine their feminism with their belief in the importance of having Jewish children and see both values as flowing naturally from a proud Jewish identity. "I continue to uphold a commitment to Jewish continuity and pro-natalism in the Jewish communal context," she writes. "But [...] our commitment to Jewish continuity should openly and honestly grapple with the fact that Jewish women are asked to bear a greater aspect of the labor to bring about Jewish continuity."[23]

As Bitton points out, it is wrong to imply that only men have cared about promoting Jewish continuity or that we men should be excluded from a discussion that affects the future of our people. This is not a conversation that can or should be suppressed. We are

---

23 Mijal Bitton, "Is Jewish Continuity Sexist?" *Sources: A Journal of Jewish Ideas* (Spring 2021), https://www.sourcesjournal.org/articles/is-jewish-continuity-sexist.

a living people, passing our identity and hopes from one generation to the next. We cannot sidestep the question of Jewish fertility, even in the face of harsh criticism.

It is a worrisome trend that Jews, especially secular Jews in affluent countries, seem to be having fewer children. Did you ever notice how much bigger even secular Israeli families seem to be than American Jewish ones? The average secular Israeli woman will, during her life, have about 3.4 children. In non-Orthodox America, by contrast, Jewish fertility rates have been around 1.9, which is below the national average. It's also below what demographers call "replacement level." To the extent that the American Jewish population has grown, it is mostly due to the high birthrate among the Orthodox as well as immigration. All our efforts to build Jewish pride, in other words, have been taking place while the demographic rug is slowly being pulled out from under us.

It is a sensitive topic, to be sure. What's more, I myself have not always been as delicate about it as I might. I have frequently employed a not-so-subtle kind of humor that not everyone appreciates. Sometimes it's gotten me in trouble.

Decades ago, I facetiously gave an entire public lecture promoting polygamy in light of the expiration of the thousand-year rabbinic ban dating back to the tenth century. I said it with a straight face, but I meant it to be taken ironically—not as a real proposal, but as a way of using humor to make a deeper point about declining Jewish fertility. To drive home the point, I called it "A Modest Proposal," invoking Jonathan Swift's satirical call for cannibalism as a way of addressing Irish poverty. It was obviously meant to be a joke. The audience didn't see it that way.

You may have noticed a recurring theme here. At various points in my life, I have felt that something untimely or unpopular needed to be said. And if I couldn't find an appropriate way to say it, I'd say it in an inappropriate way rather than remain silent. Needless to say, such comments have not always been taken in the spirit in which they were intended. But that was a price I've been willing to pay.

Over the years my passion for promoting Jewish families led me in a variety of settings to encourage Jewish young people to date and marry one another and to have children. I've never concealed my belief that it's a good thing when participants on our programs fall in love, and I've actively tried to play matchmaker for singles whenever the opportunity arose. I even offered a free Caribbean honeymoon to couples who got married after meeting on Birthright. Dozens took me up on it.

Sometimes, however, I have made comments that in hindsight I should have kept to myself. This has unfortunately created opportunities for misunderstanding. And when, in addition to this, some people have been willing to make false or embellished claims, the conditions are created for embarrassment and scandal.

In this context, I must address a series of accusations against me that appeared first in the *Jewish Week* and were then recycled in the *New York Times* in March 2019. The claim was not that I had ever touched anyone inappropriately, or made physical advances of any kind, or retaliated against anyone. It was, rather, that I had a habit of making lewd comments in a professional setting, and that this had caused hurt and discomfort among some women I encountered over the years.

While some of the complaints reported in the *Times* were simply untrue, others were more or less accurate in that I do, in fact, say things from time to time that are more appropriately said in a casual setting—or never said at all.

I vividly recall one case in which a woman who led a nonprofit organization and was asking for my help didn't take kindly to one of my inappropriate comments. "Shut up, Michael," she said.

"That's not what I'm here for. I'm here to talk about my project." I welcomed her honest response and the confidence and determination it reflected. I ended up giving her organization a generous grant, and we have had a fruitful working relationship ever since. I admired her for answering back and for her self-respect.

This in no way excuses my comments, however, and, in fact, I have apologized for them. I certainly never intended to cause harm. Moreover, I am aware that a great many excellent nonprofit leaders, male or female, would not feel as comfortable pushing back as she did. And they shouldn't have to.

But whatever one may think of my occasional missteps of speech, none of it changes the issue at stake. For me, it has always seemed natural to beat the drum for Jewish marriages. It is an impulse that flows from the same passion for Jewish life that has driven everything I've done as a philanthropist. Without more Jewish children filling Jewish homes and getting more and better Jewish education, we will simply disappear over time. That's not something I want, and if you have read this far, odds are you don't want it either.

This commitment to Jewish homes also explains my abiding focus on intermarriage as a measure of our crisis.

I do not care about the technicality of whether one marries a "halachic" Jew according to the Orthodox definition. I do not care if one's spouse is a descendant of the greatest rabbis or King David himself, or if he or she converted to Judaism through one denomination or another, or even if they didn't convert at all. Nor do I care whether we are talking about heterosexual or same-sex marriage. What I care about is the creation of Jewish homes and children who grow up seeing themselves as Jews and being encouraged to live a Jewish life. I care about a strong, proud Jewish identity that can be transmitted to the next generation.

When I first began observing the nature of Jewish life, intermarriage was essentially a writ of divorce from the Jewish people. And the rhetoric of the Jewish community as a whole reflected this concern. Many who intermarried stopped seeing themselves as Jewish, and the likelihood that children of intermarriage would call themselves Jewish and raise Jewish children themselves was small. Most Jews who intermarried were on their way out the door, so to speak, even if they didn't think so at the time. So intermarriage seemed like a good proxy for measuring assimilation.

Today, things are different. While it is still statistically unlikely that a child of intermarriage will be raised with a powerful sense of Jewish pride, it's more likely than it used to be. Unlike in the past, a majority of the children of intermarriage today express some sense of being Jewish. Jews who intermarry can more easily stay Jewish and raise children who see themselves as Jews than in the past. Nonetheless, children of intermarriage are still far less likely to live proud Jewish lives. So intermarriage remains a powerful challenge to multigenerational Jewish pride and also a proxy for measuring assimilation overall, even if it's an imperfect one.

There is no substitute for having been raised in an engaged Jewish home. An assimilated young Jew can go on Birthright and be suddenly inspired to try to lead a more involved Jewish life. But in the absence of vivid examples from one's own upbringing of the joy and excellence and mutual care that proudly identified Jews embody, changing the direction of one's life is still a challenge.

We need to recognize the importance of Jewish homes in any possible future Jewish renaissance. The examples we set for our children become the seeds we plant for the day they decide whether to lead Jewish lives as adults. And there is no escaping the importance that marrying another Jew can play in building such homes.

Again, our long-term studies showed that 55 percent of Birthright participants ended up marrying other Jews, compared with 39 percent of otherwise identical nonparticipants. That's a big difference. But why does it happen?

Birthright does not preach to its participants about whom to marry. Even if it did, it's not clear what such preaching would achieve. What Birthright does offer is an eye-opening introduction to what being Jewish can mean to us as individuals. The vibrant, modern Jewish life and rich history of Israel are so different from the experiences of most American Jews that it serves as a shock to the system, causing many to re-examine their priorities. It leads them to become more aware of what they share with other Jews and may foster a sense of duty to learn more.

Maybe some Birthright alumni make a conscious decision to marry other Jews. But I suspect that for most there is something deeper going on—an unconscious process that expresses itself in many aspects of one's life, including the friends we choose, the books we read, the hobbies or activities we engage in, and even our choice of a spouse.

As young adults, we have difficulty imagining what marriage and raising children will be like. But the decision to marry sets us on a course that has an infinite impact on the lives of the children we bring into the world.

Because at the end of the day, the question of Jewish commitment, engagement, and pride begins in the home.

IT IS ULTIMATELY IN THE home that the pillars of Jewish pride—peoplehood, excellence, and joy—come together.

It is in the home that we first become aware that we are part of something larger, important, and wonderful—a Jewish people dispersed around the world, which has crossed thousands of years to get here.

It's in the home that we learn the Jewish habits of mind and spirit and the "applied creative intellect" that allow us to excel.

It is also in the home that we may set an example for our children of an engaged and joyful Jewish life filled with learning, experiences, care for other Jews, and the rhythms of the Jewish calendar, so that when the day comes, they may draw from it to build adult Jewish lives of their own.

I don't mean to suggest that if you didn't grow up in a proud Jewish home, you can't become a proud Jew in adulthood. It's just harder. For centuries, Jewish pride was transmitted first and foremost in the home, and if we hope to rekindle a proud non-Orthodox Jewish community that can withstand the powerful forces arrayed against it, many non-Orthodox Jews must choose to create rich, vibrant Jewish homes.

In the business world, we call this a "bootstrapping" problem. The lack of proud Jewish homes in one generation makes it a lot harder to create them in the next. This is where programs like Birthright, OneTable, JECEI, Synaplex, and others play their part. Birthright offers a powerful enough experience of Jewish awakening to trigger a process that can change the Jewish trajectory of one's life. This alone is not enough to revolutionize the Jewish life of the community as a whole. But it shows that it's possible to have an effect. And when you combine it with a range of other programs keyed to different stages of the life cycle, it is possible to intervene meaningfully in the process of assimilation.

To deploy such programs on a scale that would create a surge of healthy Jewish pride in the non-Orthodox Diaspora would require far greater resources than I and my small group of friends have been able to muster. It would require an enormous, concerted, sustained communal investment. But there is at least reason to hope that one day, such resources could become available.

To understand how that might happen, though, we need to have a frank communal conversation about our relationship with what has become, by far, the largest concentration of Jewish resources in the world: the State of Israel.

CHAPTER 6

Toward a New Relationship with the Jewish State

One notable habit I developed during my career in finance is to ask troublesome questions in places where everything appears to be going wonderfully. In that spirit, I'd like to share one thing about Birthright that has concerned me.

Overwhelmingly, participants report that Israel is not like anything they ever imagined.

I can understand that sentiment. You can't really imagine a country you've never been to, especially if it's your first time abroad. But another part of me really *doesn't* understand. With all the American Jewish organizations and community institutions promoting and defending and celebrating Israel, why are Birthright participants so surprised by what they find?

Maybe it's because, for generations, Diaspora Jews have been describing Israel as a hardship case requiring the urgent mobilization of the community's resources. Israel is "surrounded by enemies," we are told. It faces "existential threats unlike any other country." Without our help, and especially our money, Israel will surely fail.

All this may once have been true. But it isn't anymore. Yes, there are security issues, there is terrorism, there is Iran. There are important, unresolved issues concerning the future of the Palestinians in the West Bank and the waves of violence coming from Hamas in Gaza. But as opposed to a common misperception in the West, these security-related issues are no longer the stories that define the country. And until we recognize this change, we will forever be confused by the smoke and mirrors of a billion-dollar nonprofit industry telling us we need to "save" Israel.

This confusion lies at the core of our inability to have a healthy relationship with the Jewish state—and ultimately, our own Jewish selves.

For starters, Israel is not a poor country. Sure, it's not as wealthy as the United States. But by a simple measure of per capita GDP—the dollar amount of total economic activity divided by the number of people—Israel is a fully-fledged, developed economy on a level with the United Kingdom, France, or Japan. With almost $400 billion in annual economic activity and a government budget of well over $100 billion, it certainly isn't being "propped up" by American government support, which is around $3.8 billion each year, or by American Jewish philanthropy, which is much less than that, at $1–2 billion a year. In short, the era of Israel's economic dependence on America is over.

Israel is not a weak country, either. It has by far the most sophisticated military in the region. According to the *U.S. News* global power rankings, Israel is the eighth most powerful country *in the world*, after Japan and before South Korea. Its biggest enemy, Iran, is much less powerful. It is also not "surrounded by enemies." It long ago made peace with Egypt and Jordan, the countries flanking its longest borders, whereas its short northern border touches Syria, a failed state mired in civil war; and southern Lebanon, which is controlled by Hezbollah, a terror army still reeling from the beating it took in the 2006 Second Lebanon War, and whose leader still hides in a bunker.

More recently, Israel has made peace with the Gulf States like the U.A.E. and Bahrain, and we may see more to come. This is a very big deal. It's not just "normalization" or even simply peace. It's more like a tacit alliance. Saudi Arabia is a silent partner in it as well. Already there are billions of dollars of trade, coordination against their mutual enemy Iran, and tourism.

Israel is, in fact, so strong and stable that it's also been able to become a world leader in certain kinds of humanitarian work. Those who believe that "repairing the world," or *Tikkun Olam*, is the essential Jewish imperative ought to take pride in the many ways Israelis do good in the world, to a degree that dwarfs the work of Diaspora organizations like the American Jewish World Service. The IDF sends its elite search and rescue teams to sites of natural disasters around the world—and does it with lightning speed and breathtaking effectiveness. Nonprofits like IsraAID and Innovation: Africa deploy Israeli technological solutions to problems of poverty, energy, and food scarcity in impoverished countries. And Israel is the global leader in exporting water technology to deal with the looming shortage in the globe's most precious resource, from desalination to agriculture to wastewater management.

Such developments do not fit the accepted narrative about Israel as a Jewish charity case. It's time we caught up with the reality of Israel as a proud, strong, and independent country playing a positive role on the global stage.

IF THE OLD STORY OF Israel desperately needing our support is simply not true anymore, what should replace it? And what are the implications for Jewish philanthropic institutions that are built on that outdated premise?

In recent years, a lot of people have talked about Israel as the "Start-Up Nation," an innovation wonderland. My good friends Paul Singer and Terry Kassel have often spoken about how central this aspect is to Israel's future and have given a lot of support to an organization called Start-Up Nation Central that connects investors with exciting new Israeli companies and government agencies. It's certainly true that Israel has become a hub of technology in a great many fields that benefit the world. But while shifting the focus in this way may be good for attracting investors and highlighting one of Israel's biggest success stories, I ask myself: How does it address Jewish identity?

If Israel is doing so well, isn't it fair to ask whether it really needs our support? Shouldn't we also ask whether we have been using the cause of supporting Israel as a way of avoiding our own, much deeper problems?

What I'm about to say may rub some people the wrong way and may even seem threatening to those who make a living off the old approach. Many pro-Israel organizations, Israeli nonprofits, and the Israeli government itself benefit from the narrative of Israeli dependency and will do everything they can to perpetuate it. After all, there's a great deal of money involved.

Every December, my inbox gets flooded with emails from organizations asking for last-minute, tax-deductible donations, many of which are focused on helping Israel. Perhaps you get them too. Even the Israeli government, through the instrument of Israel Bonds, wants American Jewish money and will say whatever they need to make us feel good about writing a check. Who can blame them? They've spent generations making a living off these pitches. It doesn't matter that their government's annual budget is more than thirty times the size of the entire American Jewish philanthropic world.

The moment we dispense with the old narratives, the logic behind the continued existence of many of these nonprofits is severely undermined. That billion dollars a year in donations to Israel—covering everything from ambulances and bulletproof vests for IDF soldiers to universities and cultural institutions to relief for the poor and hospitals and national parks—begins to look a little strange. Because these hospitals and playgrounds and parks could easily be paid for by Israeli donors or taxpayers, just as they are in any other prosperous country.

True, there may be exceptional cases. In recent decades, a small number of philanthropists have become so deeply involved in Israel, owning homes there and visiting often, that they have effectively woven themselves, along with their capital, into Israeli life. But they are few and are somewhat analogous to the small number of American Jews who choose to make *aliyah* each year. For the most part, American Jews give to Israel as a charitable cause, planting trees and building hospitals, without having a clear idea of where their help is really needed.

All things considered, Israel is doing just fine. We non-Orthodox Diaspora Jews, on the other hand, are not. And every moment we spend focusing on what Israel needs, instead of what we need, is a perilous distraction. "Supporting Israel" has in my view become a kind of narcotic, giving us a sense of self-worth and achievement that allows us to ignore the tempest that has put our own future in doubt.

CAN WE IMAGINE A DIFFERENT relationship between the world's two largest Jewish communities? Such a shift is long overdue. To make it happen, we will need to stop asking what Israel needs from us and instead ask *what we need from Israel.*

Israel no longer faces an immediate existential threat from foreign armies as it once did, but our communities in America see a daily existential threat in the form of weakened identity and lack of pride. The difference is so glaring that once we allow ourselves to see it, we are compelled to ask: Could that billion dollars a year in American donations to Israel be put to better use?

We have long painted a picture of Israel as a damsel in distress and ourselves as the savior. Now the time has come to save ourselves, and the first step is to reconceive our relationship with Israel—not as a *cause*, but as a partnership. Israelis gain tremendously from the investments, tourism, liberal values, and influential global networks that Diaspora Jews can offer. But we in turn can gain something of even greater value: Direct access to the salty determination, the creative grit, the sense of Jewish honor and self-worth that was central to the Zionist revolution and that constitutes the core of what Israel has embodied for me since I first set foot there in 1962.

I've never lived in Israel for more than a couple of months, and I've never mastered Hebrew. I am not at all "Israeli" in that sense. But I have seen a few things that tell me that we Diaspora Jews have a great deal to learn from our Hebrew-speaking cousins.

You've heard enough about the miraculous victories in wars, the absorption of millions of immigrants, making the desert bloom, and so on. But even if you look only at the last two decades, there is the story of how a small, Middle Eastern country, half-covered in desert, mastered desalination and became self-sufficient with water; how a country without any natural resources to speak of found natural gas offshore and became energy independent; how a country with relatively little domestic production ability managed to lead the world in vaccinating its citizens against coronavirus; and how, seven decades after its founding, this country never seems to stop building roads and bridges and trains and tunnels, launching new technology companies that change the world, introducing new filmmakers and musical artists and literary figures and chefs and self-help gurus and Nobel Prize-winning scientists.

All of these achievements are the products of a certain type of Jew, one who possesses creative determination, a confident courage, and a get-it-done attitude—qualities that seem a lot more prevalent in Israel these days than they do in the Diaspora. This new "Israeli" character combines a restless energy, an impulse to act with conviction and confidence, a relentless drive for excellence, a tolerance for risk, a dedication to one's people, and an unapologetic pride in being Jewish.

To know and work with these Israelis is to get a taste of the spirit driving the country. These are the sort of people who prefer to act rather than talk, who know how to drop everything and move fast, who use their Jewish minds and spirits to solve real problems and take vigorous action.

People like Teddy Kollek, the mayor of Jerusalem from 1965 until 1993. It was Teddy who transformed Jerusalem after it was united following the Six-Day War. He turned the Old City into an appealing tourist attraction, modernized the city's infrastructure, incorporated the Arab communities, and established religious tolerance as the norm in the world's most religiously divided city. Teddy was an incredible personality, a doer, with the remarkable ability to sleep through an entire meeting and then, at the end, suddenly wake up and ask the most incisive question.

Every time he came to see me at the American Colony Hotel, he would bring a bag of clementines, the sweet mini tangerines Israel produces in abundance. Teddy founded the Israel Museum in 1965, and Judy and I became involved with it over the years. The entire city of Jerusalem bears his indelible stamp.

Or take Shula Navon, who, as I mentioned, worked for Teddy for many years before agreeing to head up our family's foundation in Israel. Although she was originally from Scranton, where she knew Judy when they were young, she moved to Israel and came to embody the country's feisty, loving spirit. She once challenged me to a footrace up Madison Avenue. If I lost, she said, I'd have to give an extra-large gift that year to the foundation in Israel. She won and used the money to help children in distress and other marginalized groups in Israel.

Another is, again, Lihu Veisser, the Israeli developer with whom I partnered to build industrial parks in development towns in Israel's south, which created thousands of jobs for underprivileged immigrants, mostly from North Africa. Thanks to people like him, today Israel's southern towns are a bustling hub of jobs and industry.

Yet another is Tzaly Reshef, one of the founders of the Peace Now movement and a former member of Knesset. Tzaly believed Israel could achieve a complete end to the horrors of war through a peace agreement with the Palestine Liberation Organization. He built a political movement that drew the support of a huge number of Israelis and became an important force in Israel in the 1980s and 1990s, without which it's hard to imagine the Oslo Accords happening in 1993. We may not agree about everything, but Tzaly is a hard worker, a savvy businessman, and a great lawyer—and I'm happy that he became Birthright's lead attorney in Israel.

One final example: When I first met Tamar Dayan, esteemed scientist and wife of the former general and politician Uzi Dayan, she told me of her dream to build Israel's first serious museum of natural history. It took more than two decades, and she had to overcome a lot of opposition. But today the Steinhardt Museum of Natural History at Tel Aviv University is immensely successful, and it's all to her credit. She was the one who brought together experts from a wide range of natural sciences to present a beautiful, educational, and highly popular institution. Since its opening in 2018, it has become a major center not only of education but also of research in areas like biodiversity, conservation, and agriculture.

What these Israelis have in common is the ability to imagine something totally new for the benefit of their country, to fight for it and gather the resources, to dedicate themselves to it over many years, overcoming every obstacle. They are big-vision, no-nonsense, results-driven Jewish pioneers.

The individuals I have mentioned are, for the most part, from an earlier era, and some of them have passed on. But their pioneering spirit, which they got from the country's founding generation, has been handed down to a new generation of Israelis—young entrepreneurs, tech geniuses, artists, culture makers, and activists constantly creating new worlds.

What I've learned from my many trips to Israel and my encounters with Israelis over more than half a century is this: Whatever it is that we are lacking in the non-Orthodox Diaspora, they've got it. A fundamental will to thrive and flourish, an inner spark, a collective determination, a gutsiness, a joy, a passion, channeling centuries of Jewish excellence into building a proud, successful, secular Jewish reality.

We need this. For me, it is the key to everything. But we will never have access to it if we don't first get over our paternalistic need to "save" the Jewish state. The moment we do, we'll discover that for all of Israel's challenges and flaws, we actually need Israelis as much as, or more than, they need us.

We have already talked about how important it is for a proud Jew to care about the fate of other Diaspora communities. But that's hard to do in America. The vast majority of American Jews are of European origin, with Jews from elsewhere blending into the American fabric. Israel, on the other hand, reflects a broad mix of Jews from many different countries. As a result, their culture is alive like few other places on Earth. More than half of Israeli Jews come originally from Morocco, Algeria, Libya, Egypt, Iraq, Syria, Iran, Ethiopia, and Yemen. (As the TV talk show host Bill Maher recently put it, "Only 44 percent of the Israelis look like your dentist.") And the flow of immigrants from places like France, Argentina, Russia, and Ukraine has made Israel into an ever-evolving, vibrant hub of world Jewry.

On any given day you can walk through the Carmel Market in Tel Aviv or Machane Yehuda in Jerusalem and hear Spanish, French, Russian, Amharic, and English. Even first- and second-generation Israelis come from a much wider diversity of backgrounds than American Jews, and this has a huge impact on the culture, values, instincts, politics, and even the food of the country.

Few American Jews will ever see firsthand how the Jewish communities of Iran, Russia, Uruguay, or Morocco live. But the more you know Israel, the more you'll get a taste of what "being Jewish" means today. You can hear Persian-Jewish songs and eat in Tunisian-Jewish restaurants. You can learn about Moldovan Jews, Georgian Jews, and Jews from Azerbaijan through the people you meet. You can find yourself invited to a friend's home for *sabich*—a traditional Iraqi breakfast where the table is filled with plates brimming with roasted eggplants, eggs, tahini, salads, potatoes, sauces, and anything else you might want to stuff into a pita. This exposure to the global face of modern Jewry brings your Jewish self-awareness—and your pride in being part of this lively, diverse people—to a completely different level.

This vibrant diversity can be brought home to our communities as well. All it takes is for the people who run our Jewish educational programming, from schools and summer camps to informal contexts like OneTable dinners, to learn about it and bring it to life. You can already see it beginning to inform Jewish institutions as they try to offer their clients something new. Usually presented under the framework of "Israeli" or "Mediterranean" culture, you'll see more and more offerings of Jewish food, film, music, and dance that originated in North Africa, Yemen, Ethiopia, and other parts of the world.

The encounter with Israel is humbling, for it reveals just how deflated and provincial American Jewish life can be. But it's also immensely inspiring to discover the Jewish possibilities that have opened up for us.

To begin that journey of discovery, we need to start by creating a whole new relationship with Israel. And that begins with where we put our money.

WHAT WOULD THIS NEW RELATIONSHIP look like? Can we imagine the American Jewish community, say twenty years from now, operating under a completely different paradigm? A world where major donors have forced the big Jewish organizations to reinvent themselves in a way that benefits the Diaspora rather than Israel?

It sounds like we would be withholding a huge amount of money from worthy causes in the Jewish state. But if you push it to its logical conclusion, you'll see the benefit of this fundamental shift in how we perceive ourselves as Jews. Having shattered the illusion that we are somehow delivering vital assistance to Israel with our financial and moral support, we can focus more resources on ourselves.

Where would all that money go? I can offer a few ideas—but to be clear, these are only suggestions. There are undoubtedly many projects of a grand scale that we haven't thought of yet.

My first suggestion would be to focus on dramatically increasing familiarity with the Modern Hebrew language. Our research shows that a huge portion of Birthright participants end the program with an immediate desire to learn Hebrew. But very few have access to an effective path of study.

As a first step, we need to train thousands of teachers in the proficiency approach described earlier. We already have the beginning of an infrastructure in the project headed by Vardit Ringvald. More than a hundred teachers have been trained, but this number could expand into the thousands with the help of the consortium of university teaching programs Vardit is building with Brandeis University. With an army like that, effective courses in Modern Hebrew could be offered around the U.S. in public schools, universities, as well as private schools, preschools, charter schools, summer camps, and online learning programs, paid for by communal and public funds.

Within two decades, we could create as many as one hundred thousand fluent non-native Hebrew speakers in the Diaspora, and upwards of a million who aren't proficient but have a flavor of the language—enough to try it out on a visit to Israel. This would not only revolutionize the relationship between Israel and the Diaspora, it would also give influential American Jews direct access to Israeli culture, news, and more. A hundred thousand might not sound like a lot in a Jewish population of seven and a half million, but when you consider who these people are likely to be—disproportionately influential Jews, including those who define the programming of JCCs and synagogues, the curricula of schools, Jewish camps, and so on—their indirect influence becomes immense. They would be a critical mass that could dramatically transform the nature of American Jewish identity.

Second, I would propose a major investment in expanding travel opportunities to Israel. It is only by meeting Israelis in the context of their own lived reality that one can fully appreciate the achievements of the Israeli spirit.

One way of building on Birthright's success would be to focus on more specialized programs, internships, and professional trips. Some of these already exist on a relatively small scale or are in the early phases of development. But can you imagine if every mid-career Jewish physicist, legal scholar, jazz musician, medical researcher, novelist, economist, water engineer, filmmaker, street artist, chef, agronomist, winemaker, or defense expert had an opportunity to spend a few weeks or months with their counterparts in Israel, learning directly about the unique ways that the pioneering Israeli spirit is influencing their fields, making connections, proposing collaborations, seeing an alternative way of doing things? You could call it "Birthright Pro."

We could also invest—again, always through a process of careful planning, testing, and measurement of impact—in trip formats for a variety of ages or life situations. Many of these already exist on a small scale but could become much bigger. Bar and bat mitzvah trips, trips tailored for families with teenage children, honeymoon trips, school trips, trips for different kinds of influencers, even two-year programs offering placement for a first job after college in the high-tech sector—all of these can have a long-term impact on secular Jewish identity if done right and brought to scale.

A third target for major investment would be a concerted effort to bring Israeli culture to America and the broader Diaspora. For the great majority who have not mastered the Hebrew language, there is no better window into the soul of a people than its cultural products. This should be obvious to anyone who's seen how America has influenced the world, not just through its military and economic power, but through its movies, music, TV shows, and so on.

For many decades, Israelis really excelled in only a small number of cultural areas. The Nobel Prize-winning novelist S.Y. Agnon and the violinist Itzhak Perlman are notable examples. But as the country became wealthier, world-class cultural creativity expressed itself in more and more fields. Today, you'll find Israelis among the world's leaders in everything from new TV series to Mediterranean-inspired cuisine to architecture, music, and wine. The month-long Paris Jazz Festival devotes three full days just to Israeli jazz. TV shows like *Fauda* and *Tehran* and *In Treatment*, chefs like Yotam Ottolenghi, thought leaders like Yuval Noah Harari, actors like Gal Gadot, supermodels like Bar Refaeli, architects like Michael Arad, recording artists like Idan Raichel or Omer Adam—many of these have become household names around the world. And they are just the ones you may have heard of.

If American Jews really want to help the Jewish state, we should create a sizable fund for the translation and export of modern Israeli culture. For every cultural artist you have heard of, there are ten more potential stars who, for lack of resources at a critical juncture, never break out: The cost of translating a book, commissioning a screenplay, traveling to make distribution deals, or hiring the right people to market the product may be prohibitive.

Beyond this kind of funding, creators also need to build relationships—with agents, producers, editors, directors, and so on.

We can easily imagine a big cultural showcase that brings together Israeli creators with American industry professionals covering everything from books to movies and more. It can also work the other way, with American Jewish creators building relationships with Israelis, fostering collaborations that deepen cultural ties in both directions, and as a result inspiring more Jewish creativity in the Diaspora. More high-quality cultural products—whether Israeli, Diaspora, or a combination of the two—make expressions of Jewish identity more visible and rewarding and will instill more pride and confidence in assimilated Jews.

All this adds up to a different kind of partnership between Israelis and Diaspora Jews than what we have seen in the past. This is not about "saving" Israel or even helping it gain public support by building its brand or legitimacy. It's about helping Israel *help us* through investment in what are essentially commercial enterprises of the kind that, when successful, have the biggest impact on our own identity as Jews.

Commercial viability is often the only quantitative metric of impact in the cultural realm. If something sells, it means it's adding value to people's lives. A flood of high-quality, commercially successful books, movies, TV series, art, music, fashion, and so on would go a long way to making the Israeli cultural revolution a focus of public interest far beyond the Jewish world.

These kinds of initiatives would also be mutually supportive: Learning Hebrew makes you more likely to want to visit Israel; a trip to Israel can inspire you to study the language and enjoy its cultural products; falling in love with Israeli movies or food can make you want to visit the country or learn the language.

It would also help inspire more homegrown Jewish culture in the Diaspora. I'm old enough to remember when self-consciously Jewish writers like Isaac Bashevis Singer, Philip Roth, Saul Bellow, and Herman Wouk had an important impact on American literature, when *Fiddler on the Roof* broke records on Broadway, and when Jewish comedians dominated the art of making Americans laugh. For decades, however, we've watched our best young Jewish cultural creators become global successes in every field, without dedicating almost any of their creativity to identifiably Jewish works. With a few exceptions, like Adam Sandler or Mayim Bialik, how many famous Jewish cultural icons can you name today who are under seventy and actively involved in something that can be called Jewish culture? One effect of the successful import of Israeli culture to America could be to influence creative Jews to put at least some of their energies into rebuilding an indigenous American Jewish culture at a high level.

We could also redirect some of the money we now spend on Israel to invest in proven, sustainable, scalable, pride-building programs—including some of those I've mentioned. Programs like JECEI, Synaplex, Makor, and others like them, can be seen as successful pilots that could be rebooted and adapted for a new generation.

Perhaps the most important investment we could make, however, would be in ongoing research and development of new projects that we haven't thought of yet. Programs, for example, that reinvent classic practices for a secular audience, the way OneTable did for Shabbat dinner, or the way Aliza Kline did with the ritual *mikveh*.

One program might address the Jewish mourning practice of sitting shiva, in which traditional Jews spend a full week at home after the loss of a loved one, comforted by friends, family, and community. Today, not many American Jews sit shiva, and, as a result, they do not benefit from the emotional support, sense of community, and profound sense of closure through mourning that is embodied in the shiva experience. This is a tradition with real human wisdom built into it, regardless of one's religious beliefs and which could be modernized and made accessible to the most secular of Jews. Other traditional practices that can similarly be retooled for today's Jewish world include those celebrating child-birth, the start of the new week (*havdala* and *melaveh malka*), or the lunar cycle (*kiddush levana*). We may even invent entirely new observances, experiences, or forms of engagement.

Once the parameters have been clearly defined—scalable, sustainable, measurable impact—we can imagine the continual emergence of new projects and ideas, taking them to proof of concept, then scaling them up.

You can do a lot with a billion dollars a year.

I CERTAINLY DON'T MEAN TO suggest that the Israeli government itself should be let off the hook. On the contrary, I am baffled that they haven't invested a much larger amount in Israel-Diaspora relations than they have. The success of Birthright should be all the proof they need of its benefits. For a few tens of millions of dollars a year, they've brought more than half a million young Diaspora Jews to Israel, recouped their investment many times over, and laid the groundwork for a generation of global support, investment, tourism, and potential immigration.

Israel could easily dedicate a billion dollars out of its annual budget to the expansion of Hebrew language learning, trips to Israel, and the export of Israeli culture around the world. It may take some time for Israelis to come around to the idea. But a powerful logic suggests that they should, and eventually will, invest in many of these projects.

France, for example, runs hundreds of French Institutes and Alliance schools around the world, dedicated to promoting the French language and culture. The Qataris spend millions of dollars a year to support the study of Arabic in American public schools and universities. Even the government of Thailand, a country much poorer than Israel, has been the quiet financial force behind the proliferation of Thai restaurants all over the world.

Cultural expansion is one of the basic Zionist imperatives on which the nation was founded. A century ago, the Zionist visionary Ahad Ha'am dreamed that the Jewish community of the Land of Israel would one day become the "spiritual center" of the whole Jewish people. Theodor Herzl, who turned the dream into a political movement, imagined the Jews building a powerful and globally influential country. "The world will be freed by our liberty, enriched by our wealth, magnified by our greatness," he wrote in *The Jewish State* (1896). "And whatever we attempt there to accomplish for our own welfare, will react powerfully and beneficially for the good of humanity."

Indeed, the goal in the first stage of Zionism was to achieve independent statehood coupled with a blossoming, indigenous Hebrew culture. The second stage, beginning in 1948, was meant to firmly establish Israel as a secure, safe, prosperous Jewish homeland. When I look back on how much has changed since my first visit in 1962, when they handed me an Uzi and told me to walk the perimeter of the kibbutz—how I have seen the Jewish state transform itself from a young country under constant threat into one of the most militarily sophisticated, powerful, and secure countries on earth—it is simply astonishing.

Now, a century on, we have reached a third stage in the Zionist experiment. A new day in Israeli history—and Jewish history—has dawned. This is the moment when Israel becomes a *global force*—economically, technologically, and culturally. When every young Israeli entrepreneur, filmmaker, or author looks to markets far beyond his country's narrow borders. When every Israeli business leader who travels to the U.S., East Asia, or Europe knows that he or she is competing on a world stage. If countries like France, Greece, Spain, Japan, Italy, Qatar, Poland, South Korea, and others think it wise to invest in the worldwide study of their language and the export of their culture, why shouldn't Israel?

Once American Jews have flipped the paradigm concerning the role Israel plays in their lives, and Israelis see the value of investing in the spread of their language and culture—suddenly we are talking about billions of dollars a year potentially being put into important, pride-building projects for the Diaspora. And that amount can grow as more Jewish philanthropists see its value.

While part of that growth will come from redirecting donations toward those that build Jewish pride, that's only part of the story. The size of the pie of Jewish philanthropy is not fixed. As a new generation arises with a greater sense of Jewish peoplehood, excellence, and joy, more of them will be inclined to direct at least some of their philanthropy back into the community. The overall size of Jewish philanthropic giving can grow in direct proportion to the growing pride of the next generation of Jews.

Today, Israel seems poised to enter a new phase of its history. The decline of major military threats—at least compared with the past—will allow the Jewish state, at long last, to fulfill the promise of its founding, putting its exceptional qualities fully on display before the world.

Meanwhile, the Jews of America are largely confused about what it means to be Jewish, distracted by partisan politics, mostly ignorant of Jewish history, paralyzed by perceived threats, locked into outdated narratives, and seemingly incapable of working together as a community.

Anti-Semitism has begun expressing itself in the United States, both on the far Left and Right, and it is causing many Jews to panic. Steeped in Holocaust education, they tend to see anti-Semites as potential Nazis. In truth, most anti-Semites in America today are disorganized simpletons with no ambition beyond venting their hatreds online.

We cannot control what crazy people think, say, or even do. We can, however, decide how to focus our own efforts. The best response to anti-Semitism, now as in the past, is Jewish pride. It is to build a new future filled with the strength and confidence that our unique ingenuity and excellence provide. If we do this, then the vast majority of anti-Semitism will evaporate from our minds, for the stupidity and name-calling will no longer have the power to frighten or intimidate.

The remainder, the actually dangerous part, can be dealt with through decisive, spirited action taken by the community in coordination with relevant authorities. This is especially pertinent on college campuses, where Jewish students are increasingly intimidated. Because a proud community doesn't tolerate intimidation or violence against its people and also doesn't let hate get under its skin.

We also need to imagine what our communal institutions could look like twenty years from now. Some of them, unable to adapt to the new paradigm, will have long since shut down. Every institution that no longer serves our needs will have to shutter, replaced by new institutions that foster healthy Jewish pride. Many will be national or regional rather than local, taking advantage of new technologies to organize differently. Others will focus on the needs of Jews in other parts of the world.

Major Jewish institutions will also support the emergence of a vibrant American Jewish culture, as Jewish-themed films, books, culinary trends, and popular music become once again an indelible part of the American mosaic. And alongside all of it, there will be a massive engine to develop new projects and programs, supporting innovative forms of Jewish ritual and learning, rethinking priorities in a swiftly changing world, measuring impact, and constantly reevaluating and updating methods.

Finally, we will need to create a system of oversight to ensure that our institutional priorities are well chosen and effectively implemented, a subject I will discuss in the next chapter.

Each project reinforces the others. Each has an impact on the traditional measures of assimilation—intermarriage, Jewish practice, participation, and self-education—but the impact is cumulative and synergistic. Eventually, there could be so many effective points of engagement that we can imagine a *majority* of secular Jews choosing to live what we would call a "Jewish life," one that reflects an ongoing, lifelong commitment and a positive love of being Jewish, a commitment to peoplehood, excellence, and joy that passes from one generation to the next. Engagement begets engagement, and pride begets pride.

But make no mistake: There is *no* viable path to a thriving, proud, secular Jewish Diaspora that doesn't include a fundamental change in our relationship with the Jewish state. Our current focus on rooting for Israel like it's a baseball team, pouring money into projects that could just as well be covered by Israelis themselves, fighting off Israel's critics—all of it is a colossal distraction.

Our immediate goal should be to stop the bleeding and turn the numbers around. But beyond that, we can imagine a qualitative change in what it means to be a Jew in the twenty-first century. Culturally richer, more knowledgeable, more connected to each other and ourselves, confident, conspicuously Jewish, pioneers of a cultural renaissance, unlike anything the Diaspora has seen in centuries, sustainable over generations. A new Jewish people with Israel at its center.

Many of us have sensed for some time that something is deeply wrong with the Jewish world we live in. Something has gone awry when our most talented Jewish friends never apply their talents to enhancing Jewish life and many of the wealthiest Jews rarely give to Jewish causes. Everywhere we turn, that Jewish world seems reinforced, impenetrable, unchangeable.

I'm here to tell you that things can be different. That a completely new secular Jewish world is not only possible but necessary.

But first, we need to have one final conversation, perhaps the most difficult of all. We need to talk about how, exactly, we can go about changing the nature of our biggest communal institutions. The process will be painful—but the rewards will be worthwhile.

CHAPTER 7

How to Fix Our Broken Institutions

It's good for us to speak of Jewish pride and the kinds of projects that could foster it if we only had the funding to launch them and bring them to scale. The impulse to "save" Israel has indeed become an overwhelming distraction that leads to the diversion of enormous philanthropic resources to areas where they are mostly not needed. But Israel-facing philanthropy is not the only problem.

If we really want to transform the nature of Jewish life for future generations, the kind of shift we will need goes far beyond changing our relationship with the Jewish state. It gets to the heart of how the Jewish community in the Diaspora, and particularly in the United States, functions—from the way we set our priorities to the way we run our institutions in practice. Much of Jewish giving today is, I fear, misdirected.

I do not approach this subject lightly. I know there are many good people, committed Jews, who have dedicated their whole lives to our community. I have the utmost affection for them personally and the highest regard for their efforts. If I feel a need to focus on what I see as a potentially fatal dysfunction in the way we conduct our affairs, it comes from my own deep love and concern for the fate of Diaspora Jews.

Still, there is no way to sugarcoat it. The Jewish community in the United States is hamstrung by a vast nebula of communal institutions, a conglomeration of tired thinking and vested interests that has worked hard to prevent any major shift in our community's priorities.

The Jewish institutional world today is forlorn. This may not have always been the case, but the period of relative innovation and excitement is long gone. A bureaucratic miasma prevails in almost all of today's major institutions. There is no longer even an effort to achieve greatness or substantive communal leadership. The problem is so severe that one might be forgiven for suggesting that we could be better served by eliminating most of what's there and starting from scratch using new criteria. These criteria would include a broad, democratic format, continuous measurement of impact, and community-wide representation within major organizations.

As a Diaspora community, we do not have the benefit of a centralized government that can change, through legislation or executive action, how money is spent. Any change will come only as the result of a shift in our community's philanthropic culture—when donors, great and small, decide on change. And that will happen only if we have some difficult public conversations about our community's priorities and the practices we are willing to tolerate.

We have made such shifts in the past, especially in the wake of major historical events, such as the arrival of huge numbers of Jewish immigrants in the early twentieth century, the Depression, the Holocaust, the establishment of Israel, and the Six-Day War.

The rise of Israel as a wealthy and powerful country in the last few decades is a major historical event that should open a broad new discussion about the priorities of our community—not just about Israel itself, but about how Jewish donors are spending their money in general.

The Jewish philanthropic world comprises thousands of institutions, ranging from small local organizations to major national ones. It includes the system of federations, whose principal task is to channel the funds of Jewish donors, mostly according to the federations' own discretion, to other organizations that are themselves local, national, or international. It also includes rabbinic organizations, synagogues, and other religious entities. It includes a range of "defense" organizations, like the Anti-Defamation League (ADL) and the American Jewish Committee (AJC), founded in the early twentieth century to protect the interests of the Jewish community. It includes JCCs, Jewish Community Relations Councils (JCRCs), cultural institutions, and Jewish educational institutions at all levels as well as youth groups and summer camps. It includes campus organizations like Hillel, Chabad on Campus, and AEPi as well as political advocacy groups. And it includes Israel-focused organizations, like the Jewish National Fund (JNF) and AIPAC, as well as gifts that go to Israel through "Friends of" organizations and the Jewish Agency.

All told, we're talking about at least $4 billion per year in donations, most of which are tax-deductible.

The Jewish community is built like an archaeological site, layer upon layer. It reflects the decisions and needs of different periods over the last century or more. When you ask questions like "Why do we need JCRCs?" or "Why do we need federations?" the answer, more often than not, references problems that faced the Jewish community decades ago.

It is exceedingly rare for a major organization, once established, to decide either that it has fulfilled its mission or that it is no longer needed and, therefore, should shut itself down. Instead, they either redirect their activities to new missions or manage to convince people that their work continues to be crucial. Meanwhile, newer organizations arise, usually driven by the adrenaline of a perceived crisis—such as the fight against the "Boycott, Divestment, Sanctions" (BDS) movement that calls for the blanket rejection of Israel and those who support it.

As a result, the structure of our communal life, like the street map of a venerable European city, does not reflect careful planning from the ground up. Rather it reflects a combination of historical quirks, passing fads, and vested interests.

It is also inefficient. Unlike the business world, where companies rise and fall mostly on their ability to generate profits, nonprofit organizations in general, and Jewish ones in particular, very often are defined by opaque goals and sustained by sentiment. Fundraising often eclipses results as their highest priority. CEOs, who frequently dedicate more than half their time to fundraising, and whose salaries tend to be a function of how much they can raise, are often less motivated to ensure their organization's effectiveness than they are to convince donors that they are worthy of continuing largesse. The less obvious an organization's value to the community, the more its decision-making can be distorted by the need to protect its funding turf. In many cases, organizational leaders act intuitively, swiftly, and at times ruthlessly to prevent competition, innovation, and change.

What we have been calling the "Jewish Turf Machine" is a natural outcome of the structure of our nonprofit world, one that lives mostly without external controls. Money flows, and what happens next, in terms of dollar-for-dollar impact, goes largely unaccounted for. In other sectors—from business to government—activities take place under the watchful eye of regulators, inspectors general, rating agencies, antitrust laws, consumer advocacy groups, and so on. The nonprofit world is far behind in this regard.

The absence of effective external controls is compounded by an incentive structure that does not encourage either the crafting or the achievement of clear and compelling impact goals. In business, of course, because the goal of making money is clear and compelling, compensation is usually aligned with that end, and a web of shareholders and directors are similarly incentivized to make sure the officers of the company are achieving it. Naturally, there are disagreements about how to achieve profitability, about long- and short-term strategy. But at least there is general agreement that the goal is to make money. The nonprofit world, by contrast, does precious little to ensure the clarity of an organization's goals, to make sure they address important communal needs, or to incentivize their effective achievement.

Yes, as registered nonprofits, they are obligated to follow tax laws. Professional organizations, such as that of nonprofit fundraisers, from time to time issue "ethical guidelines" that supposedly keep them in check. But such guidelines, combined with other oversight measures—laws covering the conduct of nonprofit organizations, the filing of publicly available 990 tax forms, the emergence of "strategic planning" processes, an emphasis in some circles on metrics of impact, and the small number of investigative journalists who have revealed misconduct over the years—all these are, it seems, not enough. Far too much is still built on trust and faith.

But when decades go by and the most glaring threats facing our community go unremedied, we must reconsider whether trust and faith alone are getting the job done.

THE JEWISH NONPROFIT WORLD, IN other words, currently suffers from a severe lack of clarity as to what constitutes legitimate use of philanthropic money.

Many donors today do not actually know, and don't seem to care all that much, whether a given program is actually meeting a need. Whether that need is as urgent as the fundraisers tell them. Whether the need would anyway have been filled by somebody else. Whether recipients are providing reliable measures of impact. Whether better management could bring double the impact at half the cost. Or whether an organization has outlived its purpose.

And in the absence of a robust mechanism for external criticism or oversight, any philanthropist who really does care about these questions is left entirely to his or her own devices.

Given the state in which the Jewish community finds itself today, isn't it fair to ask hard questions about the way Jewish organizations use philanthropic money? Let's consider a few prominent examples:

- The Anti-Defamation League ($81 million annual revenue): For more than a century, the ADL has been the leader in fighting anti-Semitism in the United States. Today, they have dozens of branch offices. I have enormous personal respect for Abe Foxman, who led the ADL for decades. But we are nonetheless obliged to ask: What are the results of their efforts? We honestly have no idea. What we do know is that Jews are targeted for more reported hate crimes than any other religious group in America, and such crimes are only increasing. Although the vast majority of Americans feel positively toward Jews, it's not at all clear that the ADL has made a meaningful contribution to those views. They may have once filled an important role, but frankly today we have no way of knowing whether their efforts make a real difference in Jewish life.

+ The Jewish National Fund—USA ($95 million): This organization, founded nearly a century ago as part of the Zionist movement's institutions, had a huge impact in purchasing land for the future Jewish state. Today, JNF-USA is an independent organization whose mission is "to ensure a strong, secure, and prosperous future for the land and people of Israel." To this end, it raises enormous amounts of money, partly by convincing people to plant trees in Israel. But does Israel really need new trees? Probably not. They also raise money for playgrounds, parks, fire trucks, and other nice things across Israel that could all be covered by Israeli taxpayers or donors. Israel's government budget is today more than a thousand times the size of the JNF's, and it's unclear how these mild improvements to Israelis' quality of life actually "ensure a strong, secure, and prosperous future" for a country that already has a world-class military and a thriving economy. Their slogan is "Your voice in Israel." But I have never met an American Jew who seriously thinks they have a voice in Israel because they give to the JNF.

+ The American Jewish Committee ($92 million): They say they have thirty offices worldwide. That's a lot of offices. Their mission, as they put it, is "to enhance the well-being of the Jewish people and Israel, and to advance human rights and democratic values in the United States and around the world." (The profligate use of the word "and" in a mission statement is often indicative of calculated ambiguity.) They have historically seen themselves as the diplomatic arm of the Jewish people, representing Jewish interests with governments around the world. But does this goal actually make sense? Normally, diplomacy is what governments use to advance their nations' foreign policy objectives. Diplomats are a tool of policy, but they don't make policy—because they are neither policy experts nor directly accountable to the citizens they serve. But the Jewish people as a whole has no government—which means that not only is nobody setting policies for them, but nobody is holding them accountable if they fail to achieve them. So I cannot understand what exactly they do for the Jewish community that justifies the cost.

- The Simon Wiesenthal Center ($26 million): This organization, founded originally as a vehicle for hunting Nazi war criminals and teaching about the Holocaust, decided to build a "Museum of Tolerance" in Los Angeles, which tells the story of the Jewish role in American history. Apparently, it was quite successful, because now they're building one in Jerusalem. It's entirely unclear who in Jerusalem, a city divided into secular, ultra-Orthodox, and Arab neighborhoods that barely interact, actually will benefit from a $100-million, American-funded "Museum of Tolerance." Even if we set aside the controversy that arose after it turned out this temple to human sensitivity was built partly on a Muslim graveyard—we still are left wondering: What do we need this for?

- The World Jewish Congress ($25 million): This is smaller, but I'm including it because everything they do appears to be covered by larger, better-equipped bodies. They consider themselves "the diplomatic arm of the Jewish people," meaning their mission appears identical to that of the much larger AJC. They have hundreds of "affiliates" around the world—even in Cyprus, where only a few hundred Jews, mostly Israeli expatriates, live. What do you suppose would happen if the WJC disappeared? Much larger amounts of money are spent on Diaspora communities in distress by bodies like the JDC and the Israeli government. Larger Jewish communities, such as in France or Germany or Canada, are certainly better positioned to represent their own interests to their governments. I can't understand how this is a wise use of American Jewish philanthropic dollars.

+ The federations in general were founded as a kind of clearinghouse for Jewish donations. The assumption was, at the time, that individual donors had little access to reliable, up-to-date information about where their donations were most needed. Today, however, donors have direct access to endless information about nonprofit organizations both at home and abroad and can meet potential grantees in person or via video calls. Federations no longer have any special access to information that donors need to make their decisions. And still, the federations are raising more than a billion dollars each year. This includes an increasing share of "discretionary gifts," in which a donor has already decided to give to a different organization, but the head of the federation convinces the donor to pass it through the federation so that he can take credit for it—essentially acting as a well-paid, yet perfectly superfluous, middleman. Also, the federations' umbrella organization, Jewish Federations of North America, is permanently in search of a mission as local federations grow increasingly resentful about the exorbitant membership payments. Do we really still need the federations?

I have chosen here only a few particularly striking examples of communal bodies whose activities are, I would submit, of questionable ongoing value to the Jewish community. Similar questions may be asked of dozens or even hundreds of other organizations.

Many of these activities seem innocuous. If a wealthy Jew in Denver wants to buy a fire engine for a town in Israel, what's so bad about that? Indeed, if we in the Diaspora did not face an existential crisis of our own, it would strike me as little more than a silly gesture. The Israeli government is more than capable of supplying its fire departments with engines. But we *do* have a crisis, one of staggering proportions, and the resources we have committed to addressing it are exasperatingly limited. Misplaced philanthropic priorities are precisely the problem I am hoping to address.

Nor do I mean to suggest that Jewish organizations serve no good purpose in the context of building pride. There are many individual cases, whether synagogues or JCCs or schools or organizations like AEPi and Chabad on Campus, that happen to be led by creative, efficient, impact-minded leaders and which, as a result, really do make a difference. I mentioned the ADL's longtime leader Abe Foxman, whom I always found to be an exceptionally courageous man who led the fight against anti-Semitism consistently, tirelessly, and fearlessly for more than a generation, even if I had my doubts about the actual impact of his organization. Another example is Joy Levitt, a Reconstructionist rabbi who was once one of the movement's leaders and until recently headed up the JCC in Manhattan. She is a leader with vision, integrity, and an aversion to bullshit that competes with my own. Yet another is Daniel Landes, an Orthodox rabbi originally from Chicago who spent two decades turning the Pardes Institute in Jerusalem into one of the most important hubs of classical Jewish learning in a warm, tolerant environment. Landes took a lot of flak when he courageously performed the first ordination of an openly gay Orthodox rabbi in 2019.

But these exceptional organizations and individuals are just that—exceptions. And of course, I am far from alone in calling out some of these problems. For decades, new philanthropists, many of whom come from backgrounds in business or finance, have been astonished by the lack of efficiency and questionable value propositions that plague the Jewish nonprofit world and have looked for remedies.

Why do our communal institutions look this way? The most obvious answer is that donors want them to. This may sound strange, but in truth, nonprofit organizations live in a world of supply and demand. Donors are the main consumers, offering to pay money in exchange for a feeling—a sense of importance in the world, or social status, or being able to tell their grandchildren that they had done some good. If no one is telling them there's a problem, there's no reason for them to change their philanthropic habits.

This is a feature, not a bug. The moment you look at the incentive structure of philanthropy, you'll find that left to its own devices, the nonprofit sector will eventually turn into a kind of entertainment industry for wealthy people.

Pride reflects itself, often unconsciously, in the standards we set for ourselves and demand from those around us. Self-respecting individuals, even if they lack means, will still do their best to wear clean clothes, see to their physical hygiene, and make sure their kids do their schoolwork. As upsetting as it may be to acknowledge this, the state of our community's institutions does not currently reflect the self-respect befitting an ancient and proud people.

DOES IT REALLY HAVE TO be this way? I believe it is possible to create independent systems of oversight that will significantly change the way our community functions, bringing about a new structure that we can be proud of, and new institutions that inspire us. One in which major organizations are not only better run but also have better missions—missions that actually meet the needs of our community.

I do not claim to have all the answers, but I think it's worth suggesting a few ideas for what these forms of oversight might look like. My goal in doing so is merely to start a conversation. I hope that others will come up with additional, better ideas.

The first idea, and I think it's a rather obvious one, would be to create some kind of independent watchdog that has both the mandate and the ability to shed light on problems plaguing the Jewish nonprofit sector.

I'm sure a lot of people will oppose such a proposal, especially if they are personally invested in the existing establishment. But if we brought together a team of forensic accountants, investigative journalists, Jewish communal thinkers, legal advisors, and management experts, we could in fact create a powerful independent body dedicated to exposing questionable practices, challenging assumptions, and educating the philanthropic world about transparency, accountability, waste, turf wars, mission creep, and metrics of impact. It could offer a public rating system, establish best practices, focus on specific problem areas, publish reports, field complaints, make regulatory proposals, and make recommendations for the improvement of both individual organizations and whole sectors.

Can you imagine the effect of such a body across the whole Jewish nonprofit world? What if every time a donor were solicited by a significant organization, he or she could look them up on a publicly available website that had an independently crafted profile of that organization with star ratings for different categories based on the quality of their management, the importance of their work, the failures of their past and what they did to address them, their overlap with other organizations, and their overall impact-per-dollar? Or if every few weeks a public report was issued assessing the value and management of a different major Jewish organization?

Right now there is nothing to make a Jewish professional leader think twice about accepting a million-dollar donation for an anti-BDS campus project that's only tangentially related to the organization's mission or expertise. Yes, every nonprofit has a governing board that in theory acts as a check. But many donors, including large ones, prefer not to serve on boards, and many boards, in reality, act mainly as rubber stamps for the professionals. Can you imagine how many tens or hundreds of millions of dollars might be spent differently if there were an independent body dedicated simply to calling out such ventures?

Watchdogs are a funny thing. Nobody wants them before they are created, but everybody is grateful once they exist. Public corporations don't want to be overseen by the Securities and Exchange Commission, academic institutions don't like accreditation commissions scrutinizing them, and no government likes to be critiqued by international human rights bodies. These watchdogs exist for a simple reason: They act, with a greater or lesser degree of success, to hold institutions accountable. As Louis Brandeis famously said, "Sunlight is said to be the best of disinfectants; electric light the most efficient of policemen."

We like to imagine that nonprofit professionals, by dint of their evident self-sacrifice and their altruistic choice to commit their careers to pursue the common good, are somehow immune from the problems that justify the need for watchdogs in other sectors. They're not.

But even the most effective watchdog is, by definition, limited in scope. It can, by shedding light on an otherwise opaque process, keep organizations honest in the way they go about achieving their missions and measuring their success, and offer effective counseling to those that want to do better. What they can't usually do is ask the deeper questions that need to be raised: What are the actual needs of the community, and what kinds of initiatives would be required to meet them?

A second idea, therefore, concerns the process through which our community figures out its priorities.

YOU CAN HAVE THE MOST efficient, creative, on-mission, and impact-minded organization in the world and still be wasting an enormous amount of philanthropic money if your mission is not aligned with the actual needs of our people.

Take the state of Jewish education. The biggest problems with today's non-Orthodox Jewish educational institutions—Sunday schools, after-school programs, and the small number of non-Orthodox day schools—do not necessarily flow from mismanagement but rather from misguided priorities.

Earlier we addressed the core problems of Jewish education in America. The 1990 study *A Time to Act* revealed how low-quality educational programming had an overall effect of turning kids off. As a result, few non-Orthodox Jews bothered enrolling.

More than three decades later, little has changed. There are still, after all this time, no national bodies setting goals and standards for education in Jewish history, texts, practices, ideas, culture, or the concept of peoplehood, and few major institutions training teachers to meet such goals. As a result, Jewish schooling is just another box we check, a formality, rather than a potent formative experience in our children's lives. We know it, and our kids know it.

After all this time, in other words, we are still not taking Jewish education seriously. And this is mainly because we have not made it a communal priority. Without giving young Jews a real familiarity with the world of Jewish life, how can we expect them to become proud Jewish adults? Pride without knowledge is like driving up a mountain on an empty tank of gas: It won't go far and could end in disaster.

Education is just one example where poor results reflect ill-considered priorities. But there are others. We need a process through which we can come to agree on what the Jews of the Diaspora most acutely need and to stop wasting money on tangential, feel-good projects like some of those mentioned above.

This is not an easy fix. Alongside the lack of accountability, there is also a lack of serious community-wide conversation about the priorities of the non-Orthodox world. A proper battle of ideas needs to take place, and it's largely MIA.

In the world of government policy, for example, such a conversation is traditionally facilitated by think tanks, book publishers, public intellectuals, academic researchers, and long-form magazines like the *New Yorker* or the *Atlantic*. Such debates can influence both the broader voting public and those who make decisions in government. Laws, budgets, and elections can be swayed by ideas that have their origins in these higher debates. And when they have teeth, many smart people will choose to involve themselves in that conversation, knowing it isn't just a waste of breath. Indeed, many of the most important voices in American public policy debates are themselves highly talented, thoughtful Jews. Yet they rarely if ever direct their intellectual firepower to the challenges facing their own community.

In the Jewish community, by contrast, there is much less of an incentive to even have such a discussion, because it tends to take place in an implementational vacuum. In short, there are no teeth. There is no legislative or executive branch of our community that feels obliged to take even the most persuasive, serious discussions into account. With few exceptions, there are no "elections" through which Jews can persuade and gain power and bring change. Even when data as overwhelming as the National Jewish Population Surveys of 1990 or 2000 have come out, or the studies released subsequently by Pew and others, the real-world impact has been relatively minor.

What we need is a similar, freewheeling public debate at the highest level, enjoined by researchers, thinkers, and writers—all with the aim of asking the question: What, in fact, is "good for the Jews" today?

For that to happen, of course, the people who might engage in such a debate need to believe that their ideas and arguments might actually make a difference. This is where the watchdog comes in: Done right, such a body can give teeth to a broader debate about Jewish priorities.

Serious Jewish publications do exist, of course, and some are at a very high level of quality. But most of their energy is devoted to politics, lifestyle, religion, or the Middle East rather than Jewish communal priorities—trying, along the way, to influence the

American conversation rather than the Jewish one. Meanwhile, debates over philanthropy or institutions engage a very small audience, mainly professionals and academic scholars.

We Jews are much too afraid of "airing our dirty laundry in public" or "fanning the flames of anti-Semitism" by publicly criticizing ourselves. The result of that fear is a culture of self-censorship, insincere smiles, and self-congratulation that spends billions on feel-good efforts as our children continue to distance themselves from Jewish life. What's missing is something much more public, appealing to a broader Jewish audience, engaging the thought and writing of the smartest Jews who have reason to believe it isn't a waste of their energy.

How many popular books come out that even raise the question of Jewish priorities? How many Michael Moore-style documentaries poke fun at the shenanigans of Jewish institutions? We need to normalize and encourage such communal self-criticism. To invest in a field that we may call "Jewish public thought."

So alongside the watchdog, we will need to build up the infrastructure of Jewish public thought and criticism—scholarship, publications, books, investigative reporting, and more—aimed at helping us define, challenge, and refine the community's priorities and feed them into the oversight mechanism. We can't solve our biggest problems without allowing and encouraging our best thinkers to speak their minds and infuse our community with new ideas.

I have a third idea as well. This one may seem a little whimsical. But if we were to implement something like it, it might help change the entire dynamic of our communal life for the better. I call it "the council of thirty-six."

An ancient rabbinic legend teaches that in every generation, there are thirty-six righteous people (*lamed-vav tzadikim*), unknown and unrecognized, on whose merit the world continues to function, and without whom the world would cease to exist.

I've always been fascinated by this concept. We live in a world in which everyone is told to "build their personal brand," where people are taught from a young age to aggrandize their résumés and climb the ladder of public esteem. What if we were to harness this inspiring tradition of righteous anonymity on behalf of the secular Jewish community?

What I am suggesting is a kind of "council of sages" for the secular Jewish world, charged with assessing the health of our communal institutions, rethinking our priorities, and articulating a vision of where we should go. We could engage these individuals for limited terms and task them with delving into alternative ways to look at our institutions, formulating new approaches, and issuing periodic conclusions—all on the condition that their participation remain a secret.

Is such a thing even possible? I believe it could be done. The only place I can think of where we currently see something like it in the Jewish world is within the Israeli intelligence community. Obviously, it's a much different context. But it's still the case that for generations, thousands of secret soldiers of the Jewish state have risked their lives fighting for the nation's survival in the full knowledge that the vast majority of the Jewish people—even their own families—would never know of their contribution.

As strange as it may sound, creating an anonymous council of this sort would free its participants from the politics and struggle for advancement that characterizes so much of institutional life. It would allow them to come to an agreement about our goals, focusing entirely on what they actually believe without worrying about how others will see them. Like a sequestered jury, their anonymity would also shield them from the pressure of organizations that want to influence their conclusions. To be successful, the composition of the council would have to reflect the diversity of the community in terms of gender, geography, age, religious affiliation, and more.

The words of such a council would, I think, be taken seriously, helping us identify and agree on communal priorities and fostering a sense of collective purpose, altruistic endeavor, and shared destiny.

We can also imagine how all three of these independent bodies—a watchdog, a public debate, and an anonymous council of secular "sages"—could interact in a way that creates a whole much greater than the sum of its parts. The watchdog would both draw ideas from, and give teeth to, the public debate. The public debate, in turn, would encourage the participation of Jews from many different sectors—including those who normally don't partici-pate—into a conversation of real consequence. Both would feed into the deliberations of the council, which would draw large-scale conclusions, offer recommendations, and create a sense of impor-tance, unity, and affirmation to the community as a whole.

Such independent bodies can help us plan and change our world and chart a completely different course for the future of global Jewry.

These ideas may be a little rough around the edges, needing refinement and careful planning to ensure their effectiveness. But however you feel about these specific proposals, it should be clear that *something* must be done to address our deepest institutional problem: Namely, that too many of our philanthropic resources are directed toward purposes that are either outdated or ill-conceived and need to be rethought and redirected.

The time has come to create a system of independent bodies that can help us think things through and keep our eyes focused forward. We have the best people, the best minds, and the best resources. Together we can reinvent our world, building something of astonishing beauty, endurance, and inspiring creativity.

WE LIVE IN A TIME when a great many wealthy Jews have disconnected themselves from the fate of the Jewish community. Think of some of the top Jewish tech moguls, entertainment executives, and other industry leaders—the millionaires and billionaires who are Jews. How many of them are publicly engaged in Jewish life? How many Jewish celebrities, for whatever reason, might choose to weigh in on the conflict in the Middle East or other political issues of the day (the founders of Ben & Jerry's come to mind) but never say a word about the future of Diaspora Jewry?

I personally know quite a few people who have disengaged simply because they don't believe the Jewish institutional world, as currently constituted, is worth giving their time, energy, and money to. It's this kind of apathy, much more than the acrimony that might come from a vigorous round of debate and communal self-criticism, that will ultimately lead to our communal demise.

We should allow ourselves to dream of a better, prouder, more vibrant and engaged secular Jewish world, driven by nonprofits that are effective, creative, and clear about our needs. But we should have no illusions about the kind of work that is required to get there.

Given everything we have covered in these pages—from the Jewish world I grew up in, to nearly three decades of trial and error learning how to bolster Jewish pride through entrepreneurial philanthropy, to understanding what fosters Jewish pride, to redefining our relationship with Israel and rethinking our communal institutions and priorities—it should not be so difficult to imagine a radically different Jewish world.

Much of this book can serve as a kind of how-to manual for achieving this vision through programs that work. If we can collectively agree on the goals and methods, we can begin to muster the necessary resources.

I know that many well-intentioned people, including Jewish organizational leaders, educators, and scholars, may demur. Pride, they will argue, is all too mundane when compared with the vast intellectual riches offered by a broad and deep study of Jewish traditions, literature, religion, and scholarship.

Yet none of them have offered a compelling answer to the most obvious question: Where is the market for your product? As rewarding as deep Jewish learning may be—and I agree that it is extremely rewarding—the fact is, only a small minority of Jews have chosen to explore and enjoy it.

The methods and lessons I have suggested here, by contrast, may actually solve our most acute communal problem, which is the progressive evaporation of a huge percentage of our people while bringing about increased demand for the kind of deeper learning we would all love to see.

SOME OF YOU HAVE HAD rich Jewish lives since your childhood. Some may have come back to Jewish identity later in life. And some may consider yourselves mostly assimilated but nonetheless fascinated by the prospect of a more compelling Jewish life for yourselves and your children. What I am asking you to imagine is a secular Jewish life filled with points of entry—at home, in the community, in school, and other venues—that are fun enough, engaging enough, diverse enough, and compelling enough to attract a majority of Jewish families to get involved and stay involved.

We should allow ourselves to dream. Can we envision how, say by the year 2040, Jewish life could be revolutionized across the non-Orthodox Diaspora?

Such a life would be filled at every stage with compelling Jewish options—from early childhood until parenthood and beyond, from the schools we attend to youth groups and summer camps, to trips to Israel at different stages of our lives, to the ongoing mastery of the Hebrew language, to a reinvented synagogue experience, to rituals and holidays, to the continuing discovery of different Jewish traditions and lifestyles, to a constant flow of new cultural products from both Israel and across the Diaspora—all at a level of quality high enough to compete favorably with non-Jewish alternatives.

A new Jewish life, where most kids grow up with a great deal more than just occasional visits to synagogue, a Passover Seder, and the swirling "discourse" about anti-Semitism, Israeli policies, and the Holocaust. Where every parent and every child is motivated to choose their own Jewish path and can find what they need—socially, educationally, spiritually. Where the most creative young Jews can find a viable career contributing to a reinvigorated Jewish artistic and intellectual culture.

A Jewish life that begins with confidence and is filled with Jewish friends, a Jewish home, and a rich Jewish family experience.

Such a Jewish community would also, in all likelihood, benefit from a significantly larger base of financial resources and not just because of Israeli government support. I can't put a dollar amount on it, but I can say from my own experience that a lot more wealthy Jews would be far more inclined to support Jewish causes and institutions if they were convinced that they weren't wasting their money. Again, the size of the Jewish philanthropic pie is not fixed, and the best way to make it grow is to increase the overall performance of Jewish institutions, incentivize innovation, maximize demonstrable impact, ensure commitment to true communal priorities, and insist on excellence.

In some ways, what I am suggesting hints at a return to the prevailing spirit among the Jews I grew up with in Bensonhurst. This was an ethnically and religiously diverse community, but we had few doubts about who we were or what we had in common. "Being Jewish" was an indelible part of our secular, worldly lives. We took care of other Jews regardless of who they were or where they came from. We focused on building on our strengths rather than our fears. Underneath the hardships we encountered, we enjoyed a thick layer of collective, spiritual joy. It was not a perfect Jewish community, but it worked. Despite everything that has changed in the intervening decades, I know it can work again.

In other ways, however, I am suggesting something altogether new. A new kind of secular Jewish life, perhaps even a new phase in Jewish history, in which the Diaspora can draw strength from a powerful and prosperous Jewish state and build a Jewish world that overcomes assimilation and apathy—not through guilt or insularity but simply by offering the best products in the market. An identity that most Diaspora Jews would embrace and would not dream of giving up.

What if, by the year 2040, the *majority* of non-Orthodox young Jews enjoyed rich, engaged Jewish lives? Can you imagine how different Jewish life in America and around the world would be?

And what if I were to tell you that it's not only possible but requires nothing more than a collective decision to change our priorities—in other words, that it's entirely up to us?

Epilogue

Nestled amid rolling hills in northern Westchester County, covering fifty-six acres of lush land not far from the Croton Lake Reservoir, is my country home in Bedford, New York. Here I have built a small paradise. Perhaps you will think of it as the whimsical extravagance of a wealthy man. But I do not see it that way.

This home is my refuge and my joy. I cannot adequately describe the pleasure I take in driving up and down its swerving pathways in a golf cart or walking its trails in the light rain of spring.

From time to time we host events here, and few things give me the kind of unalloyed joy as watching children, especially my grandkids, explore its natural wonders.

One part of the estate is dedicated to horticulture. There are hundreds of different trees and plants, endless varieties of colorful Japanese maples, conifers, camellias, alpines, and ferns. There's an apple orchard with eighty different varieties, a maze-like cutting garden, and an experimental garden to test the resilience of different plants in the northeastern climate. All of it is knitted together with hidden pathways and rope and moss bridges.

The other side is filled with animals of many different kinds, from wallabies and llamas to giant tortoises and peacocks. The animals have room to run around, to interact, to rest. There are deer and zebras and serval cats and Mongolian camels—big furry ones, unlike the dry, dapper dromedaries you may see in arid countries like Israel.

Up a flagstone path between the trees, you'll find a large pavilion, almost a tower, where baby lemurs cling to their mothers' bellies under the watchful eye of half a dozen bright-colored macaws.

There are also ponds and lakes. One pond is home to grand, orange-and-white spotted koi from Japan. Another has a flock of flamingos, and an island on which dark-brown spider monkeys clamber across ropes and trees as their offspring rest in a small wooden structure high above. Yet another is home to the aviary, where peacocks and ibis call out among the trees. On a fourth pond, black swans cruise like majestic sailing ships, their red beaks glistening in the sun.

Then there are the zonkeys. A hybrid of zebra and donkey, these delightful creatures combine the speed of the former with the strength and stamina of the latter. They are extremely rare in the wild: Like mules and ligers, they are sterile, and can be found only in a few places in Africa where zebras and donkeys live close enough to have a chance to mate.

I have always taken special pleasure in the zonkeys. On some level, perhaps, they remind me of our people: Just as we Jews are neither religion nor ethnicity nor nationality alone but take advantage of the strengths of each, the zonkeys too are rare and unique and defy easy categorization. And sometimes I feel like perhaps they know something other animals do not.

This is the only place I know where time stands still. I cannot say how much time I have spent wandering its trails, lost in thought. And though it is mesmerizing, it is anything but static: Life in nature is dynamic, soaring, beautiful, and this gives me a profound sense of inner peace.

Epilogue

The quest to build our own paradise is a quintessentially Jewish endeavor. From the biblical dream of the Promised Land to centuries of exile when we endlessly searched for places we could live and thrive, we have always looked to our next golden age. Whether in ancient Babylonia, medieval Spain, Germany between the wars, or twentieth-century America, Jews have always tried to fashion their own paradise.

How odd that of all peoples, the Jews—endlessly restless, agitated, nervous, rambunctious, flighty, soaring, insecure, creative—forever have looked for a place they could call home. History often disappointed, but they never stopped trying.

How else to explain the creation of Israel—a breathtaking effort of a broken people to return to its ancient land and its place in human history? Israel today is a thriving country and consistently ranks among the top twenty happiest places on earth.

It is often hard for Jews to recognize what we have built and to enjoy it when we have it. When things are bad, we look back on better times. When things are good, we look forward, energetically imagining the future. We always fear we may lose what we have. We never rest on our laurels—though peace and rest are what we long for.

Secular Diaspora Jews of the next generation, in my opinion, will not find that peace and rest unless they fill their lives with Jewish pride. I have tried, throughout this book, to offer a few pathways to help make that happen. And while I speak often of the crisis of Diaspora life, I firmly believe we will prevail.

As I was completing this book, a new Pew Research Center survey was published exploring the identity of Jews in America. And while there is much to be worried about, there is also cause for cautious optimism. Forty-two percent say being Jewish is "very important" to them, a slight decline from 46 percent in 2013, but still quite a lot. Given that 91 percent of American Jews are non-Orthodox, this means that there are still more than a few proud non-Orthodox Jews in America.

As a percentage of the American population as a whole, the self-identifying Jewish population appears to have stabilized as well, at 2.3 percent, slightly higher than the 2.2 percent of 2013. So either more Jews are having children or more of those children are choosing to identify as Jewish. For many, it's not a matter of religion—indeed, most self-identifying Jews say that religion is not very important in their lives. Yet they remain consciously Jewish, and a lot of them are looking for secular ways to express it.

Something, it seems, is changing. Forces are in play that are pushing back against the assimilation and decline that have characterized the last generation of Jewish life. I cannot say how much of it has to do with the effect of programs like Birthright or OneTable, or the spontaneous initiatives of younger Jews and new institutions, or whether it's a response to the rise of anti-Semitism, or the crisis facing America as a whole. But the sense of a free fall in Jewish identity that has been going on for decades appears to have somewhat abated.

We have not yet turned the corner. But alongside the ongoing evaporation of disconnected Jews, there are also the beginnings of what we may one day see as a renaissance of Jewish pride.

We seldom realize just how much of our Jewish lives is up to us, a thing of our own making. Life rarely feels like the product of our choices while it's happening. But as you get older, you realize how much of who we have become is based on who we decided to be.

In Israel, Jews have built a paradise of their own. Sure, no Israeli would describe it that way. They are too busy worrying about the future, confronting the flaws in their society, protecting themselves from threats, and ceaselessly building, innovating, and creating. But overall, it is a dynamic, positive, thriving civilization built on pride.

Zionism, after all, was never just about creating a refuge for Jews. It was first and foremost about rediscovering pride as a precondition for building our own paradise.

I don't know if 95 percent of secular Diaspora Jews will ever say that being Jewish is "very important," as is the case among the Orthodox. But there is certainly growing awareness of the importance of pride and the possibility of change. We can build a thriving, creative secular Jewish world. A paradise of our own.

But paradise does not happen by itself. Every animal, every pond and garden, every stable and pavilion and winding path requires planning, curation, painstaking trial and error, an investment of time and resources and creativity as well as a thorough understanding of what every animal, tree, and flower needs to thrive.

We cannot build our paradise by wishing it but only by rolling up our sleeves, studying the problem, breaking our false conceptions, trying and failing and trying again, overcoming obstacles, and above all refusing to stop.

The challenge is exceptionally hard, and there is no guarantee of success. We will need courage, we will need to have a lot of uncomfortable conversations, and we will need to massively redirect our resources.

But given all we have been through together over the centuries, and all that we are capable of achieving in the future, it is fair to ask: What choice do we have?

About the Author

Michael Steinhardt is one of the Jewish world's most prominent philanthropists. Born in 1940s Brooklyn, following a spectacular career on Wall Street, he has spent decades inspiring Jewish pride through revolutionary programs like Birthright Israel, Makor, and OneTable, and through the Steinhardt Foundation for Jewish Life. He is the author of *No Bull: My Life In and Out of Markets*.

v